Maternal mortality, human rights and accountability

The scale of maternal mortality and morbidity today is staggering. This book focuses on a vital part of a human rights response to maternal mortality, viz accountability. Accountability encompasses monitoring, review and redress at the local, national and international levels. The book's context includes the UN Human Rights Council maternal mortality and morbidity resolutions, as well as Millennium Development Goal 5. It comes out of a roundtable conference held in Geneva during 2010 that examined maternal mortality, human rights and accountability and provided a forum where maternal health and human rights experts could listen to, and learn from, each other. As well as revised and updated conference papers, this volume includes a rich collection of additional resource material on maternal mortality, human rights and accountability.

Paul Hunt is a Law Professor at Essex University (UK), Adjunct Professor at Waikato University (New Zealand) and senior human rights advisor to WHO Assistant Director-General Dr Flavia Bustreo. He served as UN Special Rapporteur on the right to the highest attainable standard of health (2002 2008) and has an Honorary Doctorate from the Nordic School of Public Health.

Tony Gray completed his DPhil in Theology and has published in the area of philosophical theology. After working in the production of personal biographies, he now runs his own publishing services company while undertaking freelance research in topics as diverse as family history, religion and human rights.

Maternal Mortality, Human Rights and Accountability

Edited by
Paul Hunt and Tony Gray

Routledge
Taylor & Francis Group
LONDON AND NEW YORK

First published 2013
by Routledge
2 Park Square, Milton Park, Abingdon, Oxon OX14 4RN

Simultaneously published in the USA and Canada
by Routledge
711 Third Avenue, New York, NY 10017

Routledge is an imprint of the Taylor & Francis Group, an informa business

British Library Cataloguing in Publication Data
A catalogue record for this book is available from the British Library

Library of Congress Cataloguing in Publication Data
A catalog record for this book has been requested

ISBN 978-0-415-53458-1 (hbk)
ISBN 978-0-203-68421-4 (ebk)

Typeset in Garamond
by Keystroke, Station Road, Codsall, Wolverhampton

MIX
Paper from responsible sources
FSC® C013056

Printed and bound in Great Britain by
TJ International Ltd, Padstow, Cornwall

Contents

Acknowledgements

The editors would like to express their thanks to all those who contributed papers, submitted research, took part in discussions, assisted with administration and provided finance, all of which went to make the 2010 Roundtable so successful.

At the editorial stage, Genevieve Sander, Joo-Young Lee and Shannon Gough provided indispensable assistance in preparing the book.

Before and since the Roundtable, Paul Hunt has received financial support from the Ford Foundation for his human rights work. Also, since mid-2011 he has received financial support from German Development Cooperation for his work on children's health, women's health and human rights. This support enabled him to devote time to this book. He is most grateful to the Ford Foundation, the German Federal Ministry for Economic Cooperation and Development (BMZ) and Deutsche Gesellschaft für Internationale Zusammenarbeit (GIZ), for their invaluable support. Similarly, Tony Gray is thankful for the generosity and guidance of the Clemens Nathan Research Centre which has enabled him to take part in the Roundtable and the preparation of this volume.

Paul Hunt
Tony Gray

Contributors

Ximena Andión is Director of the women's rights organization Instituto de Liderazgo Simone de Beauvoir and President of the Board of the Mexican Commission for the Defense and Promotion of Human Rights. She has thirteen years of experience in the human rights field, particularly in the area of women's rights at the national and international levels. She has worked for the UN Office of the High Commissioner for Human Rights and is the Former Advocacy Director of the Center for Reproductive Rights. Currently she is professor on women's rights and gender issues at the Universidad Iberoamericana.

Flavia Bustreo was appointed Assistant Director-General for Family, Women's and Children's Health on 1 October 2010. At WHO, she served as Deputy Director and then Director of The Partnership for Maternal, Newborn & Child Health from 2006 to 2010. In 2004-2005, she served as Interim Deputy Director of the Child Survival Partnership.

Ariel Frisancho has an MSc in Health Policy, Planning and Financing from the University of London. He is CARE Peru's National Coordinator – Social Rights Programs Unit (Education, Health, Nutrition & Food Security and Water & Sanitation Programs), CARE International Maternal Health Andean Regional Program Co-ordinator and National Co-ordinator of ForoSalud – the most extended Peruvian civil society network in health.

Tony Gray completed his DPhil in Theology and has published in the area of philosophical theology. After working in the production of personal biographies, he now runs his own publishing services company whilst undertaking freelance research in topics as diverse as family history, religion and human rights, with a particular interest in religion and human rights.

Paul Hunt served as UN Special Rapporteur on the right to the highest attainable standard of health (2002-2008) and UN Committee on Economic, Social and Cultural Rights (1999-2002). He is a Professor at the Human Rights Centre, Essex University, and Senior Health and Human Rights Adviser, WHO, Geneva.

Winfred Lichuma has worked in both the public and private sectors and served the Judiciary in various capacities rising up to the position of a Senior Resident Magistrate. Commissioner Lichuma was a Legal Affairs Advisor/ Manager with the National Aids Control Council (NACC), Kenya where she was instrumental in the area of human rights and legal issues in respect to HIV and AIDS with her work culminating in the development of the HIV/AIDS Prevention and Control Act 2006. She is an expert in mainstreaming human rights, gender and HIV and Aids in development programmes.

Samantha Lobis has worked with AMDD since 2002 and is currently a senior program officer. She has over ten years of international public health and development experience, including monitoring and evaluation of programs aimed at reducing maternal mortality and the assessment of health systems in developing countries. She has a particular interest in applying a human rights approach to maternal mortality reduction and to the global movement to improve access to comprehensive reproductive health services. Prior to her work at AMDD, Samantha worked at the Lawyers Committee for Human Rights in their International Refugee Program and was a Peace Corps volunteer in the Republic of Guinea in West Africa.

Clemens N Nathan is Joint Chairman Consultative Council of Jewish Organisations (CCJO), one of the oldest non-Governmental organizations (founded by René Cassin who received the Nobel Prize for Human Rights). Clemens Nathan worked under René Cassin when he was President of the Alliance Insraelite Universelle and carried on his tradition of human rights, not only for Jewish people but for others. Clemens is also a Council Member Britain in Europe (formerly the Bow Group), is active at the UN mainly in Geneva and New York, and a Board Member of the Conference on Jewish Material Claims (dealing with all problems of restitution and indemnification of gross violation of human rights with the Federal Republic of Germany and Austria). He the Chairman of the Clemens Nathan Research Centre, and has edited, contributed to and authored over 15 books on human rights issues.

Sandeep Prasad B.A. (Hon.), LL.B., is currently the Executive Director of Action Canada for Population and Development (ACPD), a human rights organization working to advance sexual and reproductive rights within Canada and within the work of key UN bodies and mechanisms. His work at the UN Human Rights Council has included active participation in the Sexual Rights Initiative, a small South-North coalition of organizations that he helps to coordinate. In September 2012, Sandeep was appointed as a Member of the High-Level Task Force for the International Conference on Population and Development which aims to galvanize political support for sexual and reproductive health and rights, and ensure that international development efforts prioritize these issues, including within post-2015 development frameworks.

Nan Strauss is a researcher with Amnesty International USA, where she has been working on maternal health and health care in the U.S., in the context of the right to health. She is the co-author of the recently-released report, Deadly Delivery: The Maternal Health Care Crisis in the USA, and has been involved in campaigning, policy, advocacy, and media efforts associated with the project following its publication.

Francisco F. Songane, a former Minister of Health from Mozambique recognized both nationally and internationally for innovation and leadership. He was a member of Task Force 4 of the UN Millennium Project (2002-2004), analyzing the practicalities of achieving the goals related to maternal and child health, and a Member of the Board of Trustees and the Executive Committee of the International Vaccine Institute, and serves in several Advisory Committees. He was also the Director of the Partnership for Maternal, Newborn and Child Health, and later Chair of the Forum 2012 on Research for Health organized by the Council on Health Research for Development, where he served as Senior Health Advisor.

Rachel Ward is the Deputy Executive Director of Advocacy Policy and Research at Amnesty International USA and served as the Managing Director of AIUSA's Research Unit for eight years, during which time she investigated human rights violations in the United States on a wide range of issues. She has co-authored Deadly Delivery: The Maternal Health Crisis in the USA, which was published in March 2010 as part of Amnesty International's Demand Dignity Campaign. Rachel Ward is a lawyer and a member of the Law Society of England and Wales.

Hiranthi Wijemanne is a medical doctor with post graduate qualifications in Public Health. She worked for several years for UNICEF in Sri Lanka and was closely associated with the Maternal Death Audit system in Sri Lanka and the Access to Emergency care programme. She worked for several years for UNICEF in Sri Lanka. She is a consultant to the Ministry of Child Development and Womens Empowerment, the Ministry of Justice and National Child Protection Authority on Child Rights related issues. She is currently an Expert Member of the International Monitoring Committee.

Foreword

Navanethem Pillay
UN High Commissioner for Human Rights

In September 2010 I was delighted to open the international roundtable on 'Maternal mortality, human rights and accountability' and it is now my pleasure to make a few remarks to accompany the publication of the presentations made during the roundtable.

Accountability, together with equality, non-discrimination and meaningful participation, is among the key human rights principles. Maternal mortality and morbidity are often caused by violations of these principles. When authorities do not meet their responsibilities to protect, promote and fulfil women's rights, the consequences of this neglect are shamefully dire and they may be fatal. These violations continue with impunity when neither people nor institutions responsible for such violations are held accountable and, without accountability, there is practically no incentive to put in place remedial measures. When thinking of accountability, it is mistaken to think only in terms of judicial accountability. One of the merits of this book is that it explores what accountability means and highlights a wide variety of accountability arrangements for maternal mortality and morbidity.

The vast majority of the annual 350,000 deaths related to pregnancy and childbirth complications could be prevented with low-cost, targeted interventions, policies and services, all of which have been known by the medical profession and health systems for decades. Improving maternal health, Goal 5 of the Millennium Development Goals (MDGs), remains the least successful of the eight goals.

Accountability for actions taken or omitted is therefore indispensable to ensure that gaps in policy and practice are addressed and filled. Let us not forget that only in recent years has the subject of maternal mortality and morbidity been recognized as a human rights issue. This development was due, in no small part, to the efforts of civil society advocates.

The work of Paul Hunt as the former United Nations Special Rapporteur on the right of everyone to the enjoyment of the highest attainable standard of physical and mental health was significant in bringing attention to the human rights implications of maternal mortality and morbidity and placing the issue on the human rights agenda. Building on this important work as well as key civil society initiatives, my Office has consistently prioritized attention to maternal mortality and morbidity as a human rights issue. In 2008 my Office coordinated the first panel discussion on maternal mortality during a plenary session of the United Nations Human Rights Council. That discussion was a catalyst for the Council's consideration of the issue.

In March 2009 85 governments from all regions of the world reaffirmed their commitment to addressing maternal mortality and morbidity as a human rights issue and called on the Council to take action. Their pivotal joint statement, presented to the Council and delivered by New Zealand, paved the way for additional initiatives.

Three months later, the Council adopted by consensus a historic resolution entitled 'Preventable maternal mortality and morbidity and human rights' with 67 co-sponsors.[1] This resolution requested my Office to prepare a thematic study to identify the human rights dimensions of preventable maternal mortality and morbidity in the existing legal framework and recommend options for addressing the human rights dimension of preventable maternal mortality and morbidity throughout the UN system.

In June 2010 my Office's report was presented to the Council.[2] It was also the subject of a panel discussion that month. The report attracted considerable public attention, prompting 108 countries to invite me to present the study to the Millennium Development Goals Review Summit – I am seizing every opportunity to emphasize the intrinsic link between human rights and the Millennium Development Goals, using maternal mortality and morbidity as a powerful illustration.

In September 2010 the Council adopted by consensus a second resolution,[3] requesting my Office to prepare a second report, this time on good practices in adopting a human rights-based approach to eliminate preventable maternal mortality and morbidity, just a few days after the international roundtable on maternal mortality, human rights and accountability. This report was presented to the Council in September 2011.[4] The Council adopted by consensus a third resolution, requesting my Office to prepare concise technical guidance on the application of a human rights-based approach to the implementation of policies and programmes to reduce maternal mortality and morbidity.[5] Also in September 2010 the Secretary-General launched his *Global strategy on women's and children's health*, which bears the imprint of, and explicitly refers to, international human rights, as well as the Human Rights Council's groundbreaking resolution of 2009 on maternal mortality and morbidity and human rights. In its turn, the *Global strategy* led to the Commission on Information and Accountability by Women's and Children's Health, the final report of which, *Keeping promises, measuring results*, explicitly refers to international

1 Resolution 11/8 – this and subsequent UN reports cited are available at www2.ohchr.org.
2 A/HRC/14/39.
3 Resolution 15/17.
4 A/HRC/18/27.
5 Resolution 18/2.

human rights and adopts an accountability framework that draws from human rights practice.

The Council is to consider my Office's technical guidance in September 2012. Part II of this book includes extracts on accountability taken from the technical guidance,[6] the Secretary-General's *Global strategy*, the Commission's report *Keeping promises, measuring results*, as well as other documents mentioned in this Foreword.

As this progression demonstrates, we are advancing from abstract principles to their practical operationalization in relation to maternal mortality and morbidity. Of course, this journey towards practical implementation is not complete and we still have a long way to go. Moreover, the journey will not, and cannot, be completed without more interdisciplinary collaboration and effective mainstreaming of human rights across all health-related sectors. Health workers play an indispensable role in the realization of the right to health and other human rights. The medical and human rights professions share a commitment to non-discrimination and equality. To us all, every person must be equally respected, cared for and protected without distinction.

Clearly, maternal mortality and morbidity cannot be seen in isolation. In addition to the tragic loss of life, maternal mortality triggers and aggravates cycles of poverty that cause generations of suffering and despair. When mothers die, children (especially girl children) are at greater risk of dropping out of school, becoming malnourished and simply not surviving.

A key result of the human rights-based approach is that ultimately women will be able to exercise their right to participate in decision-making processes, including those affecting their sexual and reproductive health, family planning, contraception, pregnancy, childbirth and in addressing unsafe abortion.

As my Office's reports make clear, the application of a human rights approach helps us understand that maternal mortality and morbidity are not simply issues of public health but the consequence of lack of fulfilment of multiple rights. A right-based approach assists states to understand and make visible the connections among poverty, discrimination, equality and health. It also outlines their obligations to promote, protect and fulfil all human rights, including the right to health.

This timely book deepens our understanding of maternal mortality, human rights and accountability. It explains that accountability is more than monitoring and not the same as going to court. The contributions in Part I are enriched by a wide range of useful resources in Part II.

These issues are not only relevant to maternal mortality and Millennium Development Goal 5; they also closely bear on the current discussions about post-2015 aims, processes and institutions. It is critically important that human rights, including gender equality, play their part in these discussions and the post-2015 arrangements. Ensuring that human rights are fully

6 A/HRC/21/22.

integrated in the review of the Programme of Action of the International Conference on Population and Development and the elaboration of the sustainable development goals, as called for by the recent Conference on Sustainable Development in Rio in June 2012, will also be crucial to feed into the discussions towards a future vision for development in line with human rights obligations. As this volume confirms, human rights have much to contribute.

I would like to thank the Clemens Nathan Research Centre, Essex University Human Rights Centre, International Initiative on Maternal Mortality and Human Rights, SAHAYOG (an Indian non-profit civil society organization promoting gender equality and women's health), CARE Peru and Health Equity Group (East Africa) for organizing the 2010 international roundtable and I commend all those responsible for bringing this important and instructive publication to fruition.

Geneva, August 2012.

Preface

Clemens Nathan and Tony Gray

In the aftermath of the Second World War, faced with the horrors of the Holocaust, the worldwide community searched for ways in which it could ensure that 'never again' became not merely a wish, but a reality. The modern human rights movement, with its roots in eighteenth- and nineteenth-century political theory, began to take centre stage. Throughout the second half of the twentieth century, this concern for the fundamental rights of every human being has grown, developed and spread. What we have today are numerous bodies, both within and outside government, whose aims and endeavours are to clarify and implement these rights in all aspects of human life and to ensure that these rights are protected.

This volume is the result of an international roundtable that took place in September 2010 (and which was oversubscribed for its 120 participant capacity), concerned with maternal mortality, human rights and accountability. However, the rights of mothers and children are not only an issue for the twenty-first century, as only one of many possible examples will illustrate.

The Claims Conference was tasked with pursuing the human rights of those who suffered at the hands of the Nazis during the Holocaust and implementing reparations. During the tyranny of the Third Reich, over 600 women were used for medical experiments. Many of them reproduced offspring who were mentally or physically disabled. For years, many of these women never disclosed that they had these children who might have suffered disability as a result of the horrific experiments carried out on them. It was only by chance, interviewing and analysing statistics, that the Claims Conference came to the conclusion that all these children (now adults) were a direct result of the medical experiments. How does one compensate mothers for something like this? Which doctors could assess whether it was due to the experiments or to some other reason? After endless debates, it was decided that the best solution was to give every one of the mothers an additional sum of money to compensate her for her suffering – it would have been unfair to request that a doctor make a decision in each separate case.

Thankfully the issues discussed in this volume are not horrific in this way. However, they remain of the utmost importance and seriousness – as the overview chapter by Francisco Songane illustrates, the statistics for maternal mortality are staggering. In the twenty-first century, with all the world's wealth, scientific knowledge, availability of communication and travel, and with all the goodwill and effort put into government bodies and NGOs, the scale of preventable maternal deaths remains catastrophic.

This is not the only reason why this volume is so important. One of the most refreshing aspects of the roundtable, out of which this volume grew, was its focus on accountability. It is one thing to get many people to agree on what is desirable and what should be done. It is quite another to ensure that what should be done is being done. And, as the papers illustrate, there are many different forms that accountability can take. In addition, as Paul Hunt makes clear, the papers at the roundtable, and this resulting volume, are timely.

Clemens Nathan
Chairman, Clemens Nathan Research Centre

Tony Gray
Researcher, Clemens Nathan Research Centre

[The Clemens Nathan Research Centre aims to bring experts together to discuss and progress key issues in human rights. It is the research arm of the Consultative Council of Jewish Organizations (CCJO), whose first chairman was René Cassin.]

Introduction

Paul Hunt

The one-day international roundtable held in Geneva during September 2010 aimed to bring together maternal health professionals, human rights experts and diplomats to focus on one critically important component of maternal mortality and human rights: accountability. Although effective, responsive, transparent accountability lies at the heart of human rights, it is often misunderstood. Monitoring is not accountability but a step towards accountability; judicial accountability is very important, but is only one type of accountability, there are many others. Adapting Alicia Yamin's definition, human rights accountability refers to holding governments and others responsible for their conduct, in light of human rights standards of behaviour and performance, and taking remedial action when necessary.[1] Encompassing human rights standards, accountability has three key elements: monitoring, review and remedial action.

At the roundtable, we considered community, country and global perspectives on accountability, and discussed with governments, UN agencies and civil society, in the specific context of maternal mortality. The roundtable was held during September 2010 in Geneva so as to feed into discussions on both the UN Human Rights Council's groundbreaking initiative on maternal mortality and morbidity and the slow progress towards Millennium Development Goal (MDG) 5 on maternal health. However, although the Council's initiative and MDG5 formed part of the roundtable's context, the meeting was also designed to engage with developments and possibilities beyond the United Nations.

This book includes most of the presentations, suitably revised and updated, made at the roundtable (Part I). Additionally, it includes extracts from some key documents on maternal mortality, human rights and accountability (Part II). We hope that Parts I and II will serve as a lasting resource for all those interested in this field.

As the presentations were updated, and difficult choices made about what to include in Part II, two features stood out. First, this is a very dynamic area

1 Alicia Ely Yamin, Toward transformative accountability: applying a rights-based approach to fulfil maternal health obligations, *SUR International Journal on Human Rights* 7(12), 2010, 97.

of policy and practice; it has developed rapidly since September 2010. Second, it provides a rich fabric consisting of multiple threads from diverse disciplines, including public health, medicine, demography, law and public policy, as well as different areas of government involving a range of actors.

It is axiomatic that we have to find ways to strengthen appropriate forms of accountability for maternal deaths and here I mention two approaches to this challenge. *First*, by ensuring that existing accountability mechanisms give due attention to maternal mortality. Historically, human rights accountability devices have given insufficient attention to this issue. This has to change and, as several presentations and extracts in this book testify, it is beginning to change. Today, some international human rights bodies, national courts and national human rights institutions are giving renewed consideration to maternal mortality. To maintain and accelerate this momentum, existing human rights accountability devices must be willing to listen to, and learn from, maternal health professionals.

The *second* approach is by identifying existing processes that were not conceived as accountability arrangements but – suitably refined – they might be able to serve this purpose, such as maternal death audits or reviews. Processes of this sort are often designed, and primarily used, by health professionals who have to be willing to listen to, and learn from, the human rights experts.

In other words, the human rights and health communities must be open to the expertise and insights of the other. It was for this reason that an explicit aim of our roundtable in 2010 was to engender multidisciplinary discussion – and the same aim animates this book. Without multidisciplinarity, the human rights-approach to health will be a side panel at the main event.

The roundtable focused on neither maternal health nor maternal mortality; indeed, the focus was not even maternal mortality and human rights. Its focus was maternal mortality, human rights and *accountability*. The same applies to this book. We would like to have included a host of other important material on maternal mortality and human rights, but have confined ourselves to maternal mortality, human rights and accountability. One of the rare exceptions is the UN Human Rights Council's pioneering resolution of June 2009 that we include because of its historic importance in this field.[2] We abstemiously omit the Council's important follow-up resolutions.

Reviewing events and documents since September 2010, it is interesting to observe how, by an osmosis-like process, the health and human rights communities are influencing one another in relation to maternal mortality and morbidity, human rights and accountability. Consider, by way of illustration, some developments within the United Nations.

Three weeks after the roundtable, the UN Secretary-General launched his *Global strategy for women's and children's health*, which bears the imprint of human rights and explicitly refers to key international human rights treaties, the

2 See UN High Commissioner's foreword in this volume.

substantive interpretation of the right to the highest attainable standard of health adopted by the UN Committee on Economic, Social and Cultural Rights, and the UN Human Rights Council's historic resolution of 2009.[3] The *Global strategy* was strongly endorsed by many states and others, and immediately (and remarkably) generated commitments of $40 billion for women's and children's health.

However, the *Global strategy* did not establish any accountability arrangements. Instead, the Secretary-General asked WHO to take this issue forward. The *Global strategy* ends:

> The UN Secretary-General requests that the World Health Organization chair a process to determine the most effective international institutional arrangements for global reporting, oversight and accountability on women's and children's health, including through the UN system.[4]

In response, in December 2010, the WHO established the Commission on Information and Accountability for Women's and Children's Health, co-chaired by the Tanzanian President, Jakaya Kikwete, and Canadian Prime Minister, Stephen Harper. The Commission established two working groups, one of which (the Working Group on Accountability for Results, chaired by Dr Richard Horton) made recommendations to the Commission, some of which are transparently shaped by human rights law, policy and practice.[5]

The Commission received numerous submissions, including a fine report from the Partnership for Maternal, Newborn & Child Health, called *A review of global accountability mechanisms for women's and children's health*, written in large measure by Judith Bueno de Mesquita, which draws the Commission's attention to the numerous accountability mechanisms established under international human rights law since the 1960s.[6] The Partnership submitted that these precedents, commonplace in the UN human rights system, might help the Commission as it endeavoured to advise the Secretary-General on accountability for women's and children's health. Civil society organizations also urged the Commission to integrate human rights into its final report. The Commission's Working Group on Accountability for Results, and the Partnership's submission, framed accountability as consisting of three elements: monitoring, review and remedy or action.

In mid-2011 the Commission produced its final report, *Keeping promises, measuring results*, which has explicit human rights content, and adopts an accountability framework of monitoring, review and act (rather than remedy

3 United Nations Secretary-General, *Global strategy for women's and children's health*, The Partnership for Maternal, Newborn & Child Health, 2010.

4 Ibid., 15

5 Commission on Information and Accountability for Women's and Children's Health, *Working Group on Accountability for Results: final paper*, May 2011.

6 The Partnership for Maternal, Newborn & Child Health, *A review of global accountability mechanisms for women's and children's health*, PMNCH: Geneva, 2011.

or action).[7] Like the *Global strategy*, the Commission's report is incomplete from the human rights perspective. Nonetheless, as UN High Commissioner Pillay suggests in the foreword to this volume, some of its analysis and several of its recommendations are informed by human rights law, policy and practice, including in relation to accountability.

This provides one example of how human rights considerations are beginning to influence global health policy. But this is a two-way street. In the foreword, the UN High Commissioner for Human Rights outlines the progression from the Council's resolution of 2009 to her Office's technical guidance on the application of a human rights-based approach to preventable maternal morbidity and mortality, published in mid-2012, and that was discussed by the Council in September 2012.[8] The technical guidance is a document of the UN Office of the High Commissioner for Human Rights, not WHO or any other body. However, the guidance was prepared with considerable input from health professionals working elsewhere in the United Nations and beyond, and this is apparent from the text. The guidance combines health and human rights perspectives. It employs the health policy cycle and WHO's six building blocks of a health system, as well as concepts more familiar to those working in human rights, such as availability, accessibility, acceptability and quality.

In short, the traffic of concepts and experience between health and human rights is flowing in both directions.

The roundtable's revised presentations provide a range of different but complementary perspectives. Dr Songane sets the scene, reminding us of the scale of maternal mortality and its grossly uneven distribution within and between countries. He signals what needs to be done and why maternal mortality is a human rights issue. Dr Frisancho Arroyo presents citizen monitoring of healthcare in Peru. Aimed at monitoring and verifying compliance of the authorities' health and human rights obligations, can this form of community participation and citizenship surveillance effectively address the challenges of maternal mortality and morbidity?

Using emergency obstetric care indicators as an illustration, Samantha Lobis explains the roles of indicators and benchmarks. While indicators and benchmarks are monitoring tools, independent bodies can also use them to find out if the authorities are complying with their human rights obligations. Some dimensions of some human rights are subject to progressive realization, meaning that the authorities have to do all they reasonably can to make good progress in relation to the dimension of the human right in question. For example, while an effective and inclusive health system cannot be established

7 Commission on Information and Accountability for Women's and Children's Health, *Keeping promises, measuring results*, 2011.

8 Human Rights Council, *Technical guidance on the application of a human rights-based approach to the implementation of policies and programmes to reduce preventable maternal morbidity and mortality: Report of the Office of the United Nations High Commissioner for Human Rights*, UN Doc. A/HRC/21/22, 2012.

overnight, a government has to take steps to move progressively towards establishing such a health system. Thus, we need indicators and benchmarks to measure progress over time, helping to assess whether or not adequate progress is being made. If, without acceptable explanation, adequate progress is not being made, the government would appear to be in breach of its human rights responsibilities. In short, indicators and benchmarks are essential for holding authorities to account, and Samantha Lobis describes how emergency obstetric care indicators and benchmarks can be deployed and contribute to reducing maternal mortality.

In some circumstances, maternal death audits or reviews can expose the systemic causes of maternal deaths and contribute to meaningful reforms. Dr Wijemanne outlines some of the different forms of maternal death audits and explains the Sri Lankan experience. Are there circumstances in which maternal death audits may provide a vehicle for human rights accountability? Other contributors, such as Nan Strauss and Rachel Ward, also consider this issue.

Ximena Andión Ibañez shows how national and international litigation can be a powerful strategy for the promotion and protection of women's right to safe pregnancy and childbirth. She provides illustrative contemporary cases and discusses the challenges and possibilities involved in a litigation strategy. As already observed, although very important, judicial accountability – going to court – is just one form of accountability, moreover accountability of last resort. Winnie Lichuma outlines another way of holding governments accountable for their human rights commitments: public inquiries held by national human rights institutions. She describes the initiative of the Kenya National Commission on Human Rights that led to *The report of the public inquiry into violations of sexual and reproductive health rights in Kenya* published in 2012. In their case study of the United States of America, Nan Strauss and Rachel Ward remind us that African-American women are three to four times more likely to die than white women during pregnancy, a disparity unchanged for over half a century. The contributors show that weak accountability for maternal deaths is not only a problem in low- and middle-income but also in high-income countries.

In her foreword, UN High Commissioner Pillay outlines recent progress in the UN Human Rights Council on maternal mortality and morbidity; and Sandeep Prasad provides a fascinating and unique behind-the-scenes account of how this progress was achieved. As his account demonstrates, many people contributed to this achievement, including key country delegates, staff of UN agencies and dedicated civil society advocates. In her postscript, Flavia Bustreo, providing the eradication of polio as an instructive precedent, signals steps towards the elimination of preventable maternal deaths.

The extracts in Part II supplement these presentations.

In 2003 Lynn Freedman wrote a short, seminal article introducing the idea of 'constructive accountability': 'a rights-based approach to maternal mortality reduction is not primarily about enacting a system to find fault and pronounce punishment; rather it is about developing a dynamic of entitlement and obligation between people and their government and within the complex system of relationships that form the wider health system, public and private.'[9] Many of us have found very useful, and tried to apply and develop, this concept of 'constructive accountability'. When I served as UN Special Rapporteur on the right to the highest attainable standard of health (2002–2008), I found remarkably little literature on human rights accountability in the field of health. So I was delighted when, in 2008, Dr Helen Potts wrote a short accessible monograph, for both the health and human rights communities, introducing accountability and the right to the highest attainable standard of health. In 2010 Alicia Yamin, building on her earlier work on accountability, wrote an inspiring and incisive article on 'transformative accountability' in relation to maternal health. Part II includes Freedman's article and extracts from Potts and Yamin.

Part II also includes the UN Human Rights Council's resolution of 2009; some extracts on accountability from OHCHR's report of 2010 on maternal mortality and morbidity; and extracts on accountability from OHCHR's technical guidance on the application of a human rights-based approach to preventable maternal morbidity and mortality, published in mid-2012.

A third group of extracts includes some of the human rights-related passages from: the UN Secretary-General's *Global strategy* on women's and children's health; the final report of the Commission on Information and Accountability for Women's and Children's Health; the report of the Commission's Working Group on Accountability for Results; and *A review of global accountability mechanisms for women's and children's health* submitted to the Commission by the Partnership for Maternal, Newborn & Child Health.

I recommend Figure 1 of the Partnership's submission because it sets out some key definitions – monitoring, review, remedy, independent review, non-independent review, peer review and mutual accountability – which are critically important. While there is a role for non-independent review, peer review and mutual accountability, at some stage in the accountability process there must be some form of *independent* review otherwise the process lacks legitimacy, credibility and authority. The Partnership's Figure 1 helps to keep clear some of these vital distinctions.

A fourth and final group of extracts includes some passages from *The report of the public inquiry into violations of sexual and reproductive health rights in Kenya* published by the Kenya National Commission on Human Rights in 2012 and introduced by Winnie Lichuma in Part I. (I note in passing that this report urges the Kenyan authorities to implement the UN Human Rights Council resolution on maternal mortality and morbidity.) Other extracts are from two insightful articles discussing important national (i.e. Delhi High Court) and

9 Lynn Freedman, Human rights, constructive accountability and maternal mortality in the Dominican Republic: a commentary, *International Journal of Gynaecology and Obstetrics* 82, 2003, 111.

international (i.e. UN Women's Rights Committee) case law on maternal mortality; each amplifies Ximena Andión Ibañez's contribution in Part I.

Of course, this book does not provide a comprehensive survey of ideas and initiatives on maternal mortality, human rights and accountability. There is much more to be said about the oversight role of democratically elected local and national legislative bodies. While some contributions, such as Potts and Andión Ibañez in Part I and Yamin in Part II, address the question of remedies or redress, this issue deserves more attention than is possible in this volume. Also, the human rights responsibilities of donors and non-state actors in relation to maternal health receive some attention (e.g. in Yamin) but demand closer scrutiny.[10] Adopting a recommendation of the Commission on Information and Accountability for Women's and Children's Health, the UN Secretary-General has recently established an independent Expert Review Group (iERG) with responsibility to hold donors, non-state actors and others to account. The Group's work is just beginning and deserves careful attention.

Finally, there are numerous reasons for focusing on maternal mortality and human rights and I will not rehearse them all. However, I would like to emphasize one. Focusing on maternal mortality and human rights compels us to confront a wide range of issues, including family planning or access to contraceptive information and services, antenatal care, emergency obstetric care, postnatal care, unsafe abortion, international assistance and cooperation, and discrimination, inequality and other preconditions or underlying determinants of health. The maternal mortality and human rights focus brings accountability to bear on these – and other – profoundly important issues.

10 Jude Mesquita, Rajat Khosla and Paul Hunt, The human rights responsibility of international assistance and cooperation in health, in Mark Gibney and Sigrun Skogly (eds) *Universal human rights and extraterritorial obligations*, Pennsylvania Studies in Human Rights, 2010, 104–129; Rajat Khosla and Paul Hunt, *Human rights guidelines for pharmaceutical companies in relation to access to medicines: the sexual and reproductive health context*, University of Essex, 2008; Joo-Young Lee and Paul Hunt, Human rights responsibilities of pharmaceutical companies in relation to access to medicines, *Journal of Law, Medicine & Ethics* 40(2), 2012, 220–233.

Part I

Conference presentations

1 Maternal mortality: an overview

Dr Francisco F. Songane

1.1 Importance of maternal mortality

Pregnancy is not a disease; it is one of the most important experiences in the life of a woman, perhaps one of her noblest achievements. The birth of a baby is a moment of great joy for the mother, the father, the rest of the family, the village and the whole community. Childbirth is an essential part of reproduction, a condition sine qua non for our own existence as societies of human beings. Therefore, pregnancy should be protected and all the efforts made to ensure that families have good living conditions, are well informed with respect of each other, and enjoy healthy lives.

It is this context that makes a maternal death unique as compared to other deaths, particularly when it occurs in circumstances of lack of the required services and absence of social support aggravated by lack of observation to basic human rights.

Bringing the human rights element to the discussion widens the scope of our understanding and raises maternal mortality to the political level beyond the mere medical problem; it captures the complexity of its origins and underscores its importance as one of the main indicators of socioeconomic development.

A maternal death is "the death of a woman while pregnant or within 42 days of termination of pregnancy, irrespective of the duration and site of pregnancy, from any cause related to or aggravated by the pregnancy or its management but not from accidental or incidental causes."[1]

Why are we so alarmed by maternal deaths? They are a major cause of death among women of reproductive age, and progress is very slow in lowering the figures in the most affected regions. Although substantial reductions have been registered in many countries, today women continue to die in childbirth in the same large numbers as they did 20 years ago. The maternal mortality ratio (MMR) in developing countries is 15 times higher than in developed countries; more than half (55%) of the world's maternal deaths occur in

1 WHO, *International classification of diseases and related health problems*, 10th rev. edn, 1992 (ICD-10).

Table 1.1 Evolution of maternal mortality in Africa and South Asia (as per 2007 update)

	1990	*2005*
	MMR, deaths per 100,000 live births (number of deaths)	
Africa	910 (205,000)	900 (261,000)
South Asia	650 (238,000)	500 (187,000)
World	430 (576,000)	400 (536,000)

Note: 83% of world maternal deaths occur in Africa and South Asia

sub-Saharan Africa. We know where they occur, who are the most affected, and the causes of death; so how to treat and prevent them, and the interventions to achieve this, could be made available anywhere in the world. The problem is that no consequent action is taken; the issue has been neglected.

Figure 1.1 shows the distribution of maternal deaths in the world in 2010 as expressed by the maternal mortality ratio (maternal deaths/100,000 live births). Africa, particularly the regions south of Sahara, and South Asia are where most of the deaths occur, representing 85% of all deaths; the darker-tone areas represent the parts of the globe with the least favorable indicators. As illustrated in Table 1.1, little change has been registered in the first 15 years from the reference point (1990); in Africa, the number of deaths has actually increased, from 205,000 in 1990 to 261,000 in 2005. The special efforts made in galvanizing the different institutions and organizations involved in the matter did pay off, thus the lowering of the rates in the last maternal mortality estimates recently published.[2]

It is a progress that is welcome, but not statistics to rejoice about, when in a world with an annual output of US $63 trillion in 2010 we still witness huge differences among regions, in many instances shocking.[3] The number of maternal deaths in Africa is more than 75 times higher than in Europe or North America, and the risk of a woman dying in childbirth is one in 15 in Chad compared with one in 14,100 in Sweden or one in 10,500 in the Netherlands.[4] These discrepancies do convey a very important message that although the resources are available the world has not come together yet to launch concerted action to stop the tragedy, and contribute to the fulfillment of basic human rights. It is sad, and at the same time curious, to realize the rejection of the basic condition for our own existence.

2 *Maternal mortality in 2005: estimates developed by WHO, UNICEF, UNFPA and the World Bank*, WHO, 2007. *Trends in maternal mortality 1990 to 2010, WHO, UNICEF, UNFPA and the World Bank estimates*.

3 The World Bank, *2011 world development indicators*, 2011.

4 *Trends in maternal mortality 1990 to 2010*, op. cit.

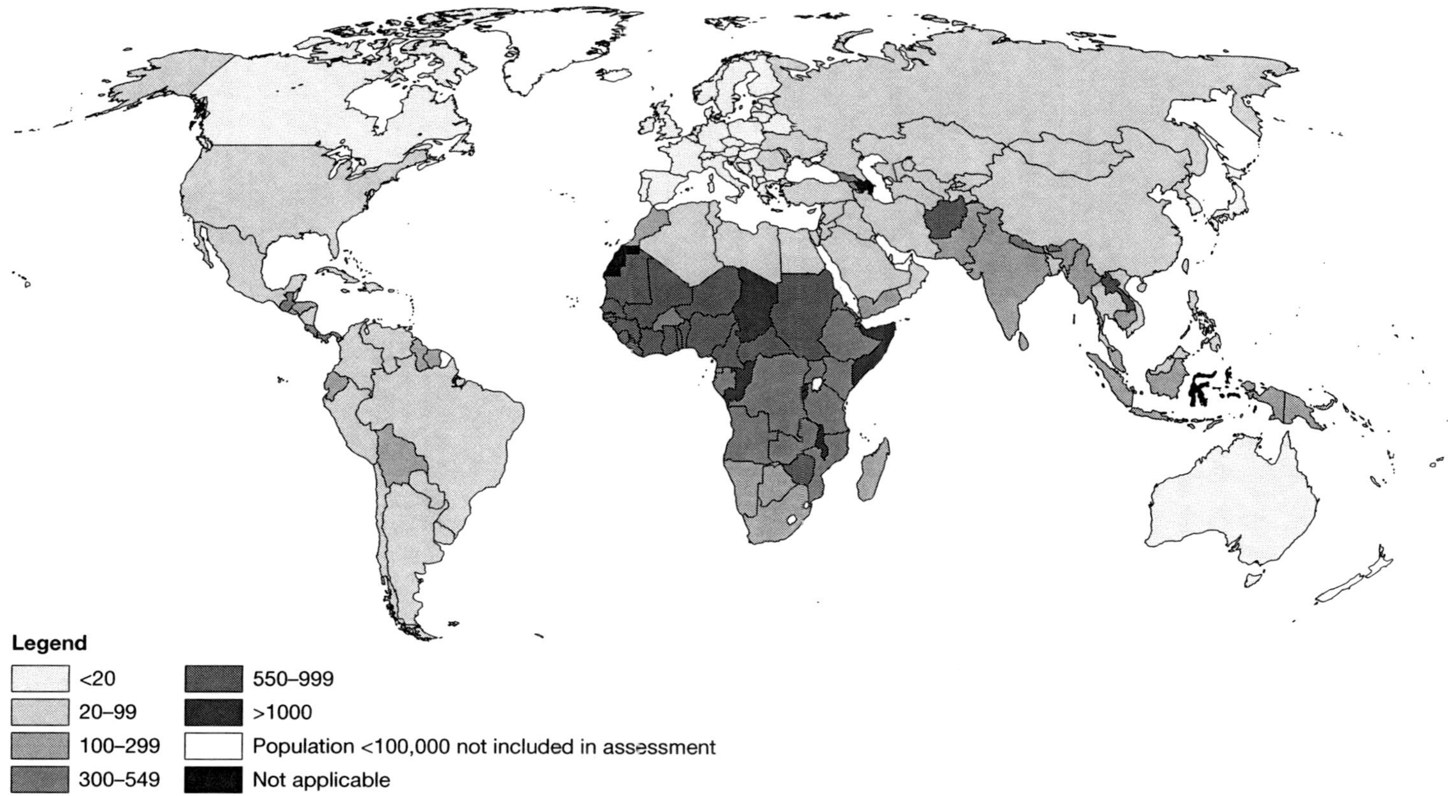

Figure 1.1 Map with countries by category according to their maternal mortality rate (MMR, deaths per 100,000 live births), 2010

Source: WHO Trends in Maternal Mortality, 1990–2010

1.2 Human rights perspective

Respect for human rights means that everyone is treated equally, and enjoys the benefits from society in an equitable manner. The global figures cannot be used to assess this; the overall national figure could be good and commendable, but not suitable to translate the reality faced by the different groups of people. Data has to be disaggregated to the subnational, regional, and sub-regional, as well as by social groupings, be ethnic, by religion, level of income, political affiliation or other forms as suited to a particular context. Analyzing the information from this angle, it becomes clear that for the case of maternal mortality, human rights violations happen everywhere, even in the countries considered exemplary for having made strides to achieve very low levels of maternal mortality. In Australia, the national figure for the MMR is 4, but it does not reflect the scenario among the indigenous minorities, where the figure is 21.5, three times higher than in the nonindigenous. In Argentina, 26% of maternal deaths are due to abortion complications, but this proportion is double in districts with poor access to services and affecting mostly teenagers; distant provinces have MMR three times higher than the national average. The US has seen the doubling of the number of women dying during pregnancy and childbirth; the current MMR is 16/100,000 live births, with African American women three times more likely to die than the white (MMR of 32.7 and 9.5 respectively). In the United Kingdom, women with a husband or partner in unemployment have an MMR seven times higher than that of women with partners in employment.[5]

Examples like this can be found in any country, and the most frequent circumstances associated with it are the following:

- poverty
- belonging to ethnic minorities
- unemployment
- those who have no chance to go to school
- very young age
- migrants
- being marginalized for political reasons.

It should be emphasized that this grouping also applies to the countries in which the problem is mostly felt, with poor indicators; amid the paucity of

5 *Improving maternity services in Australia; the report of the Maternity Services Review*, February 2009. Thomson et al., *Overview of Australian indigenous health status*, 2011. Available online at www.healthinfonet.ecu.edu.au/overview_2012. Mariana Romero, Evelina Chapman, Silvina Ramos and Edgardo Abalos, La stuación de la mortalidade materna en la Argentina; observatorio de salud sexual y reproductiva, *Hoja informativa OSSyR*, 2010, 1. Amnesty International, *Deadly delivery: the maternal health care crisis in the USA*, New York: Amnesty International Publications, 2010. Sarah Fisher, Social inequalities in maternal and perinatal mortality: a summary of research, *New Digest* 2008, 44.

services, those who do not fall under the groups listed here are much better off than the majority of people who contribute to the high MMR. The human rights approach is encompassing by taking us beyond the national figure or a simple check against a target, and looking deeper through an analysis of disaggregated data; there is still work to be done in every country, although the intensity of the work will vary depending on the level of the discrepancies. Certainly the economic condition of a country and its level of development are important factors for the provision of services, but there are other aspects that come to play and may not be necessarily linked to resources. In developed countries, there are pockets in society in which we find levels of maternal mortality resembling those of countries with very poor indicators, and, by way of contrast, in nonperforming least developed countries the better off enjoy the same safety in childbirth as in the countries with the best figures. The human rights approach compels us to look at maternal mortality globally, and not solely focused on regions and countries shouldering the highest burden.

1.3 There are solutions for the problem

We know the causes and they are clustered around the period of delivery as illustrated in Figure 1.2. They reflect poor care during labor, the delivery itself, and the immediate postpartum. Special attention should be drawn to the consequences of unsafe abortion, which, at 13%, contributes a high proportion, particularly taking into consideration the denial and the context of legal constraints that the reporting incur.

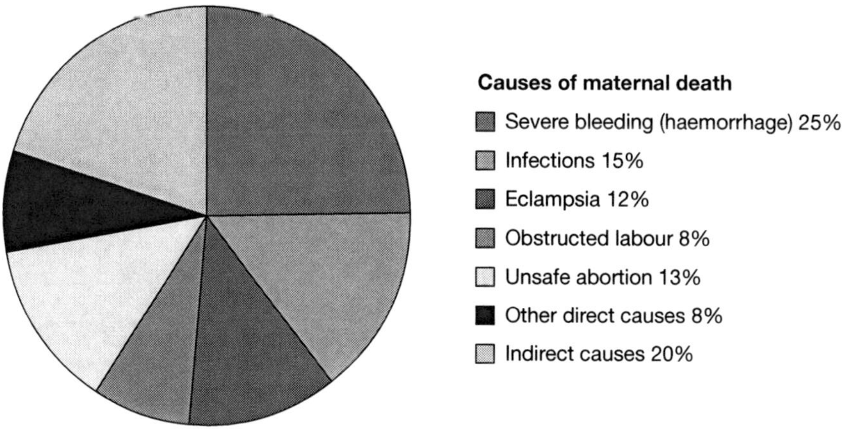

Figure 1.2 Causes of maternal death

Source: World Health Report (2005) Make every mother and child count. Geneva: World Health Organization

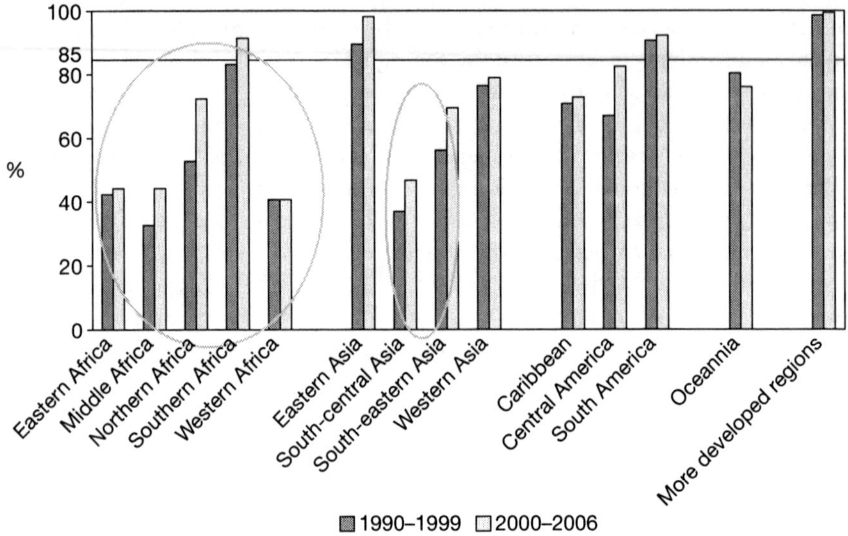

Figure 1.3 Skilled Health Worker at Birth, Blue line–ICPD target for 2010
Source: WHO skilled birth attendants, 2008 update

There are well-established effective interventions to treat and prevent these conditions, but the main issue is the weakness of the health systems, which are not responsive and with low coverage. Limited access to good-quality services is the main problem, and again the most disadvantaged as listed earlier bear most of the consequences. Taking the case of the availability of skilled birth attendants, we notice that the regions with the worst indicators have the lowest coverage of this crucial cadre to guarantee safe pregnancy and delivery, as well as a healthy newborn. Figure 1.3 does show that in some sub-regions, the number of skilled birth attendants did not increase at all over two decades.[6]

1.4 It can be done

The situation can be changed; it requires vision, leadership, and priority setting aimed at addressing the inequities. Money is important, but it is not the single determining factor. Malaysia, Sri Lanka, and Thailand have made dramatic reductions in maternal mortality in the order of 62–73% over a period of 10 years. They addressed the social aspects in a comprehensive manner, paying attention to the injustices against women, schooling extensive to women and the consistent implementation of effective interventions with

6 WHO, *Skilled birth attendants*, 2008 update.

Table 1.2 Reduction of MMR in three countries

	1960	*1970*	*% decline*
	MMR, deaths per 1000,000 live births		
Malaysia	250	150	66
Sri Lanka	260	150	73
Thailand	420	260	62

Note: Kerala (India): figures for 2006 – MMR of 95 when for the whole of India is 254. Currently, Malaysia 29, Sri Lanka 35, Thailand 48

focus on skilled attendance at birth training of midwives and adequate deployment to ensure good coverage, thus guaranteeing good access to all. The state of Kerala in India is doing extremely well, the fact that it does not feature in the group of the richest states notwithstanding; in 2010 it had an MMR of 95/100,000 live births when, for the whole of India, the figure was 254/100,000 live births. People's participation in the political process, empowerment of women, significant investment in education with special attention to girls, and strengthening of the health system centered on primary healthcare are the main factors contributing to success.[7]

In all the examples presented, political drive from the top and vision, together with consistency in policy setting and program development in a long-term perspective have been key ingredients; as shown on Table 1.2, these reductions happened between 1960 and 1970 when the three countries were still poor and not the upper-middle income countries of today. Indeed, their investment in the social sectors and health in particular were important pillars for the level of development they reached. A similar background is found in Kerala, where equity has been an important guiding principle in running state affairs.

1.5 Progress is slow: we need concerted and consequential action

One of the targets of Goal 5 of the Millennium Development Goals (MDGs) is to reduce the maternal mortality ratio by three-quarters as compared to the 1990 figure. 2015 is the critical year by which the target should be met, but the slow progress does indicate that many countries will miss the target by a large margin. Globally, the annual percentage of decline of MMR between 1990 and 2005 was 0.4% when the required rate of decline in order to reach

7 International Institute of Population Services (IIPS) and Macro International, *National family health survey (NFHS-3) 2005–06 India: volume I*, Mumbai: IIPS, 2007. Babu Patel, Where is the 'M' in MCH?, Regional Health Forum – WHO South East Asia Region, 2006, vol. 4.

the target is 5.5%.[8] The positive and encouraging figures of the new estimates showing the trend from 1990 to 2010 should be read with caution. There was a 47% decline in the MMR, but of the 181 countries analyzed for the report only 19 have either achieved the goal already or are on track.[9]

We need to accelerate change and get all the actors geared to move from the state of complacency and sometimes neglect, and take the required action to change the current situation with appalling figures. The statistics of maternal health have to be presented in a way that is easy to understand by everyone, and reflecting the level of care received, exposing the inequities. An awakening signal has to be put across to sensitize the communities and civil society organizations; in many poor communities, particularly in the least developed countries, dying in child birth is regarded as "normal" and "expected" with dozens of women passing away silently. It is this resignation that has to be overcome, and this can only happen if the information is presented in a practical way where people can easily see that in one community there are disproportionally more maternal deaths than in the advantaged communities.

Disaggregation of data is the way to achieve this, so that communities together with the civil society organizations can take matters into their own hands and demand change and the provision of the required services. By the same token, advice should be given to parliaments, so that they will understand the gravity of the problem and the dimension of human rights violation that a death of a woman in childbirth carries; maternal mortality figures should be regarded as key indicators of the level of response of governments to their people, and parliamentarians are the people's representatives and have the power to control government activities. The active involvement of the Inter-Parliamentary Union (IPU) is a welcome development that will certainly contribute to raise awareness, and eventually elicit adequate action from the lawmakers. Likewise, we are witnessing much more concerted action by important political bodies and regional organizations, as is the case with the African Union, which places health quite high on the agenda; for instance, at the Heads of State and Government Summit in 2010, maternal, neonatal, and child health was the theme of the conference.

Human rights should be made an integral component of good governance and the existing important political instruments disseminated from the Universal Declaration of Human Rights to the Resolution 11/8 of June 2009 of the UN Human Rights Council. It is the lack of progress in the improvement of maternal health that triggered the Council to pass the resolution to elicit action from the states and their governments, and provide the framework to call them to account on human rights grounds.[10]

8 *Maternal mortality in* 2005, op. cit. *The Millennium Development Goals Report*, New York: United Nations, 2010.

9 *Trends in maternal mortality 1990 to 2010*, op. cit.

10 United Nations Human Rights Council Eleventh Session Resolution 11/8: preventable maternal mortality and morbidity and human rights, June 2009.

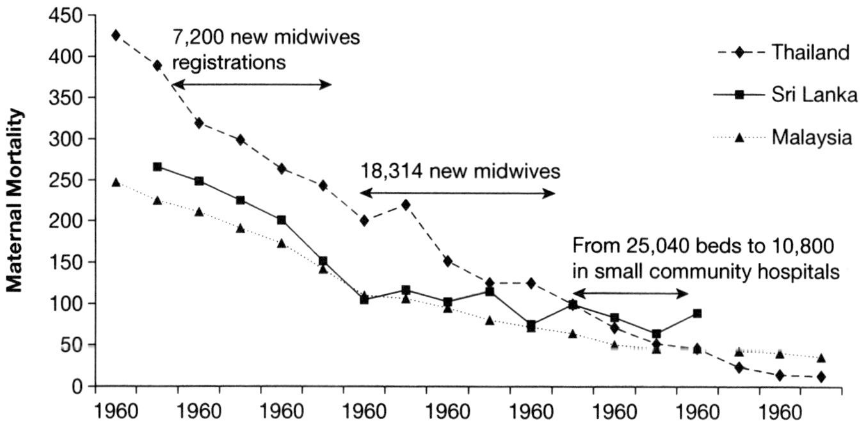

Figure 1.4 Maternal mortality since the 1960s in Malaysia, Sri Lanka, and Thailand

Source: van Lerberghe, W. and De Browere, V., cited in WHO World Health Report (2005)

International organizations can play an important role in facilitating the dissemination of these documents, as well as putting the maternal health figures in the regional and sub-regional contexts; this action can help in galvanizing action, as countries can learn from each other, and see clearly that it can be done in their own contexts with the resources available. Success stories from other regions would be an important complement to keep the momentum and provide opportunities for exchange of experiences focusing on the way change was achieved.

The situation is not satisfactory in terms of progress, but there are cases of countries making strides in the right direction, not able to go further due to limitation of resources. International solidarity is called for so that the countries in a position to assist do provide the needed resources and address the countries' development strategies with a long-term perspective. The situation is dire, and there are many countries that cannot achieve rapid change without external assistance. As we can see in Figure 1.4, change does not happen overnight; long-term sustained action is needed.[11]

Momentum has been created, however; as a result of joint effort from different partners facilitated by the Partnership for Maternal, Newborn and Child Health (PMNCH), the UN Secretary-General has added his weight to the fight in challenging world leaders to do their utmost to deliver for women and children, when he launched the *Global strategy* for women's and children's health in 2010. This will be a major lever in the complementary efforts to

11 W. Van Lerberghe and V. de Browere, Safe motherhood strategies: a review of evidence, *Studies in health services organization and policy*, Antwerp: ITG Press, 2001, vol. 17.

consolidate the activities already underway, and hopefully lead to a better expression of true solidarity rather than charity interventions.

Although we are addressing maternal mortality, it is important to interpret the suggestions presented as integrated in the overall healthcare approach in the context of the countries' development strategies.

The human rights approach to maternal mortality makes the argument more compelling, highlighting the injustice and inequities, and brings the accountability element. Advocacy to raise awareness, leadership from the top, proper monitoring to follow progress, and effective accountability at all levels is what we need to end the tragedy.

2 Citizen monitoring to promote the right to healthcare and accountability

Dr Ariel Frisancho

> When I went to the doctor at the hospital, he said: 'What is this about monitoring? We work hard here. Or would you like me to come to monitor you at home?' I told him, 'Excuse me, doctor, we are healthcare promoters and have been trained by the Ombudsman and the ForoSalud for monitoring. We know our rights. You cannot go to monitor my house, because it is private, but I can come to monitor the hospital, because it is a public institution, it is State-run. And here are my credentials.' 'Ok, come right in,' he told me. (Testimony of Nilda Chambi Monroy, healthcare monitor from Azángaro (Puno))

2.1 Introduction

In countries with as much inequality as Peru, where approximately one out of every two people is living in poverty, achieving the Millennium Development Goals (MDGs) on healthcare will not be possible with only technical interventions and increased resources allocated to healthcare. Significant and sustainable changes can only be achieved if Peruvians are more involved in the design and adjustment of social policies and the programmes that implement them, thus ensuring that their needs have been properly considered and addressed.

In general, officers and professionals who are responsible for formulating and implementing public policies to combat poverty still display a limited understanding and commitment to the right to healthcare and to citizen participation. At the beginning of this decade, according to estimates by the Ministry of Health (MOH), 25% of the Peruvian population (close to 6,500,000 people) lacked access to healthcare when it was needed.[1]

With respect to progress towards achieving the MDGs, it seems to be insufficient in terms of reducing maternal mortality to 66 per 100,000 live births,[2] despite the recent decline in the maternal mortality ratio reported by

1 Ministry of Health (2002) Sectorial policy guidelines for the 2002–2012 period, 14.
2 *The Lancet* 2008, 371.

the National Statistics and Information Institute – 265 maternal deaths per 100,000 live births in 1996, 183 in 2000 and 103 in the year 2008 (the last with a confidence interval of 50–120).[3]

The situation is aggravated by the deep and unfair differences in access to healthcare services that are capable of a comprehensive response to the needs and expectations of the population (that is, that are accessible, acceptable, culturally appropriate and of high technical quality), in the extension of knowledge and care of maternal and child health in the community, and in the absence of citizen participation of women in the design and implementation of healthcare policies. In poor rural areas, where there are heightened (high) conditions of vulnerability, maternal and neonatal death constitute a clear indicator of social exclusion faced by rural women living in poverty – especially indigenous women – but also of the structural deficiencies and the inequities that must be addressed by the healthcare system and by the national and regional authorities.[4] This requires not only technical interventions, but also placing priority on tackling these inequalities and on the effective involvement and the joint efforts of different stakeholders towards this goal.[5]

Healthcare programmes face the urgent need to be properly designed and targeted according to the real needs of the most vulnerable population. This requires new types of relationship among civil society coalitions, representatives of the poor and excluded, governmental authorities and those responsible for such programmes, which will contribute to democratic dialogue, governance, legitimacy and the sustainability of policies that are more inclusive and fair.

2.2 Description of the problem

Peru has been classified as a middle- to high-income country as a result of its economic progress during the past 20 years. However, two characteristics define the reality of its society: diversity and inequality. The interior of Peru still displays major inequities, discrimination and poverty, resulting in a high incidence of preventable disease and mortality among the poorest and most excluded, but also in the rural population living in the regions with little social and economic development.

The maternal mortality rate in Peru is among the highest in America. As indicated already, in 2000 the maternal mortality ratio was 183 maternal deaths per 100,000 live births, which in absolute numbers represents more

3 Demography and Family Health Survey (ENDES), National Statistics and Information Institute – INEI, 1996, 2000, 2009.

4 Physicians for Human Rights, Deadly delays: maternal mortality in Peru. A rights-based approach to safe motherhood, 2007. Available online at http://physiciansforhumanrights.org/library/report-2007-11-28.html.

5 A. Frisancho, Comment to the editor on the study of MC Hogan, KJ Foreman, M Naghavi, et al.: maternal mortality for 181 countries, 1980–2008: a systematic analysis of progress towards Millennium Development Goal 5, *Lancet* 375, 2010, 1609–1623.

than 1250 deaths per year.[6] However, national averages hide a discriminatory and unjust situation: there is an unacceptable gap between the regions with better socioeconomic conditions and those that are poorer: maternal mortality rates for that year in the regions of Puno, Huancavelica, Cuzco and Huánuco were 361, 302, 288 and 272 maternal deaths per 100,000 live births, respectively.[7] This correlates with the high percentages of the population living in poverty: while an average of 52% of Peru's population was living in poverty in 2007, this figure was 85.7% in Huancavelica, 67.2% in Puno, 64.9% in Huánuco and 57.4% in Cusco.[8] These higher levels of maternal mortality among poor populations in the Peruvian highlands and jungle evidence a profound social injustice and gender inequality: in Peru, the right to a healthy and safe motherhood is still denied to a share of the population that is mostly indigenous women, the poor and those in the most remote rural areas.

Despite recent progress in the increase of institutional deliveries and reducing the maternal mortality ratio, due in large part to different policies implemented by the Peruvian Ministry of Health (MoH) to address the barriers faced by pregnant women in poor and remote populations of country, the rate of decline in maternal mortality does not seem to be sufficient to achieve Goal 5 of the Millennium Development Goals related to its reduction.

In order to reduce the economic barriers that limit access to healthcare services for children and pregnant women living in poverty and extreme poverty, the MoH implemented in 1997 and 1999 so-called 'public insurance' for school-aged children, pregnant women and newborns, respectively. The two schemes were united in 2001, constituting the integral health insurance (SIS), all being cost reimbursement mechanisms for healthcare services. The current government has announced the future expansion of this modality to promote a system of 'universal insurance'. However, there are challenges related to the quality of care – and particularly the treatment of users of healthcare services – that have not been resolved. Moreover, despite the SIS having existed for 10 years, there is still a rejection by women to use healthcare services due to the mismatch between the 'western' characteristics of the services offered and the expectations of the women and men in rural communities.[9]

The insecurity and rejection to go to the health facilities is accentuated by frequent episodes of mistreatment of users of healthcare services; mistreatment is worse for female, poor, indigenous and non-Spanish-speaking users. Various studies look at the issue of abuse and illegal charges – 'fines' for not giving

6 Demography and Family Health Survey 2000, INEI, May 2001, 122.
7 Teresa Watanabe Varas, *Trends, levels and structure of maternal mortality in Peru. 1992–2000*, INEI, 2002.
8 National Statistics and Information Institute. Annual National Household Survey: 2004–2007.
9 Amnesty International Peru: *Poor and excluded women – denial of the right to maternal and child health*, 2006, 26–30.

birth in the facility[10] or charges for medicines and transport that the 'insurance' should cover – as serious problems that threaten the dignity and rights of these people, and that limit or deny the acceptability of the healthcare services.[11, 12, 13] The existence of a single healthcare provider for the poorest people, and the unequal and inequitable power relations that exist between healthcare workers and the users of such services, aggravate this situation:

> The ladies say that they cannot talk during the healthcare consultancies, because the doctor attends to them quickly and doesn't listen to what they want to say. Sometimes doctors don't even look at their face and don't know who they are treating. We have to tell them that there must be good care, asking the patient's name, talking calmly with women and, if possible, in Quechua, and asking how they feel. That is the attention we want. (Testimony of Benilda Huayta Mamani, health monitor in Azángaro)

These facts, which seem to be unknown – or in the end, accepted – by the authorities in charge, result in a poor prognosis for the proposed 'universal health insurance' if its design relies solely on efforts of the services offered. A collective, informed and organized – in sum, empowered – voice is needed to deal with these unfair situations of exclusion and the significant levels of 'leakage' in the implementation of the SIS, which ends up benefiting those who do have resources to pay for their healthcare.

Contrariwise, although the still incomplete process of decentralization has facilitated the creation of new spaces for dialogue and agreement on regional and local policies, it needs to strengthen these still limited mechanisms and contribute to a better balance of power within to promote changes in social policies that respond to the needs of the most marginalized and vulnerable groups of the population. At the same time, civil society actors should implement alternative mechanisms for dialogue: mechanisms of citizen monitoring and the promotion of accountability by state officers. They should also promote a legal framework to facilitate the demand for the right to healthcare and citizen participation.

2.3 Citizen monitoring and public policies

Citizen healthcare monitoring is a mechanism of citizen participation in which organized and informed people develop activities aimed at monitoring

10 Ibid., 26–30.
11 Ibid., 21.
12 Peruvian Ministry of Health, *Healthcare letter: listening to the voice of population. Crusade for citizenship rights and responsibilities in healthcare*, General Office of Communications – Healthcare Rights Program (CARE Peru), 2006.
13 PHR USA, *Deadly delays: maternal mortality in Peru. A human rights approach to safe motherhood*, 2007.

and verifying compliance with the duties, obligations and commitments of the state authorities and public servants in the healthcare of the population. Citizen monitoring promotes transparency and accountability, characteristics of good governance and democracy.

There has been increased international consensus in recent years on the vital importance of citizen participation to ensure the legitimacy and sustainability of social policies. It is assumed that social policies that have been generated or developed in a participatory manner will have greater legitimacy and sustainability and will better promote development and social control of their implementation. This is true not only in terms of better governance, but also for the healthcare rights approach. In this regard, and due to the realization of the third National Health Conference organized by ForoSalud (2006), Paul Hunt, United Nations Special Rapporteur on the Right to Health, issued a public statement in which he highlighted:

> The right to health not only emphasizes the importance of reducing the burden of disease and damage to health and the conditions for a healthy life, but also involves the importance of this goal being achieved through processes that are democratic and inclusive.[14]

He also stated that the right to health requires processes in which citizens exercise their right to participation, and that this participation, in turn, opens spaces for a group of processes of development and citizen empowerment.

Likewise, the World Bank, in its 2004 *World development report*,[15] presented a conceptual framework to analyse the performance of social sectors and to better understand the causes of their performance, particularly the institutional factors affecting the performance of services, highlighting the relationship between three main actors: public policymakers, the providers and the citizen-users.

Public policymakers are the different levels of government (national, regional and local), with the health facilities, including managers of the facilities and the healthcare personnel, being the providers. The population and its various groups are the citizens-users. The relationships among these three groups of actors are seen in the 'triangle of accountability' (see Figure 2.1).

According to this approach, citizens can influence better performance and responsiveness of healthcare services and facilities (and achieve health policies that better address their needs) through the so-called political 'voice' (the relationship between citizens organized into groups or networks and policymakers at different levels of government) or through the empowerment of the

14 Paul Hunt, special United Nations Rapporteur for the Right to Healthcare. Public statement for the Third National Healthcare Conference, Lima, July 2006.

15 World Bank *World development report*, Washington, DC, February 2004.

users of healthcare services and consequent social pressure placed directly on the suppliers.

Figure 2.1 adapts the World Bank's approach to Peru's healthcare sector. Added are different 'inputs' through which the different actors of the state and civil society act to encourage greater citizen participation, which is the road to better healthcare governance.

The so-called 'long route' – the construction and development of *political voice* to influence people in charge of healthcare policy nationally and regionally through citizens' coalitions or civil society networks – highlights the development that, in the last 12 years, has been shown by the Peruvian Civil Society Forum on Health, the ForoSalud, and other citizen groups (networks of patients/users of healthcare services, groups of people living with certain health conditions or diseases). The so-called 'short route' – the direct interaction of citizens with those responsible for healthcare services – in addition to CLAS (created in 1994, through which citizens elected by the population join a committee to plan and manage the resources of the local healthcare facilities) and the participatory budget, highlights the role played by initiatives of citizen monitoring of healthcare services.

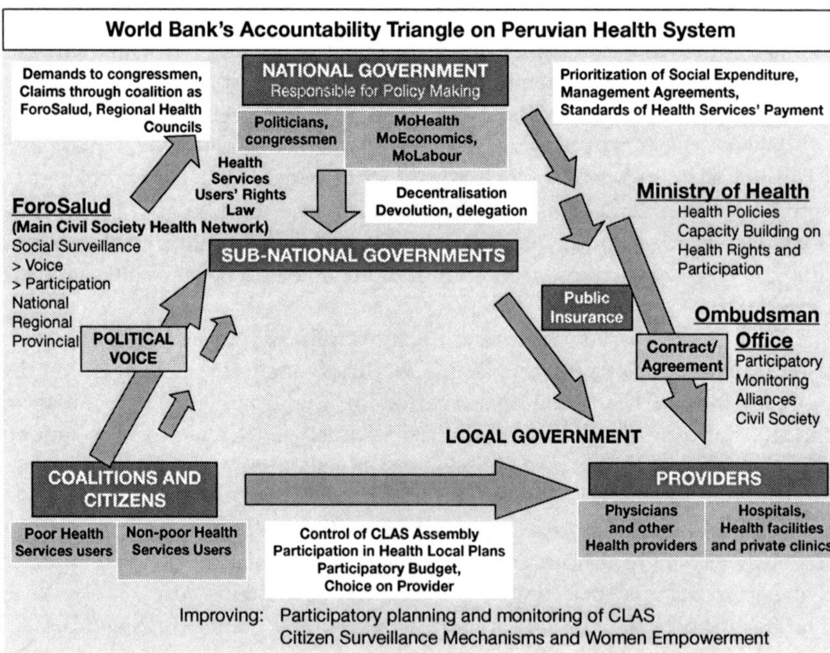

Figure 2.1 World Bank's accountability triangle on the Peruvian health system

Source: D. Fernandez Frisancho, A. Frisancho, adapting World Bank figure, in D. Cotlear (ed.) (2006) *A new social contract for Peru: an agenda for improving education, healthcare, and the social safety net*, World Bank, p. 194

2.4 An actor-oriented approach for the promotion of accountability

The Participatory Voices Project (April 2008–March 2011) was a joint effort between CARE Peru and CARE UK in the framework of a programme partnership agreement with the United Kingdom's Ministry for International Development (DFID). Its objective was 'to strengthen the capacities of national and regional civil society networks for the implementation of strategies and mechanisms of social monitoring and political advocacy to improve the policies and programs on healthcare and social development'.

The project worked with a wide range of actors, from both the public sector and civil society, seeking to strengthen governance in health and the incorporation of a rights-based approach in public actions. Its working approach prioritized four strategies:

1. Strengthening capacities of civil society networks and state officers and public authorities to facilitate improved interaction, dialogue and negotiation.
2. Identification and association with key actors at the national, regional and local levels who share the rights-based approach and who may promote the sustainability of actions.
3. Building partnerships with non-governmental organizations, international cooperation agencies, grassroots social organizations, civil society networks and key international actors.
4. Political incidence and technical assistance to the Ministry of Health, Congress, regional and local authorities and other public actors in order to improve the responsiveness of the healthcare system to the poorest and most vulnerable population.

One of the main lines of action developed by the project was to build alliances with civil society networks, grassroots social organizations and the Office of the Ombudsman to strengthen citizen participation, particularly for the implementation of mechanisms for citizen monitoring of the quality of maternal and child healthcare services that are provided to poor, rural Andean women.

The initiative began as a pilot in early 2008. It was based on the joint work experience of CARE Peru and ForoSalud – the largest civil society network on health in Peru – in the development of capacities for a greater presence and ability to impact healthcare policy. Added to this was the joint initiative with the organization Physicians for Human Rights USA. CARE Peru and PHR-USA allocated resources to promote a pilot for citizen participation in oversight and advocacy of quality in maternal and child healthcare services in two provinces of Puno (Melgar and Ayaviri), favouring: (a) building strategic alliances between CARE Peru, ForoSalud and the Office of the Ombudsman, and (b) strengthening of rural women leaders who would develop processes of citizen monitoring. The initiative looked to propel the mobilization and involvement of key actors at the local and regional levels: the regional government of Puno, the regional health directorate, the regional office of the ombudsman, ForoSalud, and the networks of Promoters and Defenders of the Sexual and Reproductive Rights.[16]

The pilot initiative culminated in April and continued in action in the context of the Participatory Voices Project until March 2011. Currently, the model of citizen monitoring of the quality of maternal and child health services has been taken by the Ministry of Health as one of the bases for the formulation of national policies to promote public healthcare monitoring[17] and it is spreading, in partnership with ForoSalud, to four regions of the country with support from CARE UK and the European Union. Likewise, the capacity-building model of citizen monitoring has been adopted by the Peruvian MoH for national extension of the experience, and by the United Nations Population Fund (UNFPA) for the promotion and implementation of citizen monitoring of maternal healthcare, in partnership with women's organizations in two other regions of Peru.

2.4.1 Stages and processes of the citizen monitoring

On the basis of the experience gained, the model of citizen healthcare monitoring comprises four broad stages (see Figure 2.2):

1 The organization and comprehensive planning of activities by the technical supporting team (in this case, CARE Peru, the ForoSalud and the Puno Office of the Ombudsman).
2 The public announcement, selection and capacity building of the members of the future monitoring committees and the planning of their activities.
3 Implementation of field activities (visits to health facilities, analysis of the findings and reaching commitments for improvement by the authorities).
4 The monitoring of the commitments and evaluation of the proceedings.

In turn, every stage can be divided into processes.

16 Regarding the last, it is noteworthy that the experience of working with sexual and reproductive rights' defenders is the product of 10 years' work by the ReproSalud Project (USAID-Movimiento Manuela Ramos), which formed promoters and defenders of sexual and reproductive rights with the aim that women know their rights, and defend them, through schemes of monitoring and negotiation with their husbands, community authorities and healthcare providers in their establishments. These networks of advocates for sexual and reproductive rights remain active.

17 Ministry of Health of Peru, *Guidelines for health policy in citizen healthcare monitoring*, R.M. 040-2011/MINSA, 14 January 2011.

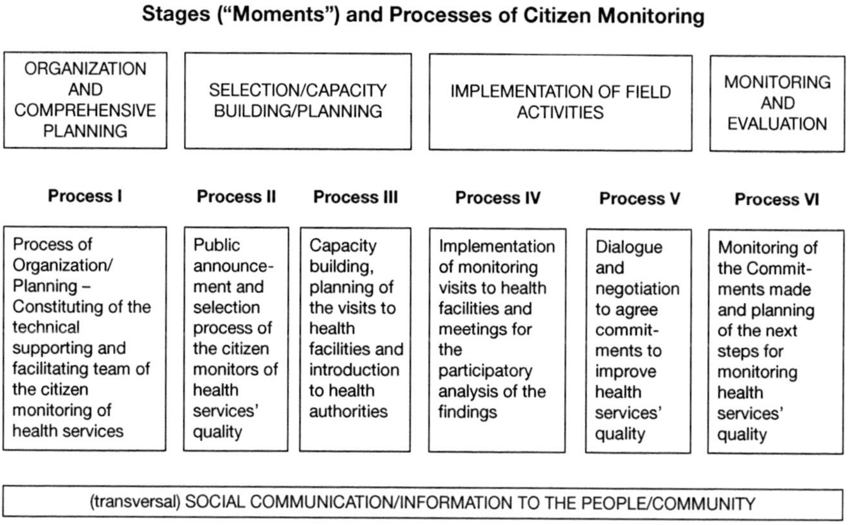

Figure 2.2 Stages (moments) and processes of citizen monitoring

2.4.1.1 Organization and comprehensive planning of the activities by the technical supporting team

In this stage, we can highlight the constitution of the technical supporting and facilitating team of citizen healthcare monitoring and the comprehensive planning of the activities.

For this, after presenting the idea of the initiative and after several joint planning sessions, an agreement was signed between the Office of the Ombudsman, CARE Peru and ForoSalud Puno. They agreed on the main components of the model, the roles of each organization in capacity building and the support for activities to be undertaken by future monitors. The various lines of action were planned, including the call for women community leaders, the visits for introducing the initiative to the authorities, the frequency of meetings to analyse the findings and presentation of the results of the monitoring to the healthcare authorities.

2.4.1.2 Public announcement, the selection and capacity building of the women members of the citizen monitoring committees and the planning of their activities

This stage includes both the public announcement, which is open to the leaders in each town of the district (radio announcement and through personal communication with the community leaders), and the capacity building for citizen monitoring, which incorporates the selection of members of the monitoring committees for each prioritized facility and the planning of its 'field' activities.

Because several female community leaders were integrated in the large regional network of the Puno ForoSalud, contact could be resumed quickly, and then design in a participatory manner how the citizen monitoring initiative could be implemented to improve the quality of healthcare services, increase the demand for timely health services and thus help reduce maternal mortality.

On the basis of the joint analysis, the women, the CARE facilitators and the Office of the Ombudsman identified the two provinces for the development of citizen monitoring, Azángaro and Melgar – these were provinces with extreme poverty, with about 95% rural population, a high number of maternal and child deaths and a history of constant complaints from the users because of the treatment received by poor women in the health facilities. Working together, the facilities in which the citizen monitoring activity would be taken, the number of people from each province who would perform these activities in their local health centers, and a possible working schedule, which included the training activities, were tentatively identified.

The topics for training were developed in modules, and the times were adapted to the convenience of the leaders (in this case, weekly meetings on two consecutive days). The meetings were held in Quechua and Spanish or in Aymara and Spanish, depending on the group, because several leaders needed to use their native language for understanding and building conceptual elements from their experience. The facilitators also used different participatory methods based on self-reflection, which allowed the participants to build, for example, the concepts of human rights, democracy and citizenship, and to analyse the role to play in promoting better treatment, a greater respect for their culture in healthcare services and respect for the right to quality in their care.

In short, the issues covered in the capacity building were human rights, healthcare rights, elements of democracy and citizenship, sexual and reproductive health and rights, organization and operation of healthcare services, the rights of SIS users, citizen participation and citizen monitoring, access to information, laws that protect citizen monitoring, ministerial norms on vertical delivery with cultural adaptation and the free issuance of the certificate of live birth. After each training workshop, practical cases were analysed on how rights were or were not respected in healthcare, what legal framework protects people in case of their not being respected and, finally, to reflect on what role the monitors would have to promote quality and rights in healthcare services.

At the end of the training workshops, the profile of the community leaders that would perform the monitoring was defined in a participatory manner; the content and shape (layout) of the formats (tools) used to gather information during the visits to the health facilities; how the monitors would self-introduce themselves within the health facilities; and also the way in which they would conduct the monitoring activity in each health facility. Once these issues were defined, the monitors were selected for both provinces. Among the *selection criteria* agreed on with them were the time available for monitoring, their proximity to health facilities, the interest shown by each participant, the knowledge gained in the training workshops, as well as their commitment and perseverance. The schedule of visits to health facilities is made with the selected monitors, as well as the frequency and dates of the meetings to discuss the findings, together with the ForoSalud, CARE Peru and the Office of the Ombudsman.

2.4.1.3 Implementation of field activities

This stage includes the visits to the facilities as well as the meetings for participatory analysis of the findings and the agreement on commitments for improvement by the authorities.

One step prior to the monitoring visits to health facilities occurs after the schedule of visits is defined: the monitors are given an ID provided and signed by the three organizations that facilitate the process. Joint visits are also planned to the regional health authorities, as well as to the hospital and health micro-networks, in order to present the initiative, explain its objectives and scope, and obtain their support.

The monitors visit the health facilities in pairs two to three times per week, and remain for approximately six hours. They perform direct observation and talk with other women in their own language. They consult and observe compliance with the schedules of the healthcare personnel, consult with the users regarding how they were treated by the staff, if they did not have to wait long, if they were given information about their condition in their own language and in a way they could understand, if their culture was respected along the healthcare provided, if rights to free care were respected, if they were given clear information on the functioning of the SIS and their rights in the program, if there were drugs in the pharmacy, and if the examinations ordered by healthcare professionals were performed, among other things – which are those most often mentioned as important by the users of healthcare services themselves.

Next, the monitors inform them about their rights as users of healthcare services or, for example, which free services they are eligible for if they are users registered with the SIS. Their observation, together with the direct and trusting dialogue with the users, and the knowledge developed in the training activities, permit them to detect erroneous and exclusionary practices – such as the lack of immediate attention of women insured by the SIS, or discrimination, neglect and extensive waiting time by the poor, Quechua-speaking, and rural women – and even illegal actions, such as improper charges (under-the-table payments) to the beneficiaries of JUNTOS Program (which provides conditional cash transfers to poor families). All these observations are registered in the formats they were trained to fill out and that they helped to design. At the conclusion of monitoring activity, they request the leaders of the facility and the health personnel they worked with, to sign the monitoring formats as proof of their visit and of their findings.

Each of the women monitors accumulates a minimum of four to eight visits a month; in some cases it may be more, depending on their time availability. Every two to three months, meetings are held among the women monitors in each province with the representative of the Office of the Ombudsman in Puno, and the members of ForoSalud and the director of the CARE Peru Participatory Voices Project to discuss the findings of the citizen monitoring, and to formulate and prioritize the proposals that are brought to the meeting by the monitors and those responsible for the healthcare service networks ('dialogue agenda'). In addition, the monitors report on how they felt while performing the monitoring, the doubts and fears they felt, the dialogues they had with the workers at the health facility, and the findings they raised in the monitoring. Each of the monitors (called 'vigilantes') presents an oral report of the most important aspects of the monitoring, report on the attitude with which the providers received the monitors, noting precisely the facts on the basis of the records made, providing names, dates and descriptions of events. The whole group shares and discusses the experiences, clarifies data that may be needed for the development of activities and makes decisions on how to improve the monitoring.

For example, given the finding by the Office of the Ombudsman in Puno on the ignorance of most healthcare teams of the rules and laws that protect and safeguard the rights of people in healthcare, a file was prepared – to be carried by each pair of monitors – with copies of the main rules and legal norms (norms on vertical delivery with cultural adaptation, free issuance of the certificate of live birth, laws that protect citizens' participation at the national, regional and local levels, etc.).

The dialogue with healthcare officials and providers is the space for discussions and agreements, non-existent until the implementation of citizen monitoring, in which the 'dialogue agenda' constructed with the participation of the monitors and the facilitating organizations is taken, together with its proposed solutions, to these internal spaces of negotiation with the local and regional healthcare authorities and with those in charge of the facilities, to agree on commitments for improvement. In these spaces, the monitors and the facilitating organizations highlight both the good findings (to strengthen and compliment them) and the bad ones (to correct them).

These spaces, initially resisted by many healthcare professionals, have become institutionalized, despite the frequent change of healthcare authorities and directors of micro-networks, which has often meant starting over with the work of sensitization and advocacy to try to ensure the fulfilment of commitments. A major breakthrough has occurred in some micro-network managers, who have even requested training for their healthcare staff on issues of health rights and citizen participation.

2.4.1.4 Monitoring of the commitments made

Monitoring is conducted on the basis of the minutes signed by the authorities present at the consultation meetings. Public hearings are being planned that will be attended by local authorities and the press media and highlight the progress being achieved. Finally, a participatory assessment is periodically performed of the initiative's achievements, progress and challenges. Recently the monitors themselves selected 10 leaders from among themselves who developed participatory research on their achievements and challenges.[18]

Finally, it is important to note that social communication and information for people about their healthcare rights constitutes a cross-cutting strategy. Simultaneous with the implementation of citizen monitoring activities, it provides information to the rural population on their right to good healthcare, particularly with respect to sexual and reproductive health. One of the initiatives developed by the community leaders, and facilitated by the Puno ForoSalud and CARE Peru, has been the production of radio messages – in Quechua and Aymara – on the rights of users of healthcare services, what to do to prevent maternal mortality, the importance of citizen participation and the role of monitoring and having the active involvement of the monitors. This material is distributed to local radio stations, and is broadcast by the local programmes with the largest audience in the rural communities of each province. In a second stage of this process, the production of radio messages aimed at the regional level is planned, with the support of the regional health directorate for their dissemination.

Figure 2.3 shows Eusebia, an Ayaviri monitor, explaining the various processes developed to implement citizen healthcare monitoring. At her side are some of the Ayaviri monitors next to the representative of the Puno Office of the Ombudsman, the coordinator of the Dialogue Assembly for the Fight against Poverty (*Mesa de Concertación de Lucha Contra la Pobreza*), and the Puno head of Integral Health Insurance (SIS), an organization that has joined to the partners of the technical supporting team.

2.5 Main results of the experience

The results were found to be as follows:

- The identification of bad practices that prevent rural women from seeking care (for example, health services that are closed at times of peak demand, long waiting times, poor care, ignorance of standards that promote culturally appropriate vertical delivery and improper charges for services and medicines that should be free).

18 R. Zapata, *Systematization of the activity-research initiative on governance with a gender focus: impact of health monitoring and participatory budgeting by women in Puno, Peru*, Lima: CARE UK, 2011.

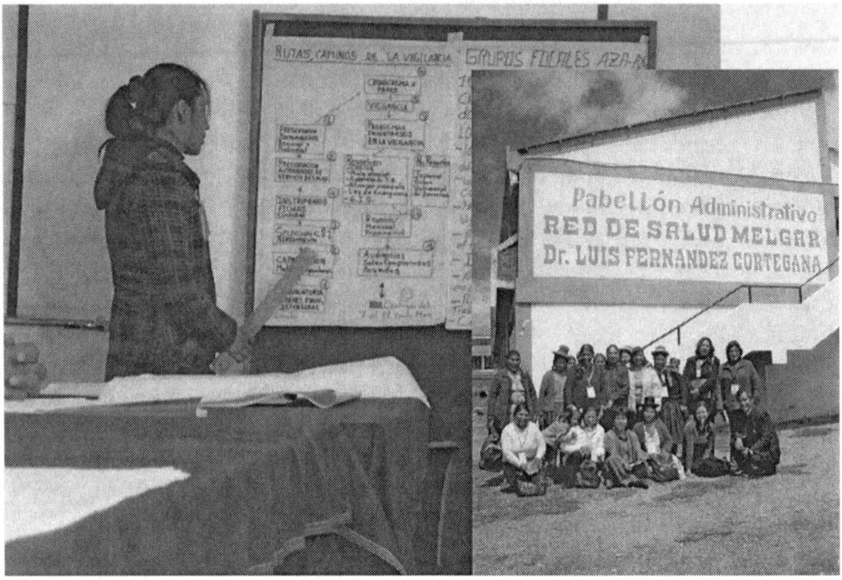

Figure 2.3 Developing implementation of citizen healthcare monitoring

- The existence of systematic spaces for dialogue and local consultation between healthcare providers and rural women, in which they express what they expect from healthcare services and the strengths and weaknesses of existing healthcare.
- The agreement of commitments for the improvement of healthcare (opportunity, treatment, information, language, culture).
- The initiative has contributed to the *empowerment* of women and to address unjust power relations between health providers and rural women.
- The initiative has contributed to a better understanding of the rights of users of healthcare services.
- Healthcare providers and authorities are accountable for their successes and shortcomings with respect to the needs of the population.

The qualitative assessment of the experience[19] has shown that those challenges in terms of the quality of service that were most frequently mentioned:

- medications missing or incompletely delivered to the SIS users
- poor treatment of the users, especially in the case of poor and indigenous women
- discrimination

19 C. Saavedra, *Evaluación cualitativa de la iniciativa de vigilancia ciudadana de la calidad de los servicios de salud en la provincia de Melgar*, Lima: CARE Peru, 2011.

- improper (under-the-table payments) charges
- healthcare services with limited cultural appropriateness.

Analysing the achievements of citizen monitoring, the most frequently mentioned changes are:

- It has improved the treatment received by women users of the services.
- Greater acceptance and promotion of culturally appropriate practices within healthcare at the time of delivery. Thus, the husband may be present, one can 'bind' the head of the women during childbirth (given the belief that there would be a 'division' of the woman's body, and they want to maintain the unity of the head).
- Not washing them with cold water (given the implications of the balance between hot and cold in the Andean region).
- The number of students entering the delivery room has been reduced (usually 8–10 medical and obstetric interns entered to learn from a single patient).
- Access to laboratory auxiliary exams has increased.

Citizen monitoring has contributed to improvements in the organization of the services:

- The citizen monitoring initiative has contributed to an increase in the allocation of healthcare workers and a better enforcement of working hours (by placing the roll of the doctors' working hours in in a prominent, visible location).
- Place the prices of medicines and procedures in a prominent location.
- Provide receipts for all payments made by the users.
- Use of the identification of the health personnel (something that is regulated, but not enforced).

Also mentioned is the improved relationship and cooperation between leaders and health personnel, especially since the monitors provide information and orient users of health services – especially rural and poor women – on the importance of their controls and the implementation of best practices in taking care of one's own health.

Highlights of other improvements include the increased attention to the right to health by health authorities, community members and public opinion. Also worth mentioning are the increased demand for institutional delivery and maternal/child healthcare, as well as a clear perception of improvement in issues that are sensitive to the population with respect to the quality of care.[20, 21]

20 Ibid.
21 R. Zapata, op. cit.

The focus groups conducted with various stakeholders show a clear perception of the benefits of citizen monitoring and the positive changes generated through its implementation over the years. These changes and benefits are not only identified by the monitors and their partner organizations and other observers, but also by the authorities and healthcare personnel themselves at different levels of the healthcare system. However, there is still a long way to go before doctors and other healthcare professionals recognize the problems faced by the healthcare users, since some only recognize the lack of drugs, while arguing that it 'does not depend on them'.

The quantitative evaluation of citizen health monitoring[22] and the participatory action research on citizen monitoring shows a variety of positive changes in the healthcare services where citizen health monitoring was implemented. The changes were evident when comparing variations in the indicators before and after the intervention and comparing these same indicators in health facilities with citizen monitoring and control facilities. The evaluation showed improved progress in healthcare indicators, both when analysed as a group of facilities with citizen monitoring and when analysed individually. The main differences are observed in (a) the opportunity of the control of the pregnant mother (early control), (b) the coverage of prenatal control, (c) care during institutional delivery, and (d) access to laboratory tests provided by comprehensive health insurance (SIS). Quantitative data showed increased access to culturally appropriate birth delivery – vertical birth delivery – from 194 in 2008 to 437 in 2009 in Azangaro Province.

Moreover, this work has contributed to the institutionalization of citizen surveillance as part of Peru's national policy and the launch in 2011 of National Policy Guidelines to Promote Citizen Surveillance.

2.6 Conclusions (lessons learned)

a. In countries with a high level of inequality, the achievement of the MDGs in health will not be possible with simply more resources and technical interventions. Significant and sustainable change will only be achieved if people have a greater involvement in the design and adjustment of social policies and programmes and in their implementation. The citizen monitoring initiative provides lessons that can be transferred to the monitoring of the implementation of universal health insurance, the actual benefits (in service) of conditional cash transfers, the implementation of participatory budgeting and the monitoring of outputs-oriented budgets (OOBs or PPR in Spanish).
b. The key importance of strategic alliances with public (ombudsman and integral health insurance) and private (ForoSalud) actors to strengthen the capacity of rural women's agency and to address unequal power relations.

22 W. Valdez, *Evaluación cuantitativa de la vigilancia ciudadana de la calidad de los servicios de salud*, Lima: CARE Peru, 2011.

c. The principles of the international human rights framework have been used at the local level in an effort to strengthen the quality of care provided in healthcare services. This is particularly important following the resolution of the United Nations Human Rights Committee (June 2009), which states maternal mortality as a human rights concern.[23]
d. The importance of implementing an accountability approach based on dialogue and the promotion of good governance, rather than on 'naming and shaming': building mutual understanding, increasing trust and credibility among healthcare officers/professionals and citizen representatives.
e. There are still major challenges ahead. Among them are the low quality of local health management (in which leadership, as well as skills to manage and monitor the national/regional policies and their enforcement, have been lost) and the lack of definition of performance indicators. This is made worse by evidence of discrimination and the undervaluation of citizens' capacity for dialogue and negotiation. As already mentioned, the high turnover of officers and public authorities in the region affects the sustainability of commitments and local policies.

2.7 Promoting the political decision to support new forms of participation

One of the greatest achievements of political advocacy that this initiative has contributed to has been its becoming a national reference point for the issue of citizen monitoring of the quality of healthcare services. As a result of a visit to Azángaro in May 2008, the Minister of Health knew the monitors and their work personally. As a result of that and the technical assistance activities of CARE Peru, a first ministerial resolution was issued in recognition and support of the citizen health monitoring committees.[24]

Since then, CARE Peru has continued with the activities of political advocacy and technical assistance to the Ministry of Health. Together with other cooperation agencies, and on the basis of the experience of Puno, in January 2011 the National Policy Guidelines for the Promotion of Citizen Health Monitoring[25] were promulgated. Still to be done is a joint effort in which the Ministry of Health, the regional and local governments and the civil society networks converge to ensure implementation of these mechanisms of citizen participation. It is hoped that the citizen monitoring process becomes a process that contributes to the improved performance of the healthcare teams at different levels of management, delivery and governance of healthcare. Its implementation makes it possible that the expectations, perceptions and demands of the people provide feedback and enrich the performance of the

23 United Nations' Human Rights Council, *Resolution on preventable maternal mortality and morbidity and human rights*, A/HRC/11/L. 16/Rev.1, 16 June 2009.
24 Ministry of Health of Peru, R.M. 422-2008/MINSA, DA 133-2008-MINSA/DEST-V01.
25 R.M. 040-2011/MINSA, op. cit.

healthcare teams. In this view, citizen monitoring is a stimulus and catalyst for healthcare services' responsiveness that contributes to the health system's governance:

> Change does not happen overnight. I think that some doctors, nurses and midwives have begun to understand why we are doing this volunteer work . . . little by little, they will see that their work also improves this way. (Eusebia Atayupanqui, citizen health monitor from Ayaviri (Puno))

3 The role of indicators and benchmarks in reducing maternal mortality: the case of emergency obstetric care indicators

Samantha Lobis

3.1 Introduction

Indicators and benchmarks, central to strong monitoring systems, play an important role in the reduction of maternal mortality. Without grasping the scope and magnitude of the problem, without knowing whether critical interventions are available, accessible, acceptable, and having the desired effect, and without having standards against which to compare achievement or performance, governments' efforts to reduce maternal mortality would be futile. With strong monitoring systems in place, critical information related to maternal mortality can be generated and utilised to track progress, inform and adjust plans, programmes and policies, and contribute to a functioning and accountable health system.

A strong monitoring system comprises indicators and benchmarks that relate directly to the critical interventions along the causal pathway that can lead to a reduction in maternal deaths. Robust indicators should tell us where to focus our efforts and whether the required services are in place, accessible, of good quality, being used by women and having the desired impact. Benchmarks are key to knowing if we are on target and making progress towards reaching all women in need – and whether current conditions are sufficient for the reduction of maternal mortality. Strong benchmarks should always be based on the best evidence available.

In recent years, consensus has been reached regarding the key interventions that must be in place to reduce maternal mortality.[1] All women must have access to and utilise good-quality and acceptable family planning services; skilled attendance at birth; emergency obstetric care (EmOC); referral systems; and safe abortion services. To ensure a sustainable, reliable and equitably distributed supply of these services, all components must be integrated

1 L.P. Freedman, W.J. Graham, E. Brazier, J.M. Smith, T. Ensor, V. Fauveau, E. Themmen, S. Currie and K. Agarwal, Practical lessons from global safe motherhood initiatives: time for a new focus on implementation, *The Lancet* 370, 2007, 1383–1391. United Nations, *Global strategy for women's and children's health*, New York: United Nations, 2010.

into a dynamic, functioning health system. Strong and relevant indicators and benchmarks must correspond directly to this strategy. If women are using the services at recommended levels and we know that these services are of good quality, we can be confident that maternal deaths are being prevented. If we find that benchmarks are not being met, good indicators will help to show where we can intervene and respond to problems.

To effectively monitor progress towards the reduction of maternal mortality, many indicators have been developed and are being used by agencies, organisations and governments worldwide to measure key components of the interventions that have proved to reduce maternal mortality.[2] Some indicators that have been developed relate to the impact of interventions (such as the maternal mortality ratio), and others relate to the inputs, outputs, outcomes or processes of moving along the causal pathway to the desired impact.

This chapter focuses on one set of indicators that has been used extensively in the past decade to measure the availability, utilisation and quality of EmOC: the EmOC indicators.[3] The EmOC indicators represent a combination of process and outcome indicators.

3.2 Overview of the EmOC indicators

Originally issued by UNICEF, UNFPA and WHO in 1997 and updated 12 years later, the EmOC indicators are rooted in the fact that to reduce maternal mortality, all women with life-threatening obstetric complications must have access to good-quality EmOC services. They are fully described in *Monitoring emergency obstetric care: a handbook*.[4]

The EmOC indicators[5] provide information about whether there are enough facilities providing EmOC; whether these facilities are well distributed; whether enough women are using the facilities and if the right

2 J. Bertrand and G. Escudero, *Compendium of indicators for evaluating reproductive health programs – vol. 1: overview, indicators that crosscut programmatic areas*, Chapel Hill, NC, Measure Evaluation, 2002. J. Bertrand and G. Escudero, *Compendium of indicators for evaluating reproductive health programs – vol. 2: indicators for specific programmatic areas*, Chapel Hill, NC, Measure Evaluation, 2002. J. Healy, K. Otsea and J. Benson, Counting abortions so that abortion counts: indicators for monitoring the availability and use of abortion care services, *International Journal of Gynaecology & Obstetrics* 95, 2006, 209–220. United Nations, Report of the Special Rapporteur on the right of everyone to the enjoyment of the highest attainable standard of physical and mental health, Paul Hunt, *Commission on Human Rights, Sixty-second session, Item 10 of the provisional agenda*, Geneva: United Nations, 2006. World Health Organization, *National-level monitoring of the achievement of universal access to reproductive health – conceptual and practical considerations and related indicators*, Geneva: WHO, 2008. World Health Organization, *Packages of interventions for family planning, safe abortion care, maternal, newborn and child health*, Geneva: WHO, 2010. World Health Organization, UNFPA, UNICEF and AMDD, *Monitoring emergency obstetric care – a handbook,* Geneva: WHO, 2009.

3 World Health Organization, UNFPA, UNICEF and AMDD, *Monitoring emergency obstetric care – a handbook,* Geneva: WHO, 2009.

4 Ibid.

5 Ibid.

Table 3.1 EmOC indicators

Questions answered	*Indicator*	*Acceptable level*
Are there enough facilities providing EmOC? Are the facilities well distributed?	Availability of EmOC: basic and comprehensive care facilities	≥ 5 EmOC facilities (including ≥ 1 comprehensive EmOC facility) for every 500,000 population
	Geographical distribution of EmOC facilities	All subnational areas have ≥ 5 EmOC facilities (including ≥ 1 comprehensive EmOC facility) for every 500,000 population
Are enough women using the facilities? Are women with obstetric complications using the facilities? Are enough critical services being provided? Is the quality adequate?	Proportion of all births in EmOC facilities	Minimum acceptable level to be set locally
	Met need for EmOC	100% of women estimated to have major direct obstetric complications are treated in EmOC facilities
	Caesarean sections as a proportion of all births	5–15% of expected births are by caesarean section
	Direct obstetric case fatality rate	≤ 1% of women with direct obstetric complications in EmOC facilities die
	Intrapartum and very early neonatal death rate	Standard to be determined
	Proportion of maternal deaths due to indirect causes in EmOC facilities	No standard can be set

women – women with obstetric complications – are using them; whether there are enough critical services being provided; and, to some extent, whether the quality of services is adequate. Most of the EmOC indicators have established benchmarks that are based on the best data and estimates currently available. All the EmOC indicators can and should be disaggregated by any meaningful level of stratification such as subnational area, language group, and whether facilities are public or private to determine if there are problems with inequitable distribution or utilisation of services (see Table 3.1).

The EmOC indicators were created based on the fact that 75–80% of maternal deaths are due to seven major direct obstetric complications, namely haemorrhage; obstructed/prolonged labour; severe pre-eclampsia/eclampsia; postpartum sepsis; complications of abortion; ruptured uterus; and ectopic pregnancies.[6] Most obstetric complications cannot be predicted or prevented but all can be treated with EmOC.

For monitoring purposes, EmOC is operationally defined as a series of life-saving medical interventions or signal functions that help to describe the level of care being provided at a given facility and a facility's capacity to treat obstetric emergencies. The choice of specific clinical interventions considered

6 K.S. Khan, D. Wojdyla, L. Say, A.M. Gulmezoglu and P.F.A. Van Look, WHO analysis of causes of maternal death: a systematic review, *The Lancet* 367, 2006, 1066–1074.

Table 3.2 EmOC signal functions

Basic EmOC	*Comprehensive EmOC*
Parenteral antibiotics	Perform EmOC signal functions 1–7, plus:
Uterotonic drugs (e.g. parenteral oxytocin and ergometrine, misoprostol)	Surgery (e.g. caesarean section)
Parenteral anticonvulsants (e.g. magnesium sulphate)	Blood transfusion
Manual removal of placenta	
Removal of retained products (e.g. manual vacuum aspiration)	
Assisted vaginal delivery (e.g. vacuum extraction)	
Neonatal resuscitation (e.g. w/bag and mask)	

signal functions relates to the services required to treat the major direct obstetric complications that lead to the majority of maternal deaths.

The use of signal functions[7] stresses actual rather than theoretical functioning and is based on recent performance of these life-saving services. To provide a signal function there must be a health worker who is trained and authorised to perform the service; requisite drugs, supplies and equipment must be available; and there must be women who present with the complications that require these services. The performance of the signal functions over the last three months determines whether basic or comprehensive levels of EmOC are available at a given facility (see Table 3.2).

3.3 Application of the EmOC indicators

The EmOC indicators have been used in more than 40 countries in Africa, Asia and Latin America to assess need, establish baselines and to monitor progress towards the availability and utilisation of good-quality EmOC services. Analyses based on the indicators have been incorporated into national and subnational planning processes, informed policy development, and used to strengthen maternal health programmes around the world. The greatest strength of the EmOC indicators is helping to focus attention on what really needs to be done to reduce maternal mortality.

With the use of the EmOC indicators – globally, nationally and subnationally – we have learned that in countries with high maternal mortality, there is a shortage of EmOC facilities.[8] In one recent assessment

7 World Health Organization, UNFPA, UNICEF and AMDD, *Monitoring emergency obstetric care – a handbook*, op. cit.

8 A. Paxton, P. Bailey and S. Lobis, The United Nations process indicators for emergency obstetric care: reflections based on a decade of experience, *International Journal of Gynaecology & Obstetrics* 95, 2006, 192–208. A. Paxton, P. Bailey, S. Lobis and D. Fry, Global patterns

conducted in Ethiopia, the Ministry of Health found that there were only 11% (83/739) of the recommended number of EmOC facilities for their population of almost 74 million (Ethiopia Federal Ministry of Health et al., 2008).[9] This needs assessment in Ethiopia also showed that the most frequently missing service was the provision of parenteral anticonvulsants (e.g., magnesium sulphate or diazepam), which is essential for the treatment of eclampsia/severe pre-eclampsia.[10] The facilities that do provide EmOC services are often distributed inequitably in countries and there is often a shortage of life-saving services in more rural areas. A needs assessment in Mauritania conducted in 2000 found that more than half of all comprehensive EmOC facilities were located in Nouakchott, the country's capital and 70% of regions had no EmOC facilities.[11]

Analysis has also shown that utilisation of EmOC services by women with obstetric complications is woefully low. One such example comes from Malawi where, in 2005, it was found that nearly 80% of women with obstetric complications did not receive EmOC services.[12] Where EmOC services do exist, they are most often used by wealthier women living in close proximity to those facilities (Gabrysch et al., 2009, Pitchforth et al., 2007).[13]

Finally, the EmOC indicators tell us that the quality of EmOC services in many countries around the world is unacceptably poor. In Ethiopia, the direct obstetric case fatality rate in almost 30% of hospitals exceeded 3%, which surpasses the recommended maximum of 1%.[14]

When used to monitor projects, the EmOC indicators have also shown that progress towards the reduction of maternal mortality is possible. From 1999 to 2005, the government of Mozambique, UNFPA and the Averting Maternal Death and Disability Program (AMDD) implemented a project in Sofala, Mozambique, that was designed to improve the access, quality and utilisation of EmOC throughout the province. After five years of interventions, the number of facilities with functioning EmOC services more than quadrupled

in availability of emergency obstetric care, *International Journal of Gynaecology & Obstetrics* 93, 2006, 300–307.

9 Ethiopia Federal Ministry of Health, UNICEF, UNFPA, WHO and AMDD, *National baseline assessment for emergency obstetric & newborn care*, Addis Ababa: Federal Ministry of Health, 2008.

10 Ibid.

11 UNFPA, Faire de la maternité sans risque une realité. Resultats de l'enquête sur les soins obstetricaux d'urgence en Mauritanie [*Making safe motherhood a reality: results of a survey of emergency obstetric care in Mauritania*], Nouakchott, 2000.

12 B. Leigh, T.G. Mwale, D. Lazaro and J. Lunguzi, Emergency obstetric care: how do we stand in Malawi?, *International Journal of Gynaecology and Obstetrics* 101, 2008, 107–111.

13 S. Gabrysch and O. Campbell, Still too far to walk: literature review of the determinants of delivery service use, *BMC Pregnancy and Childbirth* 9, 2009, 34. E. Pitchforth, E. Van Teijlingen, W. Graham and A. Fitzmaurice, Development of a proxy wealth index for women utilising emergency obstetric care in Bangladesh, *Health Policy and Planning* 22, 2007, 311–319.

14 Ethiopia Federal Ministry of Health, UNICEF, UNFPA, WHO and AMDD, *National Baseline Assessment for Emergency Obstetric & Newborn Care*, op. cit.

from four in 1999/2000 to 17 in 2005,[15] which surpassed the recommended minimum number of facilities for the population size. At the same time, met need for EmOC tripled from 11% to 33% and the direct obstetric case fatality rate was halved from 3.5% to 1.7% by the project's end.[16] While utilisation and quality improved dramatically in Sofala over five years, there was still much work to be done in order to reach the many women with obstetric complications who were still not utilising the services and to further reduce the direct case fatality rate to less than 1%.

Interpretations of the EmOC indicators have contributed to national and subnational planning processes such as the sector-wide approach[17] and, in African countries, the *Road map for accelerating the attainment of the Millennium Development Goals (MDGs) related to maternal and newborn health*.[18] They have also been used to inform policy decisions. For example, after determining a shortage of EmOC services at health centres in Malawi, the Malawian government decided to expand the scope of practice of certain cadres of nurse-midwives so that they would be trained and authorised to provide all seven basic EmOC services.[19]

At the global level, the EmOC indicators have been used to track progress in high-mortality countries by UN agencies, non-governmental organisations, donor groups and academic institutions. Since 2008 the availability of EmOC indicators has been included in the *Countdown to 2015 maternal, newborn and child survival* reports[20] and the set is now being promoted within the human rights community as important for monitoring the fulfilment of human rights obligations related to maternal health.[21]

15 C. Santos, J.D. Diante, A. Baptista, E. Matediane, C. Bique and P. Bailey, Improving emergency obstetric care in Mozambique: the story of Sofala, *International Journal of Gynaecology & Obstetrics* 94, 2006, 190–201.

16 Ibid.

17 V. Orinda, H. Kakande, J. Kabarangira, G. Nanda and A.K. Mbonye, A sector-wide approach to emergency obstetric care in Uganda, *International Journal of Gynaecology & Obstetrics* 91, 2005, 285–291.

18 L. de Bernis and Y. Wolman, *Maternal and newborn health national plans (road map) assessment*, New York: UNFPA, 2009. B. Leigh et al., Emergency obstetric care: how do we stand in Malawi?, op. cit. WHO-AFRO, *Road map for accelerating the attainment of the Millennium Development Goals related to maternal and newborn health in Africa*, Brazzaville: WHO-AFRO, 2005.

19 B. Leigh, T.G. Mwale, D. Lazaro and J. Lunguzi, Emergency obstetric care: how do we stand in Malawi?, op. cit.

20 UNICEF, *Countdown to 2015 – maternal, newborn & child survival*, New York: UNICEF, 2008. World Health Organization and UNICEF, *Countdown to 2015 decade report (2000–2010): taking stock of maternal, newborn and child survival*, Geneva: WHO and UNICEF, 2010.

21 Amnesty International, *Out of reach – the cost of maternal health in Sierra Leone*, London: Amnesty International, 2009. Human Rights Watch, *No tally of the anguish – accountability in maternal health care in India*, New York: Human Rights Watch, 2009. United Nations, Report of the Special Rapporteur on the right of everyone to the enjoyment of the highest attainable standard of health, Paul Hunt – mission to India, op. cit. Alicia E. Yamin, Toward transformative accountability: applying a rights-based approach to fulfill maternal health obligations, *Sur International Journal on Human Rights* 7, 2010, 95–121.

While the EmOC indicators have proved to be invaluable in monitoring the availability, utilisation and quality of EmOC for programmatic and political purposes, their integration into accountability mechanisms at all levels has not been fully exploited.

At the community level, the EmOC indicators could be used as an instrument for citizens to actively participate in monitoring the availability and quality of EmOC services in local health facilities. By collecting or gaining access to information about lacking services, communities could lobby for better functioning health facilities and could use the information to make informed choices of which facilities to use in case of an emergency.

Within the health system, the EmOC indicators could be more effectively used to advocate for additional resources and to determine resource allocation. For example, if certain districts had too few EmOC facilities because there were shortages of trained health professionals, decisions could be made to increase human resources in those areas.

At the national level, as is recommended in the *Report of the Special Rapporteur on the right of everyone to the enjoyment of the highest attainable standard of health, Paul Hunt – mission to India*,[22] the EmOC indicators could be used by designated independent bodies to monitor governments' progress and be used to make specific, operational recommendations for action when there is little or no progress being made.

3.4 Conclusion

The EmOC indicators demonstrate how a set of indicators can contribute to reducing maternal mortality. During the past 12 years of usage, the EmOC indicators have proved to be effective in highlighting priorities and monitoring progress towards the full implementation of good-quality, accessible and acceptable services. In the future, the EmOC indicators and related benchmarks, along with other effective indicators related to the essential components of maternal mortality reduction, should be made more accessible to civil society and to independent bodies to ensure that governments are progressively realising their obligations and that women's lives are being saved.

When data are not available to calculate the key indicators, all efforts must be made to ensure their collection. However, even when there are ample data available, indicators are only effective when they are made widely accessible and used to drive real change. Only when there is sufficient information demonstrating that appropriate, good-quality programmes and policies are in place and producing results – and when that information is universally accessible and strategically being applied – can civil society, health workers, managers, governments and independent bodies be certain that progress is being made toward reducing maternal mortality.

22 United Nations, Report of the Special Rapporteur on the right of everyone to the enjoyment of the highest attainable standard of health, Paul Hunt – mission to India, op. cit.

4 What are maternal death audits? A Sri Lankan case study

Dr Hiranthi Wijemanne

4.1 Introduction

Pregnancy is a natural, physiological condition that occurs in women by choice or otherwise. Unfortunately the state of pregnancy can pose risks, even of a life-threatening nature, if proper care is not available in a timely manner. This includes the right response during the pregnancy, at the point of delivery and after the delivery. Some situations of risk when unattended can cause not only the death of the mother and or the baby, but can also lead to long-term infirmities in one or both. What is most important is that prevention is possible if the right interventions are available. Time is of essence in preventing maternal deaths. Some women bear infirmities all their life because of the denial of maternal services. The majority of women who die or live with infirmities live in the developing world.

Although international health groups as well as women's rights organizations have advocated for action to address the many unresolved issues of maternal mortality, preventable maternal deaths still continue. Maternal health has been identified as one of the Millennium Development Goals (MDGs) (Goal 5), but the progress to attain this goal remains slow.

The growing recognition for the need to penetrate deeper into the factors that lead to maternal deaths is opportune. It is important to regard each and every single maternal death as a personal tragedy for the women's spouse and children. Denial of access to a safe delivery without loss of life and pregnancy-related complications are rights violations that must be addressed.

The systems of conducting maternal death audits (MDAs) provides a valuable opportunity to examine in depth the individual history of each mother who died and so analyse the factors that contributed to the tragic consequences of her pregnancy.

Sri Lanka shares a common culture and tradition of gender insensitivity and gender discrimination with other South Asian countries and has experienced a declining maternal mortality for over six decades since independence. Free island-wide preventive and curative healthcare with well-developed maternal and childcare was a significant factor. This included antenatal and postnatal care, as well as trained care at delivery. Over 93% of Sri Lankan women deliver in institutions. High female literacy due to free education for both boys and girls has led to high levels of health-searching behaviour by women, including seeking services during pregnancy. It is in this environment that MDAs were introduced in 1985 as a more individual rights-based approach to deaths related to pregnancy. This new approach was designed to save the lives of pregnant women and their babies, parallel to continuing to improve the quality of maternal care and access to services. MDAs provided the opportunity to go beyond the numbers, to create an understanding of each individual maternal death situation in a manner that was not possible through the death registration system.

The Sri Lankan experience as a developing country offers hope to other developing countries with scarce resources, that it is possible to reduce maternal deaths. The MDAs created the opportunity to recognize each individual mother – it made every mother count. Sri Lanka's MDAs also provided a wealth of information on individual mothers – common situations were revealed, together with general trends that could change the management of pregnancies and deliveries. Geographical variations were revealed, as well as gaps and deficiencies in the care system. One very significant feature was the undertaking of the audits in a non-threatening and confidential manner. Adherence to confidentiality also contributed to providing space for improved reporting. The focus was placed on saving lives as opposed to apportioning blame and the audits were not used for purposes of litigation or blame. Therefore the approach to maternal audits in Sri Lanka was mostly evidence based, relatively simple and integrated into the existing healthcare system.

Initially, the audits were undertaken by the Ministry of Health, supported by the Sri Lanka College of Obstetricians and Gynaecologists and the Family Health Bureau of the Ministry of Health. Other important features of the MDAs were the participation of both community health practitioners and clinicians to jointly seek solutions. The outcome was the fact that the majority of the recommendations made at the audits were collectively accepted and therefore implemented.

Sri Lanka therefore lends itself as an example of a developing country in which MDAs have been useful as an effective approach, coupled with access to safe delivery services and emergency obstetric care and quality antenatal and postnatal care, all essential for a safe and life-enhancing pregnancy.

4.2 Approaches to MDAs

MDAs include community-based/verbal autopsies; facility-based maternal death reviews, confidential inquiries, surveys and severe morbidity also known as 'near misses' and clinical audits.

The community-based approach involves examining maternal deaths that occur outside health facilities, focusing on ascertaining personal, family and community factors contributing to the death. This also includes determining medical causes that could have contributed to the death. However, the conduct of such investigation in a comprehensive and open manner requires close cooperation among family members. In addition, a considerable level of sensitivity is required to determine the true circumstances related to the death. All the necessary details may or may not be obtained, depending on each situation and the skills of the interviewer.

Community-based approaches are important in countries in which the majority of maternal deaths occur in homes. It is also important to bear in mind that the family is not under any compulsion to divulge this information. Another approach is facility-based maternal death reviews. This is the approach adopted in Sri Lanka, as over 93% of deliveries occur in institutions. The facility-based survey is composed of the conduct of an in-depth investigation on the causes of and circumstances in which maternal deaths occur in health facilities. The examination requires an identification of factors in the community and the institution that may have contributed to the death. It is necessary to determine which of these were preventable. This type of investigation requires the close cooperation of the care providers to the mother who died and their willingness to be accurate on providing details of the management of the case. Such honesty is required of the health worker involved in managing the case in the home as a home delivery.

Another approach is the conduct of confidential inquiries. This follows the format of a systematic, multidisciplinary, anonymous investigation of all or a representative sample of maternal deaths occurring in a specific area, region or even at national level. This approach includes identifying numbers, causes and preventable and remedial factors. However, this approach requires the existence of a functioning statistical system. This includes vital records of an analysis of births and deaths, human resources, etc., or dedicated staff in each facility to regularly report maternal deaths to the inquiring team.

Another is the conduct of surveys on severe morbidity ('near misses'). This approach needs the identification and assessment of cases in which the pregnant woman survives obstetric complications. Although there is no universally applicable definition, the one used in any survey must be applicable to the local situation and contribute to enabling improvements to maternal care. This approach also needs a relatively good-quality medical-record system, a management culture free of fear and blame and a strong commitment by the management and clinical staff to take action on the findings.

Finally, it is possible to conduct a clinical audit. This is a quality improvement process that aims at improving patient care and a positive outcome to the pregnancy. A systematic review is needed of all aspects, including the structure of services, processes, outcome of care against well-formulated criteria and the subsequent implementation of changes. Such changes could be effected at the individual health-worker level, team or service levels. Monitoring is necessary to confirm if improvements have occurred. This requires the possibility of identifying relevant cases from registers as well as the retrieval of notes. Open discussions need to be possible and the application of improvements to the care services being provided.

4.3 Approach to maternal death investigations in Sri Lanka – MDAs

The current maternal death audit system being implemented in Sri Lanka evolved over time. In the 1950s public health midwives investigated maternal deaths – they reported their findings to medical officers of health covering specified geographic localities. During this period, the majority of deliveries occurred in homes, attended by trained PHMS. Hospitals conducted more 'informal' and probably not that well-structured investigations. It was only in the 1960s that a maternal investigation format was first introduced. However, it lacked completeness and there was no routine reporting of deaths and formal reviews.

The first formal maternal death review in a structured manner was introduced in 1987, and it was first undertaken linked to immunization coverage reviews, established to achieve universal child immunization goals. Quarterly meetings were held under the Secretary of Health and maternal death investigations and review processes were also included. Guidelines for investigations were introduced to hospitals providing delivery care. Public health officials reported the field situation with information collected by midwives. During this period, hospital deliveries had risen, with the majority occurring in institutions.

In 1989 a further strengthening of the maternal death investigation and review processes was undertaken. In 1992 improved guidelines were developed for all institutions and maternal deaths were made notifiable, the notification being mandatory for both institution and public health staff. Each one of such notified maternal death was investigated in detail by both the field and institutional staff and at the site the death occurred.

In 1996 a further review of the maternal death audit system was undertaken, examining the estimates and causes of maternal deaths. The study aimed at obtaining accurate estimates of maternal deaths while reviewing the factors which influenced the death. Both patient responsibilities and those of the care-providing institution were included. The pooled estimate of maternal deaths was three times that recorded in the civil registration system for births, marriages and deaths, which are considered to cover over 83% of the population. This reveals the value of audits that pinpoint each individual case. In 1997 conducting of MDAs was devolved to the district level. Medical officers of health for maternal and child health were made responsible for the follow-up of what happened after the audit was conducted.

Following this, in 2000 a needs assessment study on women's right to life and health was conducted in Sri Lanka, as well as other South Asian countries. This sought to address maternal mortality and morbidity as a human rights issue. The reason was that out of an estimated 600,000 annual maternal deaths, half occurred in South Asia; and also because, for every woman who dies, a further 30 to 40 suffer from lifelong disabilities. A programme was launched on women's rights to life and health addressing leadership and management issues connected with the implementation of maternal care programmes in the South Asian region, including Sri Lanka. The other countries included Bangladesh, Bhutan, India, Nepal and Pakistan. It was a collaboration between UNICEF and Columbia University, funded by the Gates Foundation.

Since then, Sri Lanka has had annual maternal audits including reviews. It is during the review that the cause of each maternal death is established and the contributory factors are ascertained. Points at which delays occurred in seeking care are determined, particularly if a delay happened within the health institution, which should not have occurred under any circumstances.

Today numbers of maternal deaths in Sri Lanka have declined to a remarkably low level of 140. Even so, the majority are still preventable. Hence there is a need to continue to implement policies on maternal death reduction and also to reduce maternal morbidity. In 2005 there were a total of 257 maternal deaths in a population of 19,886,000 people. The maternal mortality as reported in the civil registration system in 2002 was 14.3 per 100,000 live births.

Establishing a system of MDAs in Sri Lanka has proved to be a useful tool to look beyond a total number of maternal deaths to a more individual approach that has contributed to effecting a positive change. Identifying individual women, collecting accurate information, analysing the data, recommending and following up relevant action have all contributed to a positive outcome for mothers.

The criteria adopted for maternal death notification include all deaths of women who died during pregnancy and within 42 days of the termination of the pregnancy, irrespective of the cause of death. Also included are all late maternal deaths. This includes from 42 days up to one year after the termination, following direct/indirect maternal causes of death. Since 1986 it is compulsory to notify and investigate each individual maternal death.

The three delay model in relation to maternal deaths has also been modified and applied in Sri Lanka. This includes factors contributing to seeking healthcare services that are relevant to a low socioeconomic status of the family of the woman, low educational level/lack of knowledge and inability to recognize the 'danger' signs by the mother herself/family. Although this delay occurs in Sri Lanka, it is not as common as in the rest of South Asia. The severe delay to reach a medical facility due to distance, cost, lack of transport and poor road access, although occurring in very remote areas, is also not so common in Sri Lanka. However, the third delay related to malfunctioning of the system of access to basic and comprehensive obstetric care does occur, particularly in remote localities.

4.4 Lessons learned and conclusion

Among the more important lessons learned related to the conduct of MDAs in Sri Lanka is that the audit/review information is far more accurate than that collected by the registrar general or indoor hospital morbidity and mortality statistics. The audits are useful and can lead to far-reaching changes to save women from maternal death and long-term infirmities as compared with obtaining data from the civil registration system, which, in general, tends to under-report such deaths. The emphasis on confirming the cause and addressing gaps in management is much more advantageous as compared with instituting individual action on professional negligence. High-level leadership was particularly important, as well as the participation of key policymakers in the health sector. The nexus between public health staff and consultant obstetricians was particularly useful as was the use of local protocols. Only in selected instances of negligence, if proved, did the Sri Lanka Medical Council enter into the process of establishing accountability and take action on individual cases of malpractice.

MDAs open new avenues to look beyond the numbers and avert maternal deaths. Investigating every death has also given the individual mother importance and made every mother count. It is also a recognition of every woman's right to a safe pregnancy.

Addressing maternal deaths is a moral and human rights imperative. It is directly linked to the status of women in society, their rights to a safe pregnancy and healthy motherhood. The causes of maternal deaths in developing countries bear a remarkably consistent pattern. Although poverty is regarded as dramatically increasing a woman's chances of dying during or after pregnancy, the Sri Lankan experience is that this is not necessarily so. Access to skilled care at the delivery and access to emergency obstetric care when necessary and transport can make a huge impact. Maternal death surveillance and MDAs, facilitating accessibility to medical care and combating the three delays in obtaining services are all important. All such approaches need to be simple, affordable, effective and widespread and available to all mothers on a universal basis.

I hope that the International Roundtable on Maternal Mortality, Human Rights and Accountability and this volume, which follows it, will be a rallying point for action. No woman, wherever she is, needs to lose her life or suffer long-term infirmities because of a pregnancy. The knowledge and tools to effect a positive change are well known but need wide application. Accountability for change is critical for success, as is the need for a transformation of attitudes and norms among families, communities, facilities, civil society policymakers and state authorities.

4.5 Bibliography

Annual Health Statistics, Sri Lanka 2006 – Medical Statistics Unit, Department of Health, Ministry of Healthcare and Nutrition, Sri Lanka.

Annual Report on Family Health in Sri Lanka 2006/2007 – Family Health Bureau, Ministry of Healthcare and Nutrition, Sri Lanka.

Family Heath Bureau, Ministry of Healthcare and Nutrition Sri Lanka, *Overview of maternal mortality in Sri Lanka, 2001–2005*, 2008.

Family Health Bureau, Ministry of Health, Sri Lanka College of Obstetricians and UNICEF, *Needs assessment study on women's right to life and health project/Sri Lanka*, 2001.
Ministry of Healthcare and Nutrition, UNFPA, UNICEF and WHO, *Report of the external review of maternal and newborn health, Sri Lanka*, 2007.
UNICEF, *Saving women's lives – a call to rights-based action*, UNICEF/South Asia, 2000.
WHO Department of Reproductive Health and Research, *Beyond the numbers*, 2004.

5 The role of international and national courts: human rights litigation as a strategy to hold states accountable for maternal deaths

*Ximena Andión Ibañez**

5.1 Introduction

The death of 358,000 women each year from preventable complications during pregnancy and childbirth amounts to a public health and human rights crisis.[1] In the last decade there has been a growing recognition, at both national and international levels, that preventable maternal mortality is a human rights issue, implicating the right to life, health, equality and non-discrimination, among others.[2] The development of these norms and standards, and the increasing possibility of enforcing health-related rights through courts and human rights mechanisms,[3] have fostered an enabling environment for strategic litigation on preventable maternal mortality. Thus, courts at the national and international level can play an important role as part of broader legal advocacy strategies to seek government accountability for the systematic failure to prevent maternal mortality and contribute to changing the realities of women and girls worldwide. This presentation will highlight how litigation has served as an effective strategy to promoting and protecting

* The author wants to thank Sofia Khan, Global Fellow at the Center for Reproductive Rights for her valuable support in drafting this presentation.

1 World Health Organization, *Trends in maternal mortality: 1990 to 2008. Estimates developed by WHO, UNICEF, UNFPA and The World Bank*, 2010, 1. Available at http://whqlibdoc.who.int/ publications/2010/9789241500265_eng.pdf.

2 See Center for Reproductive Rights, *Bringing rights to bear: preventing maternal mortality and ensuring safe pregnancy*, 2008. Available at http://reproductiverights.org/sites/crr.civicactions.net/ files/documents/BRB_Maternal%20Mortality_10.08.pdf; United Nations, Human Rights Council, *Preventable maternal mortality and morbidity and human rights*, Resolution U.N. Doc. A/HRC/11/L.16/REV.1, 17 June 2009; European Parliament, *Resolution on maternal mortality ahead of the UN high-level event*, 25 September – Review of the Millennium Development Goals, 2008; African Commission on Human and Peoples' Rights, ACHPR/ Res. 135 (XXXXIIII), *Resolution on maternal mortality in Africa*, 2008; Inter-American Commission on Human Rights, *Access to maternal health services from a human rights perspective*, OEA/Ser.L/V/II. Doc. 69, 7 June 2010.

3 See Human Rights Committee, Communication No. 1153/2003 (*K. L. v. Peru*), Doc. No. CCPR/C/85/D/1153/2003 (2005); Committee on the Elimination of Discrimination against Women, Communication No. 4/2004 (*A.S. v. Hungary*), U.N. Doc. CEDAW/ C/36/D/4/2004 (2006).

women's right to safe pregnancy and childbirth, and the challenges and opportunities in implementing such a strategy.

5.2 Human rights litigation and constructive accountability

In the last decade, litigation has become an attractive advocacy tool for human rights movements around the world. Human rights litigation, as the Center for Reproductive Rights understands it, is a specific form of litigation centred on promoting structural and systemic changes in order to bring about social transformations and address unequal power relations. Although human rights litigation also serves to provide redress for individual human rights violations, the broader focus is on the responsibility of the state and, to a certain extent, while not currently having been developed, on the responsibility of donors and international financial institutions to protect and promote human rights.

The role of human rights litigation in international and national courts is multifaceted. It can be used as a strategy to change laws or policies that violate constitutional protections or human rights, ensure that laws are interpreted and enforced properly, identify gaps in the law and develop civil society and mobilize communities. Moreover, human rights litigation in both the national and international forums plays a key role in both setting precedents and ensuring state accountability through the use of international human rights standards.

In the context of maternal deaths, human rights litigation serves as a form of 'constructive accountability', which focuses on system failures that threaten quality of care, as well as undermine adequate working conditions of healthcare workers.[4] Constructive accountability refers to more than the process of blame, sanction and punishment – rather, it focuses on finding out what works, so it can be repeated, and what does not, so it can be revised.[5] Accordingly, constructive accountability establishes a 'new dynamic of entitlement and obligation' that recognizes that progressive realization of human rights is inextricably linked to providing an effective health system that is accessible to all and of good quality.[6] To that end, human rights litigation is an effective tool for holding states accountable for the health system failures and discriminatory social practices that are a major impediment to successfully reducing maternal mortality.

4 Alicia Ely Yamin, Beyond compassion: the central role of accountability in applying a human rights framework to health, *Health and Human Rights* 10(2), 2008; L. Freedman, Human rights, constructive accountability and maternal mortality in the Dominican Republic, *International Journal of Gynecology and Obstetrics* 82, 2003, 111–114.

5 Freedman, op. cit., 111.

6 Ibid., 112.

5.3 National courts

At the national level, litigation in domestic courts is increasingly utilized to seek accountability and redress for violations of constitutional and international human rights law. One of the most used and successful ways of enforcing health-related rights at the national level has been through the use of public interest litigation. Public interest litigation is typically defined as legal action brought to protect or enforce a legal principle or right that is of public importance and aimed at social transformations.[7] The modalities of bringing such cases vary between the legal systems.[8] The aim of public interest litigation is to not only change the circumstances of the litigants but of all those similarly situated. Accordingly, such litigation has greater potential than private rights litigation in addressing the systemic nature of many human rights violations.[9]

Recently, advocates in India have had positive results using public interest ligation to seek government accountability for the systematic failure to prevent maternal deaths. The Center for Reproductive Rights launched a global initiative in 2004 to promote the use of strategic litigation to hold governments accountable at the national and state level for violations of women's reproductive rights.[10] In 2006 it organized the first ever training on reproductive rights for lawyers in India in collaboration with the Human Rights Law Network (HRLN), where the potential for developing constitutional litigation to address maternal mortality through the use of international norms and comparative law was discussed.

In 2008 a public health activist in India, with the legal representation of the HRLN, took the state of Madhya Pradesh to court over the staggering number of women in the state who die during pregnancy and childbirth.[11] The public interest lawsuit was brought by Sandesh Bansal, the coordinator of Jan Adhikar Manch, a network of local health NGOs. In *Sandesh Bansal v. The State of Madhya Pradesh & Others*, Mr Bansal contends that the government of Madhya Pradesh has failed to properly implement maternal health policies in the state.[12] The state has the third highest maternal mortality ratio

7 Center for Reproductive Rights, *Litigating reproductive rights: using public interest litigation and international law to promote gender justice in India*, 2006, 24. Available at http://reproductiverights.org/sites/crr.civicactions.net/files/documents/media_bo_India1215.pdf.

8 Christine M. Forster and Vedna Jivan, Public interest litigation and human rights implementation: the Indian and Australian experience, *Asian Journal of Comparative Law* 3(1), 2008, 17–18.

9 Ibid., 23.

10 Center for Reproductive Rights, *Maternal mortality in India: using international and constitutional law to promote accountability and change*, 2008, 5. Available at http://reproductiverights.org/ sites/crr.civicactions.net/files/documents/pub_br_maternal_mortality_in_india_2009.pdf.

11 Ibid., 49.

12 *Sandesh Bansal v. Union of India and Others*, W.P. (Civ.) No. 9061 of 2008, (M.P. High Court), at para. 5.13.

in India, with 498 deaths for every 100,000 live births.[13] The petition draws attention to the poor conditions of primary health centres in the state, which often lack clean water, electricity and basic sanitation.[14] It further points to the failure of the Rogi Kalyan Samiti, an oversight body created under the National Rural Health Mission, to execute its role of ensuring that government funds are spent appropriately on services most needed by women, such as emergency transportation, and highlights concern about the use of financial resources.[15] The petition requests the court to order the state government to establish health facilities where needed and ensure that they are fully functional by taking measures such as appointing staff, ensuring the availability of proper equipment and life-saving drugs, providing emergency transportation, assuring the quality of services, and monitoring the provision of services.[16] The petition also seeks a guarantee that no pregnant woman shall be denied free health services and calls for the creation of a surveillance mechanism to identify and review maternal deaths.[17] The Center for Reproductive Rights submitted a legal memorandum to the High Court of Madhya Pradesh in support of Mr Bansal's claims, describing how international human rights law supports a woman's right to safe pregnancy and childbirth.

Before the judgment was even made, the court issued interim orders calling for a visit by government officials and members of the bench to verify the claims of the petitioners and issued interim orders for the provision of blood banks to deal with emergencies and electricity for public health centres at which women seek care in the Bhind District of Madhya Pradesh.[18] The court issued another interim order asking a government official to present itself in court to explain why certain primary healthcare facilities continue to lack running water and electricity.[19]

In its final decision on 6 February 2012, the Court declared that the state of Madhya Pradesh had violated women's fundamental right to life by failing to provide proper prenatal care and maternal health services in an appropriate and timely manner.[20] It ordered the state to, *inter alia*, implement existing national policies meant to protect maternal health, and to improve conditions in health facilities by guaranteeing 24-hour delivery, make basic infrastructure improvements, ensure the 24-hour availability of emergency vehicles for all health centres and provide for the vaccination of pregnant women and their newborns.[21]

13 International Institute for Population Sciences, *National family health survey (NFHS-3): national fact sheet – Madhya Pradesh*. Available at www.nfhsindia.org/pdf/Madhya%20 Pradesh.pdf.
14 *Sandesh Bansal*, op. cit., paras 34.6–5.34.9.
15 Ibid., para. 5.15.
16 Ibid., para. 7.
17 Ibid., para. 7(d), (e) and (g).
18 Ibid., para. 7(g). Application for seeking interim direction, prayer paras 1–4.
19 *Sandesh Bansal v. Union of India and Others*, High Court Order Sheet, I.A. No. 10315/2008 (2009).
20 Ibid., para. 22.
21 Ibid., para. 23.

There has also been a recent decision in the Delhi High Court that will have major implications for future public interest litigation combating maternal mortality. In a historic decision, *Laxmi Mandal v. Deen Dayal Hari Nager Hospital & Ors*, the Delhi High Court ordered compensation for the violation of constitutional and reproductive rights of two impoverished women who died in childbirth.[22] The High Court determined two petitions simultaneously concerning deficiencies in the implementation of a cluster of government-funded schemes aimed at reducing infant and maternal mortality. In *Laxmi Mandal*, the High Court instructed the state of Haryana to pay compensation of Rs 2.4 lakh to the family of Shanti Devi who passed away during childbirth after being denied medical treatment (emergency obstetric care) from four different hospitals because she was unable to pay the fees.[23] The Court found the respondents in violation of Shanti Devi's right to life and health, reiterating that her death was preventable. Similarly, in the case of *Jaitun v. Maternity Home, MCD, Jangpura & Ors*, the High Court directed the Municipal Corporation of Delhi and Government of National Capital Territory of Delhi to pay Rs 50,000 compensation to Fatima for compelling her to give birth to her daughter Alisha under a tree, after being denied basic medical services, in violation of her fundamental rights.[24] Drawing on both national and international law, the Court underlined that women have the right to control their body and decide when they wish to conceive.[25]

In commenting on the current status of the health schemes, the High Court noted that the cases demonstrated a complete failure of the public health system and the government's implementation of programmes designed to reduce maternal and neonatal mortality by encouraging institutional delivery for poor pregnant women.[26] The High Court discussed several corrective measures in response to the shortcomings in the implementation of the government health schemes, including, among others, clarification about cash assistance for pregnant women below the poverty line, setting up health check-ups in rural areas for pregnant women, improving the system of providing safe and prompt transportation of pregnant women from private residences to hospitals and, in the event of a maternal death, providing the family with cash benefits under the government health schemes.[27]

5.4 International courts

International and regional human rights systems can also be used as a means to ensure state accountability for the alarming rates of maternal deaths

22 *Laxmi Mandal v. Deen Dayal Harinagar Hospital & Ors,* W.P.(C) Nos 8853 of 2008 and 10700 of 2009, High Court of Delhi, 4 June 2010.
23 Ibid., paras 28.10, 55.
24 Ibid., paras 29.1–29.6, 56.
25 Ibid., paras 23–4.
26 Ibid., para. 40.
27 Ibid., para. 62.

worldwide. At the regional level, cases can be brought before the Inter-American Commission and the Inter-American Court of Human Rights; the African Commission and the African Court on Human and Peoples' Rights; and to the European Court of Human Rights.[28] Each of these mechanisms can interpret regional human rights treaties and decide whether a violation has occurred and some can determine remedies or issue legally binding decision.[29] The regional systems are progressively generating an important body of jurisprudence on women's human rights and have potential to help reform current laws and policies that violate women's right to safe pregnancy and childbirth.

At the international level, United Nations' (UN) treaty-monitoring bodies (TMBs) have progressively been utilized to seek and promote state accountability for maternal deaths. UN TMBs have called on states and other actors to give increased attention to the issue of maternal mortality in their engagement with the UN human rights system, particularly through the universal periodic reviews, and as a result have played an active role in developing the recognition of maternal mortality as a human rights issue.[30] UN TMBs monitor state compliance with each of eight major UN human rights treaties.[31] Certain UN TMBs have a mandate to receive and consider individual or group complaints about specific violations of rights enshrined in the relevant treaty.[32] For example, the Committee on the Elimination of Discrimination against Women (CEDAW Committee) can consider individual communications relating to states that are parties to the optional protocol to

28 See *Charter of the Organization of American States*, 119 U.N.T.S. 3, entered into force 13 December 1951; amended by Protocol of Buenos Aires, 721 U.N.T.S. 324, O.A.S. Treaty Series, No. 1-A, entered into force 27 February 1970; amended by *Protocol of Cartagena*, O.A.S. Treaty Series, No. 66, 25 I.L.M. 527, entered into force 16 November 1988; amended by *Protocol of Washington*, 1-E Rev. OEA Documentos Oficiales OEA/Ser.A/2 Add. 3 (SEPF), 33 I.L.M. 1005, entered into force 25 September 1997; amended by *Protocol of Managua*, 1-F Rev. OEA Documentos Oficiales OEA/Ser.A/2 Add.4 (SEPF), 33 I.L.M. 1009, entered into force 29 January 1996; *Statute of the Inter-American Court on human rights*, O.A.S. Res. 448 (IX-0/79), O.A.S. Off. Rec. OEA/Ser.P/IX.0.2/80, Vol. 1 at 98, Annual Report of the Inter-American Court on Human Rights, OEA/Ser.L/V.III.3 doc. 13 corr. 1 at 16 (1980), reprinted in *Basic documents pertaining to human rights in the inter-American system*, OEA/Ser.L.V/II.82 doc.6 rev.1 at 133 (1992); *Protocol to the African Charter on human and peoples' rights on the establishment of an African court on human and peoples' rights*, 9 June 1998, OAU Doc. OAU/LEG/EXP/AFCHPR/PROT (III); *Convention for the protection of human rights and fundamental freedoms*, 213 U.N.T.S. 222, entered into force 3 September 1953, as amended by Protocols Nos 3, 5, 8, and 11, entered into force on 21 September 1970, 20 December 1971, 1 January 1990 and 1 November 1998, respectively.

29 Center for Reproductive Rights, *Gaining ground: a tool for advancing reproductive rights law reform*, 2006, 17–18. Available at http://reproductiverights.org/sites/crr.civicactions.net/files/documents/pub_bo_GG_advocacy.pdf.

30 United Nations, Human Rights Council, *Report of the office of the United Nations High Commissioner for Human Rights on Preventable Maternal Mortality and Morbidity and Human Rights*, para. 60, U.N. Doc. A/HRC/14/39, 16 April 2010.

31 Center for Reproductive Rights, *Bringing rights to bear: an advocate's guide to the work of UN treaty-monitoring bodies on reproductive and sexual rights*, 2006, 6. Available at http://reproductiverights.org/sites/crr.civicactions.net/files/documents/pub_bp_BRB.pdf.

32 Ibid., 7.

the Convention on the Elimination of All Forms of Discrimination against Women (CEDAW).[33] Individual complaint mechanisms within specific UN TMBs have great potential for holding states accountable for preventable maternal deaths. In particular, CEDAW has very specific provisions related to the right to health and non-discrimination that are critical rights in the context of safe pregnancy and childbirth.[34] In addition, the General Assembly adopted an optional protocol to the International Covenant on Economic, Social and Cultural Rights in 2008 that provides the Committee competence to receive and consider individual communications. Although fairly new, it provides an additional venue for human rights litigation in the context of maternal mortality.[35]

In 2007 the Center for Reproductive Rights and Advocacia Cidada pelos Direitos Humanos, a Brazilian organization, filed a petition before the CEDAW Committee, on behalf of the family of Alyne da Silva Pimentel, an Afro-Brazilian woman who died during pregnancy from an entirely preventable condition.[36] *Alyne da Silva Pimentel v. Brazil* is the first individual case filed before a UN human rights body to argue maternal mortality as a human rights violation and to seek government accountability for the systematic failure to prevent maternal deaths.[37]

Alyne da Silva first sought medical attention at her local health centre when she experienced vomiting and severe abdominal pain. Although these signs indicated a high-risk pregnancy, doctors performed no tests and Alyne was sent home with vitamins, vaginal cream and anti-nausea medication.[38] She continued to experience severe pain and returned to the health centre two days later. At this time, doctors discovered that there was no foetal heartbeat. Despite medical standards dictating that Alyne should have undergone an immediate curettage surgery to remove placental parts and to prevent haemorrhage and infection, she did not undergo surgery until approximately 14 hours later.[39]

Following surgery, Alyne experienced severe haemorrhaging, low blood pressure and disorientation. Despite these serious symptoms, doctors neglected to perform any tests. As Alyne's condition worsened, doctors determined

33 See *Optional protocol to the Convention on the Elimination of Discrimination against Women*, 6 October 1999, G.A. Res. 54/4, U.N. GAOR, 54th Sess., U.N. Doc A/Res/54/4 (1999), entered into force 22 December 2000.

34 *Convention on the Elimination of All Forms of Discrimination against Women*, adopted 18 December 1979, Art. 12 (2), G.A. Res. 34/189, UN GAOR, 34th Sess., Supp. No. 46, at 193, U.N. Doc. A/34/46, U.N.T.S. 13, entered into force 3 September 1981.

35 *Optional protocol to the International Covenant on Economic, Social and Cultural Rights*, G.A. res. 63/117 (2008).

36 See Center for Reproductive Rights, *Litigation briefing series: Alyne da Silva Pimentel*, 2009. Available at http://reproductiverights.org/sites/crr.civicactions.net/files/flash/LBS_alyne_09.pdf.

37 *Alyne da Silva Pimentel v. Brazil*, United Nations Committee on the Elimination of Discrimination against Women, filed 30 November 2007.

38 Ibid., paras 1–4.

39 Ibid., paras 6–12.

that she needed to be transferred to a hospital with adequate equipment to treat her condition (tertiary health facility). Doctors at the health centre located a space for Alyne at the General Hospital of Nova Iguaç, but health centre personnel refused to use the centre's only ambulance to transport Alyne to the hospital. Eventually, the general hospital authorized the use of their ambulance to transport Alyne. However, the centre did not send her medical records. As a result, doctors at the general hospital were only given a brief oral account of Alyne's medical condition and, according to subsequent medical records, they treated Alyne without knowledge that she had just delivered a stillborn foetus.[40] After arriving at the hospital, Alyne was resuscitated when her blood pressure plummeted to zero. She was later placed in an emergency room hallway where she was left largely unattended and where her mother found her with blood on her mouth and clothes. Alyne died five days after her initial visit to the health centre.[41]

A few months after Alyne's death, her family sought civil redress within the Brazilian court system. Unable to obtain any effective state relief for over four and a half years, the petition before the CEDAW Committee was filed.[42] In *Alyne da Silva Pimentel v. Brazil*, the applicants allege that due to Brazil's failure to provide Alyne with appropriate maternal healthcare, the state violated its international legal obligations under Articles 2 and 12 of CEDAW to ensure women's ability to exercise and enjoy their rights to life and the highest attainable standard of health on a basis of equality with men and free of discrimination.[43] Brazil's maternal mortality rates are disproportionately high for a country of its economic status and the chances of dying in pregnancy and childbirth are greatest among low-income and Afro-descendant women such as Alyne.[44] The petition requested that the CEDAW Committee call on Brazil to prioritize the reduction of maternal mortality, including by training healthcare providers, establishing and enforcing appropriate protocols and improving care in vulnerable communities.[45]

Following careful consideration, the CEDAW Committee, in its decision issued in August 2011, established that Brazil violated its obligations under Article 12 (in relation to access to health), Article 2 (in relation to access to justice), and Article 2(e) (in relation to its due diligence obligation to regulate the activities of private health service providers), in conjunction with Article 1, of the Convention (non-discrimination).[46] It affirmed that governments have a human rights obligation to guarantee that all women, regardless

40 Ibid., paras 14–19.
41 Ibid., paras 20–21.
42 Ibid., para. 24.
43 Ibid., paras 43–54.
44 Committee on the Elimination of Discrimination against Women, *Brazil: consideration of reports submitted by states parties under Article 18 of the Convention on the Elimination of All Forms of Discrimination Against Women*, 171 (2002), 29th Sess., U.N. Doc. CEDAW/C/BRA/1-5.
45 *Alyne da Silva Pimentel*, op. cit.
46 Ibid., para. 8.

of income or racial background, have access to timely, non-discriminatory, and appropriate maternal health services. The CEDAW Committee analysed the case from a substantive equality approach and determined that Afro-Brazilian women did not have equal access to healthcare services due to their gender, race and socioeconomic status. Furthermore it established that it is not enough for a state to have policies and programmes in place if these are not effective to reduce maternal mortality, particularly among the most vulnerable groups of women. Thus, it clearly determined that states have obligations of conduct but also obligations of result.

The CEDAW Committee ordered the state party to provide appropriate reparation, including adequate financial compensation, to Alyne da Silva Pimentel Teixeira's family.[47] Additionally, the state was instructed to, *inter alia*, ensure women's right to safe motherhood and affordable access for all women to adequate emergency obstetric care, provide adequate professional training for health workers, especially on women's reproductive health rights, ensure that private healthcare facilities comply with relevant national and international standards on reproductive healthcare and reduce preventable maternal deaths through the implementation of the National Pact for the Reduction of Maternal Mortality.[48]

Through this decision, which clarified the extent of government's obligations to reduce maternal mortality,[49] the CEDAW Committee contributed to unveiling and remedying the glaring injustices surrounding maternal mortality. This is a groundbreaking decision and the first one from a UN TMB on maternal mortality. As a precedent, the case reaffirms the state responsibility for the systemic failure to prevent maternal mortality. The case has also raised the profile of the issue and brought together experts and civil society to design and discuss strategies to address this situation of maternal deaths worldwide.

5.5 Remedies and reparations

Providing effective remedies and reparations is a critical component of utilizing international and national courts to hold states accountable for maternal deaths. Although the issue of remedies and reparations has not been particularly developed in the context of maternal mortality, international and regional human rights law requires states to provide legal remedies and redress for human rights violations.[50] The right to remedy encompasses the right to equal and effective access to justice; to adequate, effective and prompt

47 Ibid., para. 8.1.
48 Ibid., para. 8.2.
49 See Part II of this volume for more on the Committee's analysis.
50 UN General Assembly, *Basic principles and guidelines on the right to a remedy and reparation for victims of gross violations of international human rights law and serious violations of international humanitarian law: resolution/adopted by the General Assembly*, 21 March 2006, A/RES/60/147, para. 2 [hereinafter *Guidelines on the right to a remedy and reparations*].

reparation for harm suffered; and access to relevant information concerning violations and reparation mechanisms.[51]

It must be noted that violations of human rights leading to maternal deaths by their very nature are irreparable and any remedy will fail to be truly proportional to the gravity of the injury inflicted.[52] Nevertheless, reparative measures are particularly important in the context of maternal deaths, as it assures women that violation of their right to safe pregnancy and childbirth cannot be tolerated. Reparation is defined as an action or process that repairs, make amends or compensate for damages.[53] There are four generally recognized forms of individual reparation: restitution, compensation, rehabilitation and satisfaction.[54] Restitution reinstates the situation that was in place before the wrongdoing occurred, to the extent that this is possible.[55] Compensation may also be provided as reparation for victims of human rights violations.[56] Although difficult to quantify in the context of maternal mortality, compensation may include, *inter alia*, damages for physical or mental harm, loss of opportunity or costs of medical services. Rehabilitation involves measures to rehabilitate the victim and may include medical and psychological care as well as legal and social services.[57] Satisfaction refers to effective measures aimed at the cessation of continuing violations.[58] These types of reparation may include government action, such as full and public disclosure of the violation, and public apologies as well as judicial or administrative sanctions against the perpetrators of the violations.

In addition to individual reparations, there are reparations specifically targeted at preventing the reoccurrence of such harms, particularly guarantees of non-repetition.[59] In the context of maternal mortality, such reparations may include training for health professionals; implementation of monitoring and accountability mechanisms, including specific benchmarks, indicators and a timeline for achievement to effectively reduce rates of maternal deaths; and amending legislation or reversing policies that limit women's access to healthcare.[60]

Remedies continue to be one of the most challenging aspects of human rights litigation, particularly the elements of satisfaction and guarantees of non-repetition. In the context of maternal mortality, where violations are often due to systematic and institutional factors, remedies should not solely

51 Ibid., para. 11.
52 Theo van Boven, *Final report to the Sub-Commission on Prevention and Discrimination and Protection of Minorities*, UN Commission on Human Rights, E/ CN. 4/ 1997/ 104, 16 January 1997.
53 *Guidelines on the right to a remedy and reparations*, op. cit., para. 15.
54 Ibid., para. 18.
55 Ibid., para. 19.
56 Ibid., para. 20.
57 Ibid., para. 21.
58 Ibid., para. 22.
59 Ibid., para. 23.
60 Potts, *Accountability and the right to the highest attainable standard of health*, in this volume.

focus on addressing individual errors.[61] Therefore, it is critical to keep discussing and researching what remedies are appropriate and how to tailor them to specific country conditions and concentrate on identifying and correcting the failure of states to protect, respect and fulfil human rights obligations.

One of the challenges in the realm of reparations of a collective nature is the discussion of whether courts should be developing public policy through their judicial decisions with far-reaching implications.[62] Certainly, courts should not substitute the role of the government in defining public policy; however, they can have a role in redefining social arrangements and entitlements. Furthermore, courts can approach remedies in innovative ways, for instance by calling for broader stakeholder participation in decision making regarding policies and programmes and in setting benchmarks and indicators.

5.6 Challenges and opportunities

Given the complex nature of human rights litigation, there are various challenges that arise. These include a lack of trust of courts, often generated by the lack of effective, independent judicial bodies; the resource-intensive and complicated nature of litigation; and practical barriers, including language difficulties, cost, lack of information and geographical distance. Litigation in the context of maternal mortality brings additional challenges. Often it is difficult to document systemic failure by governments in order to determine whether the state is progressively realizing women's human rights related to safe pregnancy and childbirth. Another challenge is the implementation of court decisions addressing the structural inequalities and problems underlying maternal mortality.

It must be noted that, despite the challenges, human rights litigation has been fundamental to building international justice and an increasingly attractive tool for human rights movements throughout the world. As demonstrated by the cases discussed, international and national courts have the potential to affect social change; in particular litigation can be an effective tool to promote structural remedies and far-reaching changes in laws, policies

61 Physicians for Human Rights, *Deadly delays: maternal mortality in Peru, a rights-based approach to safe motherhood* 2007, 117. Available at http://physiciansforhumanrights.org/library/documents/ reports/maternal-mortality-in-peru.pdf.

62 This had been largely debated in the United States. See Daniel Butt, The courts and social policy in the United States, *The Foundation for Law, Justice and Society*, 2007. Available at www.fljs.org/uploads/documents/Butt%20report.pdf. This issue has been also extensively debated in some Latin American countries, particularly in Colombia where the Constitutional Court has issued far-reaching decisions in the area of social rights. See Uprinmy Rodrigo and Garavito Cesar, Constitución, modelo económico y políticas públicas en Colombia: el ejemplo de la gratuidad de la educación primaria, *Dejusticia*, 2005. Available at http://dejusticia.org/interna.php?id_tipo_publicacion=5&id_publicacion=178.

and practices to improve access and quality services related to safe pregnancy and childbirth. Litigation can also be creatively used as a political tool, as the mere possibility of judicial enforcement may prompt policy shifts in governments or present opportunities for negotiations with social movements related to safe pregnancy and childbirth. Additionally, even in circumstances when a court does not rule that the state has perpetrated a human rights violation, the litigation itself may create a platform for publicity regarding the issue at hand. This publicity may, in turn, promote social mobilization and empower individuals to use different accountability mechanisms to demand state action.

Human rights litigation does not happen in a vacuum; rather, it is an integral part of a larger advocacy strategy to reduce maternal mortality. The decision to utilize international and national courts must be individually assessed to determine whether the strategy can play a positive role in promoting social change. Nevertheless, litigation plays a critical role in the multifaceted efforts to eliminate preventable maternal deaths worldwide.

6 The role of national human rights institutions in monitoring human rights: a case study of the Kenya National Commission on Human Rights

Commissioner Winfred Lichuma

6.1 What are national human rights institutions (NHRIs)?

National human rights institutions (hereinafter NHRIs) are state-funded public organizations that are established in line with the UN Paris Principles[1] that require governments to establish the entities through a legislative framework. Most NHRIs are established and entrenched through a country's constitution or acts of parliament. Basically, NHRIs are set up with broad mandates and objectives to promote and protect human rights at both domestic and international level, including the regional level. NHRIs have increasingly been recognized by the international community as mechanisms that are integral to ensuring respect for, and effective implementation of, international human rights standards at national level.[2]

On establishment of NHRIs, different countries have given different names to these entities; however, their broad mandate is similar. Some of the common references to NHRIs are: human rights commissions, office of the ombudsman, independent human rights commission, committee of human rights, centre for human rights and human rights defenders. As at June 2010 the International Coordinating Committee of National Human Rights Institution for Promotion and Protection of Human Rights (ICC) had accredited about 67 NHRIs globally.

1 Principles relating to the status and functioning of national institutions UN Doc. E/CN.4/1992/54.Annex (1992).

2 UN international human rights instruments, 7 February 2007, during the sixth inter-committee meeting of human rights treaty bodies, Geneva, 18–20 June 2007.

6.2 Mandates of NHRIs

Depending on their constitutive legal frameworks, NHRIs have been given different mandates and powers. The roles are basically twofold: first, a watchdog role and, second, an advisory role. Specifically, the roles are:

- monitoring and documenting situations of violations of human rights
- advisory to the government, parliament and any other competent body on specific violations, on issues related to legislation and on state compliance with international and regional human rights obligations
- promotion of education with mandate to educate and inform citizens on human rights
- quasi-judicial powers where they are empowered to hear and consider individual complaints and petitions. These they can do through non-legal methods such as mediation, negotiations and conciliation or setting up inquiries
- they can initiate their own investigations to address systemic human rights violations. These they do through public inquiries and recommendations to government. These form a basis to hold governments accountable to their obligations to promote, protect and fulfil human rights.

6.3 Independence of NHRIs as key to promotion and protection of human rights

The key element of NHRIs is the independence from government. NHRIs are accredited by the ICC in accordance with how independent they are from the government. This independence is in terms of resources and infrastructure, including staffing. Independence has been categorized in legal terms, in order to allow independence in decision making without direct or indirect interference by the government. It also includes operational independence, where each entity established formulates its own rules of procedures and regulations. At policy level, in terms of making recommendations, NHRIs reports and recommendations should emanate from its members and not from any other external person or body, including the government. Similarly, the reports of the findings should not be subject to review by any other body. Finally, the infrastructure requires that NHRIs should have financial independence with adequate funding from the state so as not to be subjected to control by the government or any other third party providing the funds.

6.4 The KNCHR establishment and mandate

The Kenya National Commission on Human Rights (KNCHR or 'Commission') is an NHRI that was established in July 2003 following the publication of the KNCHR Act of 2002.

The KNCHR Act spells out the Commission's key mandate areas and powers that broadly include protection, promotion, respect and fulfilment of human rights in Kenya. The Commission is the chief agent of the government of Kenya in ensuring the latter's compliance with its obligations under international human rights instruments.[3] It has a wide mandate to investigate human rights violations, visit prisons and other places of detention, carry out human rights education, advising government agencies on human rights issues and a broad function of performing, 'such other functions as the Commission may consider necessary for the promotion and protection of human right'.[4] For purposes of making the Commission accountable to taxpayers, the Commission is enjoined to submit annual reports or other 'special reports' to the president and to parliament through the responsible minister.

The Paris Principles call for vesting a NHRI with 'as broad a mandate as possible' that must be set forth in the institution's founding legislation.[5] The KNCHR Act sets out 16 specific functions for the Commission that can be broadly clustered under four headings:

1 protective
2 monitoring
3 advisory
4 educational or educative.

The KNCHR is created by statute as an independent body, and is not answerable to either the executive or to the judiciary, but to the legislature only to the extent that it is required in section 21 of the enabling Act to submit annual reports to parliament. The Commission's mandate is quite broad, as stipulated in the UN standards. It has powers 'to investigate, on its own initiative or upon a complaint made by any person or group of persons, the violation of any human rights'.[6] Also, sections 17 and 18 of the Act provide for the objects and principles of the Commission and its general powers respectively. Interestingly, the novel and most radical provision of the Act is the investment of the Commission with the powers of a court.[7]

The Commission is empowered to issue summonses, order the production of documents, question any person in respect of any matter under its investigation and require the disclosure of relevant information.[8] Of utmost importance, if the Commission is satisfied that human rights or fundamental freedoms have been infringed, it has powers to order the 'release of any unlawfully detained or restricted person', 'payment of compensation' or 'any other

3 Section 16(1) (f), KNCHR Act. Available at www.kenyalawrepot.org.
4 See section 16 of the KNCHR Act.
5 The Paris Principles UN Doc. E/CN.4/1992/54.Annex (1992).
6 Section 16(1) (a), KNCHR Act.
7 Section 19(1), KNCHR Act.
8 Section 19(1) (a)–(c), KNCHR Act.

lawful remedy'.[9] In this regard, the Commission may be deemed fundamentally empowered to deal with human rights issues effectively and expeditiously. The Commission's *suo moto* powers are an important aspect of its protective functions that have not been fully utilized.

In terms of its monitoring and advisory mandate, the Commission is entrusted with visiting police stations, prisons and other places of detention, studying their conditions and recommending measures for improving them.

The Commission's mandate is also educative.[10] A valuable component of protecting human rights is to spread awareness about it among the public. This task takes on special urgency in Kenya, a country in which a substantial tranche of the citizenry is ignorant of their rights and the avenues available for their vindication. The Commission has been carrying out human rights education and spreading human rights literacy through working with the media, releasing publications, conducting seminars and workshops and encouraging the activities of CSOs and other human rights institutions.

Kenya has been undergoing a constitutional review process for over 20 years – this came to an end on 4 August 2010, when, in referendum, Kenya's voted in a new constitution, promulgated on 27 August 2010. Under the new constitutional dispensation, the KNCHR has been elevated to a constitutional body with broad mandate of promotion and protection of human rights. The new entity will now be known as the Kenya National Human Rights and Equality Commission. A great boast for the human rights agenda in Kenya is the entrenchment of economic, social and cultural rights in the constitution. Among key achievement is the guarantee of the right to health, including the right to reproductive health.[11] The constitution includes right to health services, including reproductive healthcare and the assertion that no person shall be denied emergency treatment – in that sense, the public inquiry is helping to make that rights guarantee a reality.[12]

6.5 National inquiries into systemic patterns of human rights violations

NHRIs have powers to deal with individual complaints or initiate their own investigations in undertaking their mandates of promotion and protection of human rights. One way of doing this is through national public inquiries, which KNCHR, like other NHRIs, has in the past used successfully to address systemic problems and make recommendations to the government and other stakeholders. A national public inquiry is one in which there is systemic human rights problem in which the public in general is invited to

9 Section 19(6) (a)–(c).
10 Under section 16 it may 'inform and educate the public as to human rights for the purpose of enhancing respect for such rights by means of research, publication, lectures and symposia and by such other means as the Commission may deem fit'.
11 See Article 43 (f) of the new constitution available at www.kenyalawreport.org.
12 See Article 43 of the new constitution.

participate. It is a very useful mechanism for investigating violations of economic, social and cultural rights.[13]

KNCHR has successfully had two other inquiries since inception. The commission has used public inquiries to give recommendations in form of advisories to the government, government institutions, civil society organizations, private entities and individuals. To a larger extent, the commission's recommendations have been complied with and the commission has continuously made follow-ups to ensure successful implementation.

6.5.1 The reproductive health inquiry

The Federation of Women Lawyers (FIDA(K)) working in partnership with the Center for Reproductive Rights (CRR) submitted a complaint to the KNCHR on alleged violations of women's human rights in Kenyan health facilities. They had undertaken preliminary investigations into Pumwani maternity hospital[14] and other facilities also situated in the capital city of Nairobi, serving middle-level citizens and the very poor and vulnerable. The report dubbed 'Failure to deliver' made findings that the Kenyan government was responsible for very severe reproductive health rights violations for the following reasons:

- The facilities were underfunded and lacked the necessary equipment and supplies.
- There was delay in access to services for various reasons, including lack of qualified personnel.
- The user fee charged was a barrier to the poor seeking services, resulting in serious delays or denials of care in some cases leading to women's deaths. Detention of patients who could not pay their medical bills was an ongoing practice.
- Women often failed to get assistance during delivery. In cases in which assistance was offered, the nurses used very abusive language and sometimes others were physically abused.
- There was lack of accountability for violations occurring in healthcare facilities and the government was not providing redress or remedy for these violations.

6.5.2 Processing of the complaint

Preliminary processing of the complaint concluded that violations of reproductive health rights existed not only in Pumwani maternity hospital,

13 A training manual of 'National inquiries into systemic patterns of human rights violations: Asia Pacific forum', RWI Lund University.

14 It is a maternity hospital based in the capital city in Nairobi run by the local authority and catering mainly for the poor and mid-level citizens.

but also in almost all government hospitals/institutions. Due to the poor healthcare services, many women opted to have deliveries at home, either unaided or with the assistance of traditional birth attendants (TBAs). The Kenya Demographic Health Survey of 2008 affirmed that 56% of women delivered at home. The desk review pointed to the fact that about 7000 women die annually from complications related to pregnancy. The KDHS put the deaths per 100,000 at 488.[15]

The KNCHR satisfied itself that indeed there were various allegations of violations of the right to health, including reproductive health. The allegations amounted to systemic violations. These included many reported deaths of women and children; many cases of complications of unsafe abortion and cases of medical negligence that were not adequately addressed. There were also cases of rampant detention of mothers and their newborn babies on failure to pay the maternity charges.

Further, there was indication that home deliveries were unsafe and many women died due to complications related to breached or prolonged labour or in cases of haemorrhage. The government failed to provide adequately for the poor and the marginalized communities to access the services. The background study also pointed to other possible violations that included unwanted pregnancies caused by inaccessibility and unaffordability of family-planning services, poor infrastructure preventing quick access to the services, non-availability of ambulances at community facilities for emergency services and general lack of information and education in the area of sexual and reproductive health.

In line with its mandate and due to the fact that KNCHR has a larger mandate than FIDA(K) and CRR, the Commission deemed it right to have a public inquiry on reproductive health rights sampling all eight regions of Kenya. The Commission planned to investigate both violations at the hospital and/or institutional levels, while allowing citizens as members of the public to discuss other related violations. The public option was found suitable because it would enable citizens to audit the government's performance in providing the right to health, including reproductive health. It was decided that the public inquiry would be open to all people to come forward and state/swear/affirm what they knew about the issues being investigated.

6.5.3 Objectives of the inquiry

The objectives of the inquiry included:

- To provide a forum to discuss the situation of reproductive health services for women in Kenya and identify root causes of poor-quality and

15 Kenya Demographic Health Survey (KDHS) of 2008–2009. Available at www.measuredhs.com/ pubs/pdf/FR229/FR229.pdf.

inadequate healthcare service in government and other public hospitals and clinics.

- To provide people affected by mistreatment and neglect in prenatal and postnatal treatment in Kenya an opportunity to express their opinions and describe their experiences.
- To provide a framework for understanding the linkages and interfaces between budgetary allocations for government hospitals, recruitment of gynaecologists, quality of medical care for maternity patients and redress of complaints; and formulate feasible recommendations for improved quality of reproductive and maternity care in public hospitals.
- To raise public awareness and promote public debate on state obligations vis-à-vis reproductive health as a human right.
- To assess how the user policy is working towards promoting or inhibiting the right to women to access healthcare services.
- To investigate and document the violations of reproductive health rights broadly and to reveal systemic shortcomings in the healthcare system.

6.5.4 The process

The inquiry was managed by a secretariat from KNCHR and a coordinator was appointed to facilitate the process. Altogether, the inquiry took approximately one and a half years, with the panel hearings being conducted in sampled areas of all eight regions. A panel of five experts consisting of three Commissioners of the KNCHR and two consultants, one health expert and another gender expert, carried out the hearings, while a team of six experts, referred to as the reference group, provided support. The coordinator and the secretariat were responsible for acquiring background information, undertaking reconnaissance visits to identify victims and their relatives, witnesses to the violations, any public officials responsible, any perpetrators and academic experts on the issues arising. Those wishing not to appear in public were able to participate in in-camera hearings, which guaranteed their confidentiality. The KNCHR provided a support team, including counsellors, to prepare witnesses and offer counselling services after testifying. This in itself was a healing process.

Government officials were also engaged in the process. They provided information on available data, communicated government policies and responded to the accusations that were made against the government. The hearings were open to NGOs, private sector and public officials, who were also invited to present official submissions. Finally, media, and especially health-related reporters and commentators, were also present during the hearings.

6.5.5 Partnerships

The KNCHR partnered up with civil society organizations working on reproductive health issues in the areas where the inquiry was undertaken.

Partnerships with the Ministry of Health and other relevant ministries and government departments were also instrumental in the process. The Commission had successful engagement with the division of reproductive health under the Ministry of Health of Kenya to become part of the entire process. It is important to note that the process was not set to be a fault-finding one, but rather a constructive process aimed at correcting the situation and reducing maternal mortality.

6.5.6 *Participation*

The National Commission was keen on ensuring that people living in the country were able to have access to these processes including those with disabilities and marginalized communities. In that regard, therefore, the methodology applied by the Commission facilitated the attendance of marginalized groups at the hearings. Notices regarding the hearings were delivered through electronic and print media in all eight regions. The secretariat made advance visits to prepare the witnesses. In addition, interpreters and translators were engaged to ensure that participating communities had access to the proceedings. The venues hosting the panel were chosen based on the criterion that they had adequate facilities for persons with physical disabilities. Measures were taken to enable visually impaired persons to access the panel, as well as documents and other communicative material generated from this process. It is important to note that the Commission also gave effect to its gender mainstreaming and disability policies.

6.5.7 *Consultative process*

The process was entirely consultative and stakeholders were involved at every stage of the inquiry. This was because the Commission recognized and appreciated the role played by everyone involved in the reproductive health sector.

6.5.8 *The public inquiry report*

The findings of the public inquiry were published in a 210-page report in April 2012.[16] The report confirms that the sexual and reproductive health rights of Kenyans, particularly those belonging to marginalized and vulnerable groups, are being violated. Accordingly, the report includes a number of important recommendations for the government and stakeholders relating to family planning, maternal health, sexual violence, the sexual and

16 Kenya National Commission on Human Rights, *Realizing sexual and reproductive health rights in Kenya: myth or reality?* Report of the public inquiry into violations of sexual and reproductive health rights in Kenya, April 2012. Available at www.knchr.org/ReportsPublications/ThematicReports/ EconomicSocialandCultural.aspx.

reproductive health rights of sexual minorities and other marginalized and vulnerable groups, as well as the financing of sexual and reproductive healthcare services.

The report will be submitted to the president of the Republic of Kenya in line with the requirements of the KNCHR Act. The report will also be submitted to parliament for discussion and adoption for implementation. Copies will be made available to all stakeholders, victims and other witnesses, as well as to the public at large for both accountability and educational purposes.

6.6 Conclusion

The public inquiry process is one way of holding the government accountable. The Kenyan government has made numerous commitments to international and regional instruments protecting sexual and reproductive health rights. The Commission used the inquiry as a mechanism to hold the government accountable to the commitments made in, *inter alia*, CEDAW, ICPD Cairo Platform of Action of 1994, the Beijing Platform of Action of 1995, the Maputo Women Protocol of 2003, together with the Maputo framework on sexual and reproductive rights and the Millennium Development Goals of 2000.

7 A human rights-based approach to maternal mortality in the United States

Nan Strauss and Rachel Ward

7.1 Introduction

With 99% of maternal deaths occurring in developing countries, preventable maternal mortality in developed nations is an often overlooked subject. Yet preventable maternal deaths persist in wealthier countries, often signalling systemic failures and significant health disparities. In the United States, where more money is spent on healthcare than in any other country,[1] women are more likely to die of complications resulting from pregnancy or childbirth than in 49 other countries.[2] The maternal mortality ratio is higher in the US than in nearly all European countries, as well as several countries in Asia and the Middle East.[3] Despite UN data showing a 34% decrease in global maternal mortality between 1990 and 2008, with maternal death rates declining in 147 countries, the US was among just 23 countries to see an *increase* in maternal mortality.[4]

In the United States, two to three women die each day from complications of pregnancy and childbirth,[5] and approximately 34,000 women a year experience a 'near miss' (a maternal complication so severe that the woman nearly died).[6] Near misses have increased by 27% between 1998 and 2005 and now affect one woman every 15 minutes in the US.[7] Well over 1 million women a

1 Organization for Economic Co-operation and Development, *OECD health data 2011: frequently requested data*. Available at www.oecd.org/document/16/0,3343,en_2649_34631_2085200_1_1_1_1,00.html.

2 World Health Organization, et al., *Trends in maternal mortality: 1990 to 2008*. 2010, WHO: Geneva. Available at http://whqlibdoc.who.int/publications/2010/9789241500265_eng.pdf.

3 Ibid. Also M.C. Hogan, et al., Maternal mortality for 181 countries: 1980–2008: a systematic analysis of progress towards the Millennium Development Goal 5, *The Lancet* 375, 2010, 1609–1623.

4 See n.2.

5 J. Xu, K.D. Kochanek, et al., *Final data for 2007*, National Vital Statistics Reports, Hyattsville, MD: National Center for Health Statistics; 2010. Available at www.cdc.gov/nchs/data/nvsr/nvsr58/ nvsr58_19.pdf.

6 E.V. Kuklina, et al., Severe obstetric morbidity in the United States: 1998–2005, *Obstetrics and Gynecology* 113(2 Pt 1), 2009, 293.

7 Ibid.

year suffer complications or adverse health effects related to pregnancy and childbirth.[8] Between 2003 and 2007 (the most recent data available), the average maternal mortality ratio has remained close to 13 deaths per 100,000 live births, approximately double the low of 6.6 deaths per 100,000 live births recorded in 1987. Although partly a result of data-collection improvements, this substantial increase remains a cause for concern.[9]

Countries with similar economic, cultural and social characteristics as the US, including Australia, Canada and the United Kingdom have maternal mortality ratios half of or less than half of that of the US.[10] The comparatively high rate of maternal deaths in the US is an indicator of the failure of the US government to ensure that women have guaranteed lifelong access to equitable, quality healthcare including reproductive health services.[11]

7.2 Maternal mortality and human rights

Preventable maternal mortality can result from or reflect violations of a variety of human rights, including the right to life, the right to freedom from discrimination and the right to the highest attainable standard of health.[12] The United States has ratified two key international human rights treaties that guarantee these rights: the International Covenant on Civil and Political Rights and the International Convention on the Elimination of All Forms of Racial Discrimination. It has also signed two international treaties that address these rights – the International Covenant on Economic and Social Rights and the Convention on the Elimination of All Forms of Discrimination against Women – and so has an obligation to refrain from acts that would defeat the object and purpose of these treaties.

Governments are obligated to respect, protect and fulfil these and other human rights and are ultimately accountable for guaranteeing a healthcare system that ensures these rights universally and equitably. According to

8 C.J. Berg, et al., Overview of maternal morbidity during hospitalization for labor and delivery in the United States 1993–1997 and 2001–2005, *Obstetrics and Gynecology* 113(5), 2009.

9 C.J. Berg, et al., Pregnancy-related mortality in the United States, 1998 to 2005, *Obstetrics and Gynecology* 116(6), 2010, 1302. G.K. Singh, *Maternal mortality in the United States, 1935–2007: substantial racial/ethnic, socioeconomic, and geographic disparities persist. A 75th anniversary publication*, 2010, Health Resources and Services Administration, Maternal and Child Health Bureau, U.S. Department of Health and Human Services: Rockville, MD. Available at www.hrsa.gov/ourstories/mchb75th/mchb75maternalmortality.pdf.

10 See n.2.

11 Amnesty International, *Deadly delivery: the maternal health care crisis in the USA*, 2010, New York: Amnesty International USA. Available at http://www.amnestyusa.org/our-work/campaigns/demand-dignity/maternal-health-is-a-human-right/maternal-health-in-the-us?id=1351091.

12 United Nations Office of the High Commissioner for Human Rights, *Report of the Office of the High Commissioner for Human Rights on preventable maternal mortality and morbidity and human rights*, UN Doc. A/HRC/14/39. Available at http://www2.ohchr.org/english/bodies/hrcouncil/docs/14session/A.HRC.14.39_AEV-2.pdf.

human rights principles, the healthcare system must provide healthcare services that are available, accessible, acceptable and of good quality.[13] In addition, the healthcare system must be accountable, free from discrimination, and ensure that women are actively involved in health policy and healthcare decision-making processes.[14]

The human rights framework provides a practical tool to monitor and hold governments accountable on ensuring maternal health and eliminating preventable maternal mortality and morbidity. In June 2009 the UN Human Rights Council issued a resolution explicitly recognizing preventable maternal mortality as a human rights issue.[15] The UN Office of the High Commissioner on Human Rights followed the resolution with a report further elaborating on the application of a human rights-based approach to maternal mortality and making recommendations on how a human rights analysis can add value to existing maternal health initiatives.[16]

Amnesty International has applied a human rights framework to research and analyse maternal health in the United States as well as other countries, including Burkina Faso, Peru and Sierra Leone, in an effort to help identify solutions to the problems that exist and to develop an example of how a human rights framework can be used to address human rights violations in developed as well as developing nations.

7.3 US maternal mortality data

The most recent data from the US Centers for Disease Control and Prevention, released in 2010, put the US maternal mortality ratio at 12.7 deaths per 100,000 live births.[17] Maternal mortality remains approximately three times as high as the 'Healthy People 2010' goal – the target established by the US government to reduce maternal mortality to 4.3 deaths per 100,000 live births.[18]

There is wide variation in risk and outcomes across the 50 states.[19] The maternal mortality ratio for the District of Columbia (41.6 deaths per 100,000 live births) is almost 30 times higher than in Maine (1.4 deaths per 100,000 live births), and 10 times higher than Indiana (4.3 deaths per 100,000 live births).[20] Ten states had particularly high maternal mortality ratios of 18.5 or more, while only five states met the government's goal of

13 United Nations Committee on Economic Social and Cultural Rights, *The right to the highest attainable standard of health. General comment no. 14 E/C.12/2000/4*. 2000: Geneva.

14 Ibid.

15 United Nations Human Rights Council, Resolution 11/8, *Preventable maternal mortality and morbidity and human rights*, UN Doc. A/HRC/RES/11/8, 11th Session, 17 June 2009.

16 See n.12.

17 See n.5.

18 See n.9.

19 Ibid. See n. 11.

20 See n.9.

4.3 deaths per 100,000 live births.[21] This considerable variation may reflect the significant differences in healthcare access, funding, policies and staffing in different areas.

7.4 Inequities in maternal health

In the United States, women of colour, low-income women, indigenous women, immigrant women and women with limited English all face additional risks to maternal health.[22] African American women are three to four times more likely to die than white women during pregnancy, a disparity that has been unchanged for six decades.[23] While no racial or ethnic group came close to meeting the 'Healthy People 2010' goal, the maternal mortality ratio for American Indian/Alaska Native women is four times higher and for non-Hispanic black women it is eight times higher than the target, respectively.[24] Recent government data show that for 2005–2007, the maternal mortality ratio was highest among non-Hispanic black women (34.0), followed by American Indians/Alaska Natives (16.9), Asian/Pacific Islanders (11.0), non-Hispanic whites (10.4) and Hispanics (9.6).[25]

Women from lower socioeconomic backgrounds are more likely to be exposed to risks during pregnancy, with women living in the lowest-income areas twice as likely to suffer a maternal death compared with women in the highest-income areas.[26] Higher poverty rates increased the risk of maternal mortality for both white and black women and racial disparities were seen at all income levels, with black women facing approximately three times higher maternal mortality risk compared to white women in low-, middle- and high-income areas.[27] These disparities reflect the inequitable access to healthcare and information, discrimination and inappropriate treatment, and socio-economic inequalities that low-income women and women of colour face.[28]

Studies have demonstrated that the greater risk of death for black women does not simply reflect a greater risk of an underlying complication occurring. In a national study of five complications that are common causes of maternal death and injury (pre-eclampsia, eclampsia, obstetric haemorrhage, abruption and placenta previa), black women were not significantly more likely than white women to suffer from any of these conditions.[29] However, the black women in the study were two to three times more likely to die than white

21 See n.9.
22 See n.11.
23 See n.9.
24 Ibid.
25 Ibid.
26 Ibid.
27 Ibid.
28 See n.11.
29 M.J. Tucker, C.J. Berg, et al., The black–white disparity in pregnancy-related mortality from 5 conditions: differences in prevalence and case-fatality rates, *American Journal of Public Health* 97, 2007, 247–251.

women who had the same complication.[30] This discrepancy suggests that disparities in the quality of care may be a factor contributing to the increased risk for black women. Likewise, a study comparing maternal outcomes for Mexican-born women and white non-Latina women in California found that while Mexican-born women were less likely to suffer complications overall, they did face a greater risk of particular obstetric complications such as postpartum haemorrhage, major puerperal infections and third- and fourth-degree lacerations, suggesting that the care they receive may be of poorer quality.[31]

While women of colour face particular barriers and risks, reflected in their significantly higher rates of maternal death, all women in the US face an unacceptably high risk. By the most conservative estimate, the maternal mortality ratio for US white women alone would rank 32nd in the world, behind *31 other countries*.[32] The disparities and the overall high rates of maternal deaths together indicate the need for strategies to improve maternal health for the entire population of women.

7.5 Barriers to care

Approximately half of US maternal deaths could have been prevented with better access to good-quality maternal healthcare.[33] The US government has failed to address the obstacles that stand in the way of women getting the care that they need and have the right to. Women in the US face a range of systemic barriers that prevent them from obtaining the services, care and assistance required for a safe and healthy pregnancy and childbirth.

The UN Committee on Economic, Social and Cultural Rights has established that in order to fulfil the right to health, health systems must meet the following criteria:

- Health facilities, goods, services and information on health must be physically and economically *accessible* to everyone without discrimination.
- A sufficient quantity of health facilities, trained professionals and essential medicines must be *available*.
- Health facilities, goods, services and information must be acceptable – that is, respect medical ethics, be culturally *appropriate* and sensitive to gender requirements.

30 Ibid.

31 S. Guendelman, et al., Social disparities in maternal morbidity during labor and delivery between Mexican-born and US-born white Californians, 1996–1998, *American Journal of Public Health* 95(12), 2005, 2218–2224. Available at www.pubmedcentral.nih.gov/articlerender.fcgi?artid=1449510.

32 See n. 2. See also n. 3. See also n. 5.

33 S. Bacak, C.J. Berg, et al. (eds), *State maternal mortality review: accomplishments of nine states*, Atlanta: Centers for Disease Control and Prevention; 2006. Available at www.cdph.ca.gov/data/statistics/Documents/MO-CDC-ReportAccomplishments9States.pdf.

- Health facilities, goods services and information must be scientifically and medically appropriate and of *good quality*.[34]

Amnesty International documented failures in each of these areas that must be remedied in order to ensure that all women in the US can enjoy their right to the highest attainable standard of health in pregnancy and childbirth.

7.5.1 *Accessibility*

For many women in the US, the high cost of healthcare means that effective and comprehensive maternal care is out of reach. Challenges to ensuring maternal health emerge even before women become pregnant. Low-income women are more likely to begin a pregnancy uninsured and, as a result, are more likely to enter pregnancy suffering from undiagnosed or untreated chronic health conditions that increase the risk to themselves and their babies during pregnancy.[35] Increase in unemployment as a result of the recent economic recession has resulted in a growing number of uninsured women, because most individuals in the US obtain their health insurance through their employer.[36] The recession has had an especially large impact on women of reproductive age, with 2.3 million losing private health coverage between 2008 and 2009. While some of these newly uninsured women were able to obtain coverage through Medicaid, the number of reproductive age women not covered by any insurance has risen to 13.7 million, 22.3% of that segment of the population.[37] Among women living below the federal poverty level ($18,310 for a family of three), four in 10 women of reproductive age were uninsured because of the lower percentage who are offered or can afford private insurance and because in many states Medicaid only covers individuals who are not pregnant if their income falls well below the poverty level.[38]

Having a baby is the most costly health event families are likely to encounter during their childbearing years.[39] Approximately 99% of women give birth in hospitals where facility fees alone average between $8900 and $11,400 for a vaginal delivery and between $14,900 and $20,100 for a

34 United Nations Committee on Economic Social and Cultural Rights, *The right to the highest attainable standard of health. General comment no. 14 E/C.12/2000/4*. Op. cit.

35 D. D'Angelo, et al., *Preconception and interconception health status of women who recently gave birth to a live-born infant – pregnancy risk assessment monitoring system (PRAMS), United States, 26 reporting areas, 2004*. MMWR Surveill Summ 56(10), 2007, 1–35.

36 Kaiser Family Foundation, *The uninsured, a primer: key facts about Americans withouth health insurance*, October 2011. Available at www.kff.org/uninsured/upload/7451-07.pdf.

37 A. Sonfield, Evidence mounts of recession's impact on women of reproductive age, *Guttmacher Policy Review* 13(4), 2010.

38 Ibid.

39 Jennifer L. Howse, March of dimes study unveils cost of having a baby, *Law & Health Weekly* June 2007, 887.

caesarean, depending on whether complications occur.[40] This does not include the health professional fee, which can include an additional $4350 to $6000:[41]

> Trina Bachtel died from complications of pre-eclampsia after giving birth to a stillborn baby in August 2007. Trina began to feel ill during her pregnancy. She did not immediately seek care at a local clinic because she had previously incurred a medical debt there, and she believed she would be required to pay a $100 deposit to get care.[42]

Women of colour face particular barriers to accessing healthcare. While women of colour account for one-third of all women in the US, they account for half of the uninsured.[43] Low-income workers are less likely to be offered employee insurance, but many do not qualify for Medicaid and cannot afford to buy private insurance.[44] About one-third of Hispanics (32%) and Native Americans (30%), and 22% of African Americans are uninsured, compared to 14% of the white population.[45] Undocumented immigrants are by far the group most likely to be uninsured, with approximately 60% of adults lacking health insurance in 2008.[46]

Women with no prenatal care are three to four times more likely to die of pregnancy-related complications than women who receive prenatal care.[47] That risk increases even further for women with high-risk pregnancies.[48] Native American women are three and a half times more likely and African American and Latina women are two and a half times as likely as white women to receive prenatal care beginning in the third trimester or not at all.[49] The 'Healthy People 2010' goals set a target that 90% of women receive adequate prenatal care beginning in the first trimester.[50] However, data suggest that, for approximately one in four women, her care falls short of this goal.[51] This

40 Childbirth Connection, *Charges for giving birth by facility and mode of birth*. 2011. Available at www.childbirthconnection.org/article.asp?ck=10463.

41 Thomson Health, *The healthcare costs of having a baby*, June 2007, p. 8, Table 3. Available at www.kff.org/womenshealth/upload/whp061207othc.pdf.

42 See n.11.

43 Ibid.

44 L. Clemans-Cope, et al., *Access to employer-sponsored health insurance among low-income families*, The Urban Institute, 2007. Available at www.urban.org/UploadedPDF/411533_fringe _ benefits.pdf.

45 Ibid.

46 J. Passel and D. Cohn, *A portrait of unauthorized immigrants in the United States*, Pew Hispanic Center, 14 April 2009, 8.

47 J. Chang, et al., *Pregnancy-related mortality surveillance – United States, 1991–1999*, MMWR Surveill Summ 52(2), 2003, 1–8.

48 D. Rosenberg, S.E. Geller, et al., Disparities in mortality among high risk pregnant women in Illinois: a population based study, *Annals of Epidemiology* 16, 2006, 26–32.

49 National Center for Health Statistics, CDC, Health, United States, 2010, Table 5. Available at www.cdc.gov/nchs/data/hus/hus10.pdf.

50 Healthy People 2010: midcourse review. US Department of Health and Human Services. 2000.

51 Ibid.

figure rises to 32% for African American women and 41% for American Indian and Alaska Native women.[52]

For those who are eligible for publicly financed care on becoming pregnant, complicated bureaucratic hurdles also stand in the way of women receiving early prenatal care. Such hurdles can include in-person interviews prior to receiving prenatal care, burdensome and costly documentation requirements and long waiting times to make an appointment or to be seen on the day of the appointment, due to staff shortages.[53] In addition, providers' unwillingness to accept patients with Medicaid due to low reimbursement rates increases the likelihood that a woman will not receive timely or sufficient care.[54]

Barriers to accessing timely healthcare during pregnancy include problems obtaining or paying for transportation to medical care, childcare and time off work,[55] all of which particularly affect women from low-income groups. Language barriers also persist. A lack of interpreter services, bilingual caseworkers and materials not written in English limit a woman's ability to access services and treatment, express concerns about her health and pregnancy and restricts her ability to make informed decisions. It is also important for health providers to understand that language is not the only barrier to effective patient–provider communication.[56] Cultural beliefs and values can influence how a person understands healthcare information, but are often not taken into account by healthcare providers, resulting in ineffective communication and preventing women from participating in care decisions.[57]

Many women face a lack of access to information about family-planning and affordable contraceptive services. Approximately half of all pregnancies in the United States are unplanned.[58] The rates are significantly higher for low-income women and women of colour. For example, black women are nearly three times as likely as white women to experience an unintended pregnancy.[59] Women with unintended pregnancies face greater risks to their

52 Ibid.

53 Betsy Gotbaum, *Hurdles to a healthy baby: pregnant women face barriers to prenatal care at city health centers*, Office of the New York City Public Advocate, May 2007. I. Hill and A. Westpfahl Lutzky, *Getting in, not getting in, and why: understanding SCHIP enrollment*, Urban Institute, Assessing the New Federalism Occasional Paper No.66, 16 May 2003, 8–9. Available at www.urban.org/uploadedPDF/310793_OP-66.pdf.

54 See n.11.

55 B.M. Aved, et al., Barriers to prenatal care for low-income women, *Western Journal of Medicine*, 158, 1993, 493–498. R. Milligan, et al., Perceptions about prenatal care: views of urban vulnerable groups, *BMC Public* Health 2(1), 2002, 25. Available at www. biomedcentral.com/ 1471-2458/2/25. See also n. 11.

56 See n.11.

57 K. Singleton and E. Krause, Understanding cultural and linguistic barriers to health literacy, *OJIN: Online Journal of Issues in Nursing*14(3), 2010.

58 L.B. Finer and S.K. Henshaw, Disparities in rates of unintended ppregnancy in the United States, 1994 and 2001, *Perspectives on Sexual and Reproductive Health* 38(2), 2006, 90–96. Available at http://www.guttmacher.org/pubs/psrh/full/3809006.pdf.

59 Ibid.

health: they are more likely to start prenatal care late, receive inadequate prenatal care, develop complications and face worse outcomes for themselves and their babies.[60] In addition, women are two and a half times more likely to die if they become pregnant again within six months of giving birth.[61]

Of the estimated 17.5 million women in the US estimated to be in need of publicly funded family planning services and supplies, Medicaid and government funded clinics cover only just over half of this demand,[62] leaving many without the necessary coverage. The problems accessing reproductive healthcare have become even more serious as a result of the recession. Family planning centres have reported an increase in low-income and uninsured clients seeking low- or no-cost care. At the same time, family planning clinics are facing budget crises due to state budget shortfalls and cutbacks, resulting in cutbacks in the services and contraceptive options offered, as well as staff being stretched thin due to lay-offs and hiring freezes.[63]

Recognizing these serious failures of the healthcare system, the UN Committee on the Elimination of Racial Discrimination has recommended that the US: '[C]ontinue its efforts to address persistent racial disparities in sexual and reproductive health, in particular by improving access to . . . family planning; facilitating access to adequate contraceptive and family planning methods; and providing adequate sexual education aimed at the prevention of unintended pregnancies.'[64]

7.5.2 *Availability*

Shortages of trained maternal healthcare providers and inadequate staffing at facilities, particularly in low-income inner-city and rural areas, contribute to a lack of available healthcare providers. Contrary to expectation, the US has a relatively small number of obstetricians (9.6 per 1000 births) and the lowest number of midwives to births (0.4 per 1000) among industrialized countries,[65] which has created an acute shortage of maternal care providers in some areas.

In December 2011 healthcare provider shortages, including maternal healthcare providers, affected 58.4 million people, most of whom were living

60 Ibid.

61 A. Conde-Agudelo and J.M. Belizan, Maternal morbidity and mortality associated with interpregnancy interval: cross sectoral study, *British Medical Journal* 321, 2000, 1255–1259. Available at www.bmj.com/cgi/content/full/321/7271/1255.

62 Guttmacher Institute, *Contraceptive needs and services, 2006*, 2009. Available at www.guttmacher.org/pubs/win/allstates2006.pdf.

63 Ibid.

64 CERD, Consideration of reports submitted by states parties under Article 9 of the Convention, concluding observations of the Committee on the Elimination of Racial Discrimination, United States of America, February 2008. Available at www2.ohchr.org/english/bodies/cerd/docs/co/CERD-C-USA-CO-6.pdf.

65 Organization for Economic Co-operation and Development, *Midwives and ob/gyns per 1,000 births, OECD Countries, 2006*. 2009.

in inner-city and rural areas.[66] Of these medically underserved areas, only about 20% of these areas are served by community health centres (also known as federally qualified health centres – FQHCs) that provide 'safety net' care in underserved areas and communities.[67] Community health centres face significant barriers in recruiting and retaining healthcare providers, with especially severe shortages of obstetricians.[68]

Understaffing, a problem especially prevalent in low-income communities, can result in substandard care and may lead to an increased likelihood of errors made by healthcare professionals.[69] Understaffing creates the need to care for a high volume of patients, making it difficult or impossible to provide good-quality care.[70] The current economic downturn is likely to exacerbate the problem of understaffing, as state budgets are being reduced, resulting in services and positions being eliminated:

> Trudy LaGrew, a Native American woman living on the Red Cliff reservation in Wisconsin, died of an undiagnosed heart condition following the birth of her son. Although her pregnancy was high risk, she was unable to seek care from a specialist, which would have required a two hour drive each way.[71]

Women have reported particular shortages among providers who accept Medicaid, with the most severe shortages affecting specialists, such as cardiologists or obstetricians specializing in high-risk pregnancies. This is likely due to the fact that maternal healthcare providers face high malpractice insurance premiums and receive very low fees for the services they provide to women covered by Medicaid, which results in a disincentive to practising in this area and to treating low-income women.[72]

66 Health Resources and Services Administration, *Shortage designation: HPSAs, MUAs & MUPs*. 2011. Available from http://bhpr.hrsa.gov/shortage/.

67 Health Resources and Services Administration, *Health centers: America's primary care safety net, reflections on success, 2002–2007*, 2008, US Department of Health and Human Services, Bureau of Primary Health Care: Rockville, MD.

68 H. Andrilla and G. Hart, *Health center expansion and recruitment survey 2004: results by health and human services regions and health center geography*, Technical Report, March 2007, 19 and 23, Figures 4a and 4e. Available at http://depts.washington.edu/uwrhrc/uploads/HC_Survey_Report.pdf.

69 M. Regenstein and J. Huang, *Stresses to the safety net: the public hospital perspective*, Kaiser Commission on Medicaid and the Uninsured, report no. 7329, June 2005. Available at www.kff.org/medicaid/7329.cfm.

70 Institute of Medicine, Keeping patients safe: transforming the work environment of nurses, Institute of Medicine Committee on the Work Environment for Nurses and Patient Safety Board on Health Care Services. Washington, DC: National Academies Press; 2004, 229 and 386. Association of Women's Health, Obstetric and Neonatal Nurses, Guidelines for professional registered nurse staffing for perinatal units, Washington, DC: 2010.

71 See n.11.

72 Ibid.

7.5.3 *Acceptability*

Discriminatory attitudes that prevent or discourage women from accessing the healthcare they need when they need it can have serious health consequences. Discrimination and culturally inappropriate care greatly affect a woman's chance of being healthy prior to as well as during pregnancy and childbirth.[73] The failure to provide culturally competent and gender-sensitive care can significantly impact a women's ability and willingness to access services and care.[74] Discriminatory attitudes towards women who speak little or no English can also exacerbate barriers. Amnesty International has had reports of discrimination on the basis of gender, race, indigenous status, immigration status, language and poverty,[75] resulting in women's needs and rights being routinely disregarded.[76]

Amnesty International received reports of inappropriate behaviour and care experienced by women of colour in a variety of healthcare settings, affecting both access to and quality of services. Amnesty International's research documented accounts where women who were, or were assumed to be, uninsured or insured through a public health programme, were treated with indifference or a lack of respect and sometimes dissuaded from seeking services. Latina women reported experiencing unusually long delays in waiting rooms and feeling that they were ignored or treated with disdain by staff. Native American and Alaska Native women also reported culturally inappropriate and discriminatory treatment. This was a particular problem for the many women who must seek healthcare services at some distance from their communities.[77] Measures that women perceive as punitive or which penalize those with substance abuse problems or undocumented immigrants can also deter some women from seeking healthcare services.[78]

Reports from women, health providers and advocates suggest that the information women are given is often inadequate and undermines their right to informed consent. In particular, women of colour, women who are uninsured or receive Medicaid and women who do not speak English are less likely to be involved in decisions about their care.[79]

73 United Nations Office of the High Commissioner for Human Rights, *Report of the Office of the High Commissioner for Human Rights on preventable maternal mortality and morbidity and human rights*, UN Doc. A/HRC/14/39, op. cit.

74 J.R. Betancourt, et al., Defining cultural competence: a practical framework for addressing racial/ethnic disparities in health and health care, *Public Health Reports* 118(4), 2003, 293.

75 K. Singleton and E. Krause, *Understanding cultural and linguistic barriers to health literacy*, op. cit.

76 See n.11.

77 Ibid.

78 Ibid. M.A. Jessup, Extrinsic barriers to substance abuse treatment among pregnant drug-dependent women, *Journal of Drug Issues* 33, 2003, 285–287. Available at www.nnvawi.org/pdfs/alo/ Humphreys_barriers_substance_treatment.pdf.

79 See n.11. E.R. Declercq, et al., *Listening to mothers II: report of the second national US survey of women's childbearing experiences*, 59 and 68, table 27. Available at www.childbirthconnection.org/pdf.asp?PDFDownload=LTMII_report.

The intersection of discrimination on the basis of gender, race, indigenous status, immigration status, language and poverty may create a climate in which women's needs and rights are routinely disregarded.[80] Only six states had legislation requiring or strongly recommending that medical students or physicians complete cultural competency courses as part of their licensing or accreditation programmes.[81] The Office of Minority Health within the Department of Health and Human Services has developed 14 national standards for culturally and linguistically appropriate services in healthcare (CLAS) in order to provide a consistent approach to cultural and linguistic competence in healthcare, but these are not implemented nationwide.[82]

7.5.4 *Quality*

Currently there is an inadequate implementation of guidelines and protocols, as well as a lack of information and participation in maternal care. Furthermore, the quality of care provided is highly variable, with many women receiving substandard care, particularly those in low-income areas where clinics and hospitals are more likely to be overcrowded and understaffed.[83]

Seven leading potentially fatal complications of pregnancy and childbirth together account for approximately three out of four of maternal deaths: embolism (blood clots); haemorrhage (severe blood loss); eclampsia/pre-eclampsia (pregnancy disorders associated with excessively high blood pressure); infection; cardiomyopathy (heart muscle disease); cardiac conditions; and other medical conditions.[84] There is a need for implementation of guidelines on preventing, recognizing and treating these conditions, in order to reduce the preventable deaths and to ensure that all women receive quality, evidence-based care:[85]

> Linda Coale died of a blood clot a week after giving birth to her son, Ben, by C-section. The infant welcome packet included extensive information about acclimatizing pets to a new baby, but had failed to adequately alert her to warning signs of complications, despite the heightened risk due to her surgery.[86]

80 See n.11.
81 Office of Minority Health, Cultural Competency Legislation. Available at www.thinkculturalhealth.hhs.gov/Content/LegislatingCLAS.asp. (WA, CA, CT, NJ, NM mandate cultural competence training and MD strongly recommends it.)
82 US Department of Health and Human Services, Office of Minority Health, National Standards for Culturally and Linguistically Appropriate Services in Health Care, March 2001. Available at www.thinkculturalhealth.hhs.gov/Content/clas.asp.
83 See n.69.
84 See n.8.
85 C. Sakala and M. Corry, *Evidence-based maternity care: what it is and what it can achieve*, Childbirth Connection, the Reforming States Group and the Millbank Memorial Fund, October 2008, Figure 2. Available at www.milbank.org/reports/0809MaternityCare/0809MaternityCare.html#figure3.
86 See n.11.

Currently in the US there are no nationally implemented, evidence-based protocols for promoting safe and quality maternal care and for preventing, identifying and managing obstetric emergencies.[87] The failure to establish and ensure the adoption of such standards can result in high variability of services and procedures and increased risk of error, preventable complications and deaths.[88]

Research has shown that the use of medical procedures when they are not needed carries unnecessary health risks that may put women and their babies at risk.[89] For example, caesarean section is a life-saving intervention for both baby and mother that remains one of the most essential components of emergency obstetric care needed to prevent unnecessary maternal mortality globally.[90] However, a woman's risk of death is over three times higher with caesareans and they carry a greater risk of a number of complications including infection, hysterectomy and kidney failure.[91] The increase in 'near misses' has also been associated, in part, with rising caesarean rates.[92]

The US caesarean rate, 32.8% in 2010, has increased nearly 60% since 1996, when it was just 20.7% of all births.[93] It is now more than double the World Health Organization's recommended rate of between 5 and 15%.[94] African American women have the highest caesarean rates. On average, costs are higher for caesareans, even though they take less time, and studies have found that caesarean rates are higher at for-profit hospitals and among women with private insurance.[95]

87 Ibid.

88 Ibid. See also n. 11.

89 See n. 6. M. Knight, Peripartum hysterectomy in the UK: management and outcomes of the associated haemorrhage, *BJOG: An International Journal of Obstetrics & Gynaecology* 114(11), 2007, 1380–1387. J.M. Belizán, F. Althabe, and M.L. Cafferata, *Health consequences of the increasing caesarean section rates. Epidemiology* 18(4), 2007, 485.

90 L. Gibbons, et al., *The global numbers and costs of additionally needed and unnecessary caesarean sections performed per year: overuse as a barrier to universal coverage*, in *World Health Report. Background Paper 30*, 2010, WHO: Geneva.

91 C. Deneux-Tharaux, et al., Postpartum maternal mortality and cesarean delivery, *Obstetrics & Gynecology*, 2006, 108(3), part.1. Available at www.acog.org/from_home/publications/green_journal/2006/v108n3p541.pdf. J. Villar, et al., Maternal and neonatal individual risks and benefits associated with caesarean delivery: multicentre prospective study, *BMJ* 335, 2007, 1025, 5. Available at www.bmj.com/cgi/reprint/335/7628/1025?maxtoshow=&HITS=10&hits=10& RESULTFORMAT=&fulltext=Caesarean+delivery+rat es&searchid=1&FIRSTINDEX=0&resourcety pe=HWCIT.

92 See n.6.

93 B.E. Hamilton, et al., Births: preliminary data for 2010, *National Vital Statistics Reports*60(2), 2011, National Center for Health Statistics, table 8. Available at www.cdc.gov/nchs/data/nvsr/nvsr60/ nvsr60_02.pdf. J.A. Martin, et al., Births: final data for 2006, National Vital Statistics Reports 57(7), 2009, National Center for Health Statistics, table 28. Available at www.cdc.gov/nchs/data/nvsr/ nvsr57/nvsr57_07.pdf.

94 WHO, *Baby-friendly hospital initiative: revised, updated and expanded for integrated care*, 2009, 58. Available at www.who.int/nutrition/publications/infantfeeding/9789241594967_s1/en/index.html.

95 C.A. Russo, et al., *Hospitalizations related to childbirth, 2006*, Statistical Brief No.71, April 2009, 7, table 1. Available at /www.hcup-us.ahrq.gov/reports/statbriefs/sb71.pdf. N. Johnson, For profit hospitals are performing more C-sections, *California Watch*,

Recent data have indicated that in US states with higher than average caesarean rates (over 33%) were associated with a 21% higher maternal mortality risk than states with a lower than average caesarean rate.[96] Despite this correlation between maternal mortality and rising rates of medical procedures, no national efforts are yet under way to establish guidance for providers regarding the appropriate circumstances for the use of medical procedures:[97]

> Valerie Scythes died in 2007 from an embolism soon after giving birth by C-section to her daughter, Isabella Rose. Despite having a heightened risk of developing a blood clot, simple preventative measures were never taken to prevent a clot from forming, including ensuring that Valerie got out of bed as soon as possible following surgery or providing compression devices to prevent the development of a clot.

Providing quality postpartum care will reduce the risk of complications and will contribute to the overall health of the women and the baby. Postpartum care in the US is generally limited to a single office visit approximately six weeks after childbirth, unless the woman has a recognized complication. Most health insurance plans do not cover home visits by a nurse or mid-wife or other trained professional who could help the woman to recognize complications that may develop and could educate women about how they can best ensure their health and the health of their babies. By contrast, in many countries in Europe, multiple home visits following birth are the standard of care for all women. Providing quality postpartum care to all women in the US would help reduce maternal deaths and improve maternal health by helping women to recognize complications, such as infection, blood clots and haemorrhage, that can develop after women have returned home:[98]

> Tameka McFarquhar bled to death alone in her apartment in Watertown, New York. She was discharged a day after giving birth to her daughter. Family members became alarmed when they could not reach her, but by the time they could access her apartment, they found her and her baby already dead. According to one expert, Tameka's death may have been prevented with a post-partum home visit.[99]

11 September 2010. Available at http://californiawatch.org/health-and-welfare/profit-hospitals-performing-more-c-sections-4069.

96 See n.9.

97 See n.11.

98 Ibid.

99 Ibid.

7.6 Lack of data, oversight and accountability

A lack of recent, quality data is masking the full extent of the problems with maternal health in the US. Currently, there is no comprehensive, nationwide system through which to collect and analyse data on maternal deaths, complications and performance measures. With incomplete data, it is difficult to analyse and address problems and develop evidence-based programmes and policies.[100] There is no nationwide requirement to separately report maternal deaths and only six states require such separate, mandatory reporting. While other states track maternal deaths using other methods, including data linking through birth certificates and death certificates, under-reporting of pregnancy-related deaths remains a pervasive problem.[101] The lack of consistency in reporting from state to state results in wide variation in the classification and reporting of maternal deaths.

The US also lacks effective mechanisms to review maternal deaths that are reported and to ensure accountability regarding such deaths. Enquiries and investigations into the circumstances and causation of maternal deaths are fundamental to the assessment of the safety and effectiveness of maternity and healthcare services and are essential to preventing future deaths.

Maternal mortality review procedures provide an effective way of identifying problems, developing recommendations and establishing key priorities for addressing gaps in service provision. Such procedures also ensure accountability and can develop targeted interventions. Efforts have been made by a number of states to establish maternal death review processes. However, funding shortages and issues around implementation continue to plague the development of such processes. Despite the positive effects maternal mortality review processes can have on reducing pregnancy related deaths,[102] as of 2010, 29 states and the District of Columbia reported to Amnesty International that they had no review process at all.[103] As a result of increased advocacy on maternal health, in 2011 three additional states (Georgia, New Hampshire and New Mexico) have been able to initiate or re-establish maternal mortality review boards. Efforts in other states to pass legislation to establish review boards are ongoing.

100 K.S. Khan, et al., WHO analysis of causes of maternal death: a systematic review, *The Lancet* 367(9516), 2006, 1066–1074.

101 D.L. Hoyert, Maternal mortality and related concepts, National Center for Health Statistics, *Vital Health Stats* 3(33), 2007.

102 Centre for Maternal and Child Enquiries (CMACE), Saving mothers' lives: reviewing maternal deaths to make motherhood safer: 2006–08. The eighth report on confidential enquiries into maternal deaths in the United Kingdom, *BJOG: An International Journal of Obstetrics & Gynaecology* 118(Suppl. 1), 2011, 1–203.

103 See n.11.

7.7 Impact of healthcare reform

On 23 March 2010 President Obama signed into law the Patient Protection and Affordable Care Act of 2010, the most extensive healthcare reform to be enacted in the US in decades, which promises to substantially improve healthcare coverage. A number of provisions begin to address barriers to obtaining quality healthcare documented by Amnesty International, although significant gaps and obstacles remain.[104] Healthcare reform is an important step to increasing women's access to maternal care, but the proposed legislation will not solve the maternal health crisis nor adequately address the human rights violations many American women are facing. Moreover, these expected improvements are at risk of not ever being fully implemented due to legal, legislative and financial challenges.

Because reform is primarily focused on healthcare coverage, it would leave largely unaddressed the issues of maternal health disparities, accountability and the quality of maternal care. It is expected that 23 million will remain uninsured[105] and 60% of medically underserved areas will remain without essential services. Furthermore, the reform does not adequately address the institutionalized unacceptable treatment of women and marginalized groups and does not include a strategy or plan to develop national guidelines for evidence-based maternal care.

Some of the expected results of the reform will likely have a positive effect on maternal care and health in the US. It is estimated that 32 million individuals will gain healthcare coverage, including an estimated 4.5 million women who will become eligible for Medicaid prior to pregnancy.[106] The availability of healthcare facilities and services will be improved by increased funding that has been committed for community health centres operating in provider shortage areas.[107] Barriers to accessing midwives, birth centres and home healthcare have been reduced through healthcare reform provisions allowing for Medicaid reimbursement for those services. The introduction of programmes on a small scale to support the training of a diverse workforce and promote cultural competence trainings of healthcare professionals are among provisions addressing disparities generally.

Various challenges put expanded access and other improvements promised by healthcare reform at risk. In 2011 legislation was introduced by Congress to repeal healthcare reform entirely or partially and, although it is considered

104 Patient Protection and Affordable Care Act, Public Law 111–148, 23 March 2010. Available at http://democrats.senate.gov/reform/patient-protection-affordable-care-act-as-passed.pdf.

105 Congressional Budget Office. *Cost estimate for the amendment in the nature of a substitute for H.R. 4872, incorporating a proposed manager's amendment made public on March 20, 2010*, 2010. Available at www.cbo.gov/ftpdocs/113xx/doc11379/AmendReconProp.pdf.

106 Ibid.

107 National Association of Community Health Centers. *Community health centers lead the primary care revolution*, 2010. Available at www.nachc.com/client/documents/Primary_Care_ Revolution_Final_8_6.pdf.

unlikely to pass, it reflects efforts to limit the effectiveness of the reforms. Financial constraints and proposed deep budget cuts are likely to have a damaging effect on maternal health in the US. Funding for existing healthcare programmes as well as planned expansions face the threat of significant cuts, including eliminating all funding for publicly funded family planning clinics and significantly reducing funding for community health centres, maternal child health grants to the states and the CDC. The proposed funding cuts could have a devastating impact on maternal health.

As efforts to reform the US healthcare system are developed and implemented, it is imperative that human rights standards are applied, so that all have equal access to affordable, quality healthcare, including maternal healthcare, and in order to avoid backsliding.

7.8 Next steps

7.8.1 National solutions

Amnesty International is calling on the US government to prioritize and establish accountability for improving maternal healthcare and outcomes. The Department of Health and Human Services should designate an individual, agency, or interagency committee charged with monitoring maternal health and healthcare and improving access to and the quality of maternal care. Critical steps include: expanding comprehensive data collection regarding deaths, complications and performance measures; establishing nationwide review of mortality and severe morbidity; ensuring that all women have access to timely prenatal care and home visits after birth; and developing and creating an implementation plan for evidence-based guidelines to prevent, recognize and respond to leading complications that cause maternal deaths.

The US must immediately take steps to eliminate maternal health disparities, including by vigorously enforcing federal anti-discrimination laws.

7.8.2 State-level solutions

All states should take measures to establish and improve maternal mortality review boards to investigate maternal deaths, complications and inequities and to implement changes to improve care. Review boards are essential to identifying gaps in maternal care and ensuring accountability to prevent deaths and complications in the future. Steps must also be taken to ensure that all women have prompt access to prenatal care, particularly for women seeking care under Medicaid.

7.8.3 Federal legislative developments

Amnesty International is working with a number of partners representing a wide variety of stakeholders to ensure that its recommendations are translated into policy and legal frameworks and to increase efforts to achieve change. Several federal bills have been introduced in Congress in 2011 and 2010 that would directly address a variety of the concerns identified and recommendations made by Amnesty International.

The Maternal Health Accountability Act of 2011, HR 894, was introduced on 3 March 2011 to help establish a maternal mortality review board in every state and improve existing review boards by creating a new grant programme. In addition, it would establish programmes to address disparities in maternal health for women of colour, those living in poverty, and indigenous and immigrant women, and it would also expand data collection and analysis.

The Maximizing Optimal Maternity Services (MOMS) for the 21st Century Act of 2010, HR 2141, introduced on 7 June 2011, would: establish an inter-agency coordinating committee in the US Department of Health and Human Services with responsibility for improving evidence-based maternal healthcare and practices; expand best practice maternity care; establish mechanisms to measure and reduce shortages of maternal care providers; and improve workforce diversity. The legislation also authorizes a public awareness media campaign to educate the public on maternal health and best practices in maternal.

On 8 December 2011 the Quality Care for Moms and Babies Act, HR 3620, S. 1969, was introduced to establish a core set of maternity care quality measures for Medicaid; to support the use of state and regional quality collaboratives to improve maternity care; and to create a woman-and family-centred maternity care home demonstration project.

In addition to the bills introduced in 2011, a bill was introduced into Congress in 2010 that would need to be reintroduced in the current Congress in order to move forward. The Maternity Care Improvement Act of 2010, HR 6318, was introduced on 28 September 2010. This legislation would increase government accountability on maternal health by improving the coordination of maternal health efforts and improving data collection; improve the maternity care workforce by making it more interdisciplinary; and improve the diversity and cultural competency of the maternity care workforce.

Federal legislation aimed at reducing global maternal mortality, the Global MOMS Act, HR 5268, was also introduced in 2010 and would support activities that help expand access to better-quality maternal health services by authorizing new assistance, better aligning existing programmes and improve coordination among US government agencies. This act would also remove barriers to such services ensuring that the US meets its international human rights standards.

7.9 Conclusion

Over the last 20 years the US has seen no improvement in maternal health and indications suggest that maternal health is actually deteriorating. Women continue to suffer preventable maternal deaths at rates that are unacceptable, particularly when the US is expending more resources on healthcare and maternal care than any other country in the world. To reverse these trends, the US government must commit to implementing a robust, systematic response to the issue of maternal health, incorporating input from multiple stakeholders. Steps must be taken to ensure that all women have access to timely and quality maternal healthcare before, during and after pregnancy, and to ensure that a system exists to maintain accountability.

Amnesty International recognizes a number of positive developments during 2010 and 2011, which suggest that, with a concerted effort, progress can be made in reducing maternal mortality and improving maternal health. Yet much more work must be done to ensure that all women have equal access to good-quality healthcare throughout their lives, that health disparities are addressed and eliminated, and that the government is accountable for ensuring specific improvements in the quality, safety and effectiveness of maternal care for all women in the US. In order to ensure women's right to a safe and healthy pregnancy and birth in the US, additional legislation and policy changes need to be put in place. Achieving these goals will require the prioritization and coordination of efforts specifically targeted to improve access to and the quality of maternal healthcare and outcomes for all women.

8 Enhancing international accountability for maternal mortality and morbidity: the work of civil society at the United Nations Human Rights Council

Sandeep Prasad

8.1 Introduction

It is not surprising that there has been a great deal of work by civil society to bring issues of maternal mortality and morbidity within the global human rights agenda and discourse – violations of human rights are always meant to entail accountability, which is the cornerstone of a human rights approach. Much of this effort has focused on using international expert bodies to hold governments accountable to their international human rights obligations related to maternal mortality and morbidity. In the process, this has led to the development of a large body of jurisprudence that interprets various international human rights treaties and establishes a variety of entitlements and obligations that governments are meant to provide for and discharge, respectively. However, this chapter tells the story of civil society bringing this issue into the intergovernmental human rights agenda and seeking to enhance international accountability for maternal mortality by advocating for the UN Human Rights Council, in particular, to play a key role in ensuring governments live up to their human rights obligations in this area. This work has enhanced and will continue to enhance international accountability through providing greater attention to how human rights principles need to be integrated into efforts to address maternal mortality and morbidity. This ongoing work has a strong potential to complement accelerated efforts led by the UN Secretary-General to meet commitments in the area of reproductive health found in the Millennium Development Goals (MDGs) by the 2015 deadline.

8.2 Background

Since about 2007 there has been an unprecedentedly high level of international attention on the issue of maternal mortality. Despite the inclusion of a goal on maternal health within the MDGs, which governments were agreed on in 2000, the period of time after this was marked by very slow improvements towards realizing this goal. In fact, in spite of various safe motherhood campaigns since 1987, overall levels of maternal mortality had reduced only slightly. High maternal mortality and morbidity rates have in fact been referred to as 'one of the shameful failures of development'.[1] Many attribute this failure to a lack of political will to prioritize and appropriately address women's health issues. In the words of one commentator: '[M]aternal care rarely gets the priority or attention it deserves. Partly that's because the victims tend to be faceless, illiterate village women who carry little weight in their own families, let alone on the national or world agenda.'[2] In speaking of the lack of progress on maternal and child health, another commentator stated: '[D]espite isolated examples of welcome progress, national and global attention to maternal, newborn, and child health is still strikingly inadequate. Children and mothers are dying because those who have the power to prevent their deaths choose not to act. This indifference – by politicians, policy makers, donors, research funders, and civil society – is a betrayal of our collective hope for a stronger and more just society.'[3]

8.3 Initial attention to maternal mortality as a human rights issue

Action to bring maternal mortality into the intergovernmental human rights agenda was fundamentally motivated to address this lack of political will to make concerted efforts towards the elimination of preventable maternal mortality and morbidity. It was intended to reinvigorate energy among governments and to encourage them to build a new perspective for themselves on this issue – one that moves away from seeing this from public health and development perspectives to one where it is viewed as a clear human rights issue.

Work specifically at the UN Human Rights Council to advance maternal mortality as a human rights concern began with work by the Special Rapporteur on the right to enjoyment of the highest attainable standard of physical and mental health, who is mandated to report to this intergovernmental body as well as to its parent body, the UN General Assembly. In his September 2006 annual report to the UN General Assembly, the Special

1 Kirstan Hawkins, Karen Newman, Deborah Thomas and Cindy Carlson, Developing a human rights-based approach to addressing maternal mortality: desk review, 2005, DFID Health Resource Centre. Available at http://hurilink.org/tools/Developing_aHRBA_to_Maternal_Mortality–DFID.pdf.

2 Nicholas D. Kristof, Terror of childbirth, *New York Times*, 20 March 2004. Available at www.nytimes.com/2004/03/20/opinion/terror-of-childbirth.html.

3 Richard Horton, Countdown to 2015: a report card on maternal, newborn, and child survival, *The Lancet* 371, 2008, 1217–1219.

Rapporteur called for a human rights campaign to be mounted against maternal mortality. In his words:

> [T]he human rights community should be challenged to mount a global human rights campaign against maternal mortality. The human rights community must be urged to remonstrate and demonstrate about maternal mortality just as loudly as it complains about extrajudicial executions, arbitrary detention, unfair trials and prisoners of conscience. Persistently high maternal mortality rates, coupled with the fact that all states are committed to reduce by three quarters the maternal mortality ratio by 2015, suggests that the time is ripe for such an initiative.[4]

During his following address to the Human Rights Council in March 2007, Paul Hunt suggested a key concrete step for the Council to begin to lead efforts within the UN system to address maternal mortality from a human rights perspective. He called for the Council to hold an urgent special session to address the insufficient attention being paid to maternal mortality as a human rights failure and a global health emergency.[5] This was a call that was reiterated one year later in his March 2008 address to the Council in discussing the Council's role in mainstreaming human rights, including the right to health, throughout the UN system: 'As I have argued before, one way for the Human Rights Council to encourage such mainstreaming is by holding a Special Session – or thematic panel – on a right to health issue of global importance, such as maternal mortality and MDG 5 . . . It would not be a technical meeting. But it would have major symbolic and political significance.'[6]

The symbolic and political significance of the Council's holding a debate on maternal mortality was not lost on civil society actors working at the Council. As of late 2007 Action Canada for Population and Development (ACPD) and its partners in the Sexual Rights Initiative,[7] all NGOs active at the Human

4 Report of the Special Rapporteur on the right of everyone to the enjoyment of the highest attainable standard of physical and mental health, Paul Hunt, to the United Nations General Assembly, 61 Sess., Item 66(b), 13 September 2006, UN Doc. A/61/338 at para. 34.

5 See Address of the Special Rapporteur on the right of everyone to the enjoyment of the highest attainable standard of physical and mental health, Paul Hunt, to the United Nations Human Rights Council, 28 March 2007. Available online at Human Rights Council Extranet http://portal.ohchr.org/ portal/page/portal/HRCExtranet.

6 Address of the Special Rapporteur on the right of everyone to the enjoyment of the highest attainable standard of physical and mental health, Paul Hunt, to the United Nations Human Rights Council, 11 March 2008. Available online at Human Rights Council Extranet http://portal.ohchr.org/portal/page/ portal/HRCExtranet, at p. 4.

7 The Sexual Rights Initiative is a coalition of global south and global north organizations working together to advance sexual rights (broadly defined as including all issues in the intersection of sexuality and human rights, including reproductive rights and sexual and reproductive health) at the UN Human Rights Council. The SRI partners at the time of writing are: Action Canada for Population and Development (ACPD), AKAHATA, Creating

Rights Council, began pushing for the Council to hold a half-day debate on maternal mortality. When it became clear that this debate was going to occur within the context of the Council's annual consideration of the human rights of women, ACPD and the Sexual Rights Initiative drew in the Center for Reproductive Rights to begin working together and to build a civil society coalition with the partners needed to support the advancement of this work, including many organizations in the International Initiative on Maternal Mortality and Human Rights, such as Sahayog and CARE Peru, numerous sexual and reproductive rights organizations, such as Ipas, and mainstream human rights organizations, such as Human Rights Watch. The June 2008 session of the Council saw not only the Council's first annual 'Human rights of women' day, but also, within that, the first discussion of maternal mortality as a human rights issue by an international political body mandated to address human rights. Thus maternal mortality was one of the first women's human rights issues that the young Council – established in 2006 – took up.

8.4 Civil society goals for work on maternal mortality at the Human Rights Council

It should be understood that the UN Human Rights Council is the primary intergovernmental body responsible for strengthening the promotion and protection of human rights around the world. It has a mandate to set norms and policies, to monitor and provide guidance on human rights issues to governments and to mainstream human rights throughout the UN system. As such, it was felt that the Council was the natural body to bring maternal mortality and morbidity onto the intergovernmental human rights agenda and that it had a role to play to strengthen international accountability in this area. Besides reinvigorating political will and having governments make a paradigm shift in how they view maternal death and disability, it was believed that there were many other ways in which having the Council take action on maternal mortality and morbidity at the international level could enhance accountability.

First, it was hoped that the Council would recognize preventable maternal mortality and morbidity as a violation of human rights, that it would specify which rights were often violated and that it would recognize that maternal mortality and morbidity occurred *as the result of* violation of or failure to realize other human rights obligations. Such recognition by an intergovernmental body would undoubtedly enhance accountability, as it would mark recognition by governments themselves that they are responsible for preventing maternal deaths and injuries, and that specific human rights are violated in the lead-up to and occurrence of such tragic events. Such an admission

Resources for Empowerment in Action (CREA; India), the Egyptian Initiative for Personal Rights (EIPR) and the Federation for Women and Family Planning (FWFP; Poland). ACPD is the current coordinator of the SRI.

could then be used within national or regional courts or by international treaty-monitoring bodies to help establish responsibility for failure to prevent maternal deaths and disabilities. Even simply having an intergovernmental body acknowledge it as a human rights issue, without even using the term 'violation', though not as clear cut, would have much the same effect. The clear message would be that women and girls are rights holders who are failed when they die or are severely injured from pregnancy or childbirth. As human rights entail accountability for their violation, having something recognized as a human rights matter is a clear recognition of the need for greater accountability of various actors, including governments themselves, for patterns of violations of or failures to uphold rights that result in maternal mortality and morbidity.

With respect to ensuring that governments acknowledged that maternal mortality implicated a range of human rights, the goal among civil society organizations was to ensure that maternal mortality was not just seen as a right-to-health issue. A clear and explicit link with the human right to life was felt important in part to make clear that maternal mortality should not be subject to the doctrine of 'progressive realization', which (though not intended to be) can often be invoked as an excuse for lack of progress. The right to life is not subject to this doctrine and its immediate effect entails numerous obligations with respect to accountability.

Further work highlighting discrimination and marginalization and its impact on maternal mortality and morbidity was also seen as indispensable in giving attention to the human rights dimensions of the issue. In that, it was seen as important to show that the injustice is not simply that women of reproductive age die at an alarmingly high rate from preventable causes, but that women experiencing multiple forms of discrimination – women in minority communities, indigenous women, poor and rural women, and young women entering their reproductive years – disproportionately die or suffer from reproductive ill health. Such attention was also important to make it clear that all countries can benefit from examining the human rights dimensions of maternal mortality and morbidity, not just developing countries – even many richer countries with low overall rates of maternal mortality show higher rates when these data are appropriately disaggregated in these key ways.

Second, in bringing the issue of maternal mortality and morbidity into the intergovernmental human rights agenda, civil society organizations wanted to have governments legitimize and recognize the work of international human rights bodies and mechanisms in this area. Human rights treaty-monitoring bodies – such as the UN Committee on the Elimination of Discrimination against Women and the UN Committee on Economic, Social and Cultural Rights – have interpreted the respective treaties for which they oversee compliance as imposing legal obligations to prevent maternal deaths and to uphold underlying sexual and reproductive rights whose violation underlie these. This body of substantive legal obligations and entitlements is well developed.[8] By having governments acknowledge this work by international expert bodies, it promotes buy-in by governments for the recommendations of these bodies and gives them added political weight.

While these goals focused on a reinforcing and legitimizing a 'violations' approach – that preventable maternal mortality and morbidity is a violation of and a result of violations of existing human right standards – there were other goals for civil society in pursuing this work. For example, it was hoped that the increasing visibility generated by this work at the international level on the scope and nature of maternal mortality and morbidity, and on the failures to respect, protect or fulfil human rights in these areas, would enhance accountability through ensuring greater awareness of the problem and its human rights dimensions. Furthermore, for civil society organizations, work on maternal mortality at the international level – much like in many national contexts – could serve as an important entry point for further work on sexual and reproductive rights. Violations of these rights often underlie and contribute to maternal mortality and morbidity, including lack of access to sexuality education and necessary sexual and reproductive health services, such as contraceptive services and HIV treatment and care, and the criminalization of particular health services, such as abortion.

Civil society was also very clear in its goals that work on the human rights dimensions of maternal mortality and morbidity cannot be focused only on violations of international human rights, the substantive obligations of states, and using the international legal framework to hold governments accountable. While that is a key part of a human rights-based approach, human rights principles also need to be actively used in shaping strategies to address preventable maternal mortality and morbidity. As human rights approaches lead to more sustainable and meaningful improvements, these fundamental human rights principles – *in addition to* the substantive legal standards – need to ground reduction efforts. This has been a major area of focus in which civil society has desired to see further work happen. It was strongly felt that in this area international accountability needed to have a constructive component to it. A great deal of international accountability involves ensuring that governments are provided with expert advice that is sufficiently specific to help them: identify gaps in the implementation of obligations; identify options to strengthen implementation; and assess the effectiveness of their chosen approaches. Such recommendations are important tools for advocates to use in national-level efforts to spur governments into action.

It was envisioned that the Human Rights Council could and should play a role to lead efforts to better understand how human rights principles could be effectively incorporated into efforts to address maternal mortality

8 See Center for Reproductive Rights, Preventing maternal mortality and ensuring safe pregnancy (briefing paper) in bringing rights to bear, October 2008. Available at http://reproductiverights.org/ sites/crr.civicactions.net/files/documents/BRB_Maternal%20 Mortality_10.08.pdf.

and morbidity and to urge governments to centre these principles in their programmes and policies related to this issue. For example, it was felt that accountability, as the cornerstone of a human rights-based approach, could use greater systematic analysis to increase understanding of, in particular, the concept of 'constructive accountability'. As the Special Rapporteur on the right to health, in addition to numerous scholars, has made clear, not all accountability is in the form of judicial action or 'naming-and-shaming'. There is tremendous scope for constructive approaches to accountability at national and local levels, which can be effective and which need to be transparent and participatory. However, there is a knowledge gap in this area among governments and other stakeholders alike that could be addressed with focused expert analysis and advice. Governments would be more likely to heed this advice if an intergovernmental body such as the Human Rights Council had mandated it. It was felt that such work led by the Human Rights Council could directly result in the strengthening of accountability systems domestically, including the creation or use of constructive accountability mechanisms, such as reproductive health councils, no-fault public hearings into maternal deaths, community-based maternal death audits that look at underlying causes leading to the death rather than strictly the medical cause and having national human rights institutions play a role in evaluating compliance with human rights standards in this area.

It was felt that the international community needed such useful, operational guidance and advice as an urgent matter and that this was a significant part of the constructive accountability needed at the international level. The Human Rights Council could play a lead role in guiding governments to integrate human rights-based approaches into their programmes and policies, including their work as international donors. The Council could also play a lead role in mainstreaming these approaches within the UN system, encouraging UN agencies and technical bodies working in the area to integrate human rights into their work.

The goals identified here were developed, in the lead-up to the June 2008 Council, by the coalition of civil society organizations just mentioned as a short- to medium-term set of advocacy goals for work with the Human Rights Council. In summary of this discussion, these goals consisted of the following:

- Having an international intergovernmental body with a human rights mandate acknowledge that maternal mortality and morbidity is a human rights issue, thus shifting government perspectives on the issue worldwide, helping to address lack of political will, and increasing visibility on the scope and nature of the problem.
- Having the Council recognize preventable maternal mortality and morbidity as a violation of human rights.
- Ensuring that the Council recognized that maternal deaths and injuries occur as a result of violations of or failures to realize other human rights obligations, including specifically discrimination and marginalization.

- Ensuring that the Council would explicitly recognize that maternal mortality and morbidity is linked to an array of specific human rights, including the right to life.
- Ensuring that the Council recognized the work of international human rights bodies and mechanisms related to this issue.
- Having the Council lead efforts, through its seeking expert advice on the topic, to increase understanding of how human rights principles, such as accountability, can be effectively incorporated into efforts to address maternal mortality and morbidity.
- Ensuring that the Council plays its role to urge governments to integrate human rights-based approaches into their programmes and policies, including in their international cooperation and assistance work.

These goals, set at an early stage in the process, represented the focus of civil society efforts at the Human Rights Council to enhance human rights accountability for maternal mortality and morbidity. Despite resistance on the part of governments, many of these goals have been achieved to varying degrees or are in the process of being achieved as a result of the three resolutions that have been adopted by the Human Rights Council on 'Preventable maternal mortality and morbidity and human rights' (in June 2009, September 2010 and September 2011) or through work of the Office of the High Commissioner for Human Rights that has been commissioned by the Council.

8.5 June 2008 – Council debate on maternal mortality and human rights and the goal of establishing an international accountability mechanism

In response to the call by the Special Rapporteur on the right to health, and relentless pressure by a few civil society groups, for a debate on maternal morality at the Human Rights Council, there was an unsuccessful attempt to schedule a three-hour (a half-day in the UN context) debate in the programme of work for the March 2008 session.[9] While the debate clearly appeared on the first draft, it did not remain on the schedule beyond that. With further pressure from civil society organizations on governments who had led the development of the Council's gender framework and the suggestion of bringing the debate within the Council's annual full-day discussion on the human rights of women, a half-day discussion of maternal mortality was set for and took place on 5 June 2008. This represents the first intergovernmental debate on maternal mortality by a human rights-mandated body at the

9 See Address of the Special Rapporteur on the right of everyone to the enjoyment of the highest attainable standard of physical and mental health, Paul Hunt, to the United Nations Human Rights Council, 11 March 2008. Available at http://portal.ohchr.org/portal/page/portal/HRCExtranet, at p. 4.

international level and a historic moment as all of the expert panellists leading the debate observed in their comments.

Despite this moment, many governments were unsure of how to engage in the expert panel-led Council debate and so only 12 delegations took the floor at the time, leaving a great deal of time for commentary by the expert panel. There was significant focus within panellists' comments on the need for accountability at local, national and global levels; examples of the sort of accountability mechanisms needed at these levels; and particular focus on the Council's role in addressing maternal mortality within its human rights mandate.

The boldest recommendation from the experts on the panel came from the Special Rapporteur on the right to health himself:

> At the international level, a simple mechanism is needed to hold states – and others – to account in relation to maternal mortality. Perhaps an interdisciplinary working group of five independent people with expertise in public health and medicine. They would consider what all states – and others – are doing in relation to maternal mortality. They would come to conclusions and make sensible recommendations. Those states that need help to address the recommendations would go to the experts – [the] Partnership [on Maternal Newborn and Child Health], WHO, UNFPA, and so on – for advice and assistance. [. . .]
>
> The new, changing human rights landscape demands new, imaginative, appropriate, independent accountability mechanisms.
>
> I encourage the Council to rise to this human rights challenge – just as it has risen to human rights challenges in the past.[10]

These comments by the Special Rapporteur actually contain a number of key thoughts: that an accountability body beyond existing mechanisms was needed; that the Council needed to establish it under its own aegis; that the structure of existing mechanisms were not necessarily suited to the type of body envisioned, thus requiring some creativity; that it would need to give advice to states from a human rights perspective on how to improve on their practices in addressing maternal mortality; and that its relationship to existing UN agencies would need to be considered carefully.

For a number of organizations from the civil society coalition, this commentary by the Special Rapporteur struck a positive chord. One could see the need and utility of such a mechanism looking at these characteristics identified.

Some of the current international and regional human rights mechanisms, including the treaty-monitoring bodies and the system of UN 'special

10 Address of the Special Rapporteur on the right of everyone to the enjoyment of the highest attainable standard of physical and mental health, Paul Hunt, to the United Nations Human Rights Council, 5 June 2008. Available at http://portal.ohchr.org/portal/page/portal/HRCExtranet, at p. 4.

procedures', had undoubtedly made and continue to make tremendous contributions in holding governments accountable in relation to maternal mortality and morbidity. For example, the UN human rights treaty bodies – the set of UN expert committees, each established to monitor compliance with a particular human rights treaty through interpreting provisions of that treaty and evaluating states parties' compliance with it – have laid out many substantive obligations states must fulfil to prevent maternal deaths and ill health. They continue to hold governments to account when information related to substantive human rights violations in relation to maternal mortality and morbidity are brought to their attention.[11]

Other newer mechanisms, such as the UN Human Rights Council's Universal Periodic Review, have the potential to make valuable contributions. This is a relatively new mechanism of the Human Rights Council whereby the HR record as a whole of every state is evaluated every four to four and a half years. Its major strength is that it is primarily a state-to-state process and thus there is a significant political weight that attaches to each recommendation. In the first three years of the process, over 50 recommendations were raised by governments to other governments on improving maternal mortality and morbidity. Many dozens of recommendations on related or broader aspects of reproductive health were also raised.

However, many of these recommendations suffer from an extreme generality. In the seventh session of UPR, for instance, Turkey recommended to Bolivia to: 'continue to implement measures to reduce maternal mortality'.[12] The helpfulness of similar recommendations is clearly lacking, except to tell the government being reviewed that one of its peers, or perhaps an ally, is concerned about maternal mortality in their country and hopes that they are continuing their efforts to address it. Sometimes UPR recommendations simply and unfortunately lack criticism altogether; for instance India, Honduras and Djibouti all recommended to Cuba to 'share its experiences and good practices with regard to the right to health, in particular the primary, maternal and child care programs'.[13]

Stronger UPR recommendations in the area of maternal mortality and human rights are certainly plentiful. In the sixth session of UPR, Portugal recommended to Equatorial Guinea to 'ensure that public hospitals and other health-care facilities and services are both affordable and accessible, in

11 See, e.g., *Alyne da Silva Pimentel Teixeira v. Brazil*, Committee on the Elimination of Discrimination against Women, 49th Sess., UN Doc. CEDAW/C/49/D/17/2008, Communication No. 17/2008, 10 August 2011; Concluding observations of the Committee on the Elimination of Discrimination against Women: Kenya, CEDAW, 48th Sess., UN Doc. CEDAW/C/KEN/CO/7, 2 February 2011.

12 Report of the Working Group on Universal Periodic Review: Bolivia (Plurinational State of), UN Human Rights Council, 14th Sess., Item 6, Universal periodic review, UN Doc. A/HRC/14/7, 15 March 2010.

13 Report of the Working Group on Universal Periodic Review: Cuba, UN Human Rights Council, 11th Sess., Item 6, Universal periodic review, UN Doc. A/HRC/11/22, 5 October 2009.

particular making provision for child maternal health services [sic] and for the prevention and treatment of preventable diseases'.[14] And in the eighth session of UPR, Germany recommended to Grenada to 'develop comprehensive policies and programmes to reduce the incidence of infant and maternal mortality'.[15] What is clear from these examples is that even when UPR recommendations are more critical and point to specific actions that need taking, they tend not to give comprehensive or detailed enough guidance, including on how human rights principles and norms can underpin the steps to implement these specific actions or how they can more broadly be used in the country's policies and programmes related to maternal mortality and morbidity. Treaty body recommendations, which are often the source of the more-specific UPR recommendations, similarly do not have this comprehensiveness and detail that could be useful in these circumstances.

Within both UPR and treaty body reviews, there is no guarantee that any specific issue with respect to maternal mortality and morbidity will be raised due to the broad mandates of these processes and bodies and the weight of other business. These existing mechanisms are rarely able to provide governments with detailed, specific and sustained expert guidance on the human rights dimensions of maternal mortality and morbidity. They are not sufficient to be able to identify for governments their specific shortcomings in using a human rights-based approach to preventing maternal deaths and disability and to offer specific and comprehensive advice to states to remedy these. In addition, they would not be able due to their broad mandates to develop further policy guidance for all states in terms of what a human rights-based approach to eliminating maternal mortality and morbidity requires and how to base policy and programming in these areas on human rights principles. Such policy guidance was viewed as and remains a missing but important contribution towards greater accountability for maternal mortality. Such guidance was also particularly needed for the further establishment and strengthening of local and national-level accountability mechanisms, as the concept of accountability was seen as and remains a newer topic for the international community, which still understands it narrowly as involving 'naming and shaming' or judicial accountability. Laying out the range of what is involved in constructive accountability at local and national levels would be an important part of such policy guidance.

Looking at these gaps in what treaty bodies and other review bodies such as the Human Rights Council's universal periodic review would be able to offer in terms of detailed, specific and sustained guidance for all states in this area,

14 Report of the Working Group on Universal Periodic Review: Equatorial Guinea, UN Human Rights Council, 13th Sess., Item 6, Universal periodic review, UN Doc. A/HRC/13/16, 4 January 2010.

15 Report of the Working Group on Universal Periodic Review: Grenada, UN Human Rights Council, 15th Sess., Item 6, Universal periodic review, UN Doc. A/HRC/15/12, 16 June 2010.

many civil organizations within the civil society coalition were attracted to the recommendation to create an independent expert body or mechanism on maternal mortality and human rights.

Among these organizations, the vision for what could be created to fill this gap was modelled on what are known as the 'special procedures'. This is the generic name given to the system of over 40 Special Rapporteurs, special representatives, independent experts and working groups that are tasked with reporting to the HRC on a variety of human rights issues. They offer expert advice generally to all states through thematic reports exploring specific topics within their mandate and to specific governments when they undertake a country visit. Through their work, they give visibility to problems and put pressure on governments to change laws, policies and practices. The Special Rapporteur on the right to health is an example of a special procedure and quite an important one in this context, as it was this Special Rapporteur who first started bringing the human rights dimensions of the issue of maternal mortality to the attention of the Council as a global health and human rights crisis.

For these organizations, when looking at existing mechanisms and special procedures, there was a critical point that needed recognition – that the incidence of maternal mortality far exceeds the number of disappearances and arbitrary detentions, and there is a working group mandated to address each of these issues. Thus, these groups suggested, as the Special Rapporteur had already done, that a specific mechanism – in fact, another working group – on maternal mortality and morbidity was warranted.

It was felt that the Human Rights Council needed to, at the very least, give serious consideration to the establishment of an independent working group of three to seven independent experts from various backgrounds and key disciplines. It would offer expert advice to individual states but also more generalized expert advice directed at all states on eliminating maternal mortality and morbidity from a human rights perspective. In this respect, it would increase international accountability by helping to guide governments in their domestic policies and programmes and it would also scrutinize the fulfilment of donor commitments and obligations for international assistance and cooperation to ensure their accountability. It would monitor and hold states accountable for implementing human rights obligations in relation to maternal mortality and morbidity and it would tender independent, pragmatic, constructive, sensible and evidence-based advice to states. In these ways, the body would operate much like a special procedure. Unlike special procedures, however, the body would clearly have to be multidisciplinary and would have to have a multiplicity of reporting relationships. Diverse expertise would be important for this body. For example, if it were constituted as a three-person working group it would need to have the following advantage: it could consist of one clinician, one public health expert and one human rights expert. All three dimensions are very important in relation to maternal mortality and morbidity and it would be difficult if not extremely rare for all three dimensions to reside in one person. Last, there would be advantage in the working group reporting to both the Council and the World Health Assembly as well as having appropriate liaison with WHO and UNFPA. Such a reporting relationship would be consistent with the Human Rights Council's duty to mainstream human rights throughout the UN system.

Moving forward from the June 2008 Human Rights Council debate on maternal mortality and human rights, the establishment of such a mechanism became a further goal of a number of civil society organizations working to support efforts to advance the issue at the Council. Their view of the characteristics of this working group was very much in accord with the Special Rapporteur's vision. While not all organizations within the coalition supported the creation of this mechanism and advocacy towards that goal (some feeling its creation would further the proliferation of human rights mechanisms) it was certainly agreed that, regardless, the establishment of such a mechanism was not for the immediate – it was not a feasible first step. Given the limited participation of states in the June 2008 debate, it was clear that this issue was not yet fully or properly on the intergovernmental human rights agenda. There were numerous other goals to be achieved in this work and the first step was to clearly have the Human Rights Council speak out as a unified voice on the issue, through a resolution.

8.6 March 2009 – joint intergovernmental statement to the Human Rights Council

With increased pressure on governments in Geneva from civil society to have a resolution presented, negotiated and adopted by the Human Rights Council, two delegations, New Zealand and Colombia, decided to take things further towards this. On 16 March 2009 83 governments in a joint statement delivered to the UN Human Rights Council reaffirmed their commitment to addressing maternal mortality as a human rights issue and called on the Human Rights Council to take decisive action to contribute to the existing efforts to address maternal mortality. Under the leadership of New Zealand, which delivered the statement, and Colombia, this joint statement included countries from all regions as signatories and represented one of the largest joint intergovernmental statements delivered to the Council, or to its predecessor body, the Commission on Human Rights, and it was the first with respect to maternal mortality at these bodies. The statement followed directly from the June 2008 debate and the 85 governments – far more than the 12 that actually participated in the debate – recognized the importance of that panel in bringing to the Council's attention that there are human rights implications of maternal mortality.

The statement also made the link between human rights and maternal mortality more explicit and used the phrase 'violation of human rights'. The 85 governments stated:

> It is estimated that more than 500,000 women die each year as a result of pregnancy or childbirth. Most of these deaths are preventable. The failure to prevent them is an impediment to the universal realisation of human rights and could constitute a violation of human rights, including women's right to health, life, education, dignity, access to information and appropriate healthcare.[16]

The governments called for renewal of political will to address the unacceptably high number of maternal deaths and the stagnation of improvement in this area. And more concretely, they identified a few specific ways that the Council could begin to address the issue, including: identifying the human rights dimensions of preventable maternal mortality and morbidity; bringing focus to how discrimination impacts access to health services for women; integrating consideration of the human rights implications of maternal mortality and morbidity into the UPR and in dialogues with treaty bodies; and requesting governments to ensure women's participation in decision making about maternal health. Last, the governments signalled their intent to ensure that the Council would take collective and concrete action on the issue during its subsequent session in June 2009.

Consistent with their goals, members of civil society organizations working on this issue at the Council had been seeking language unequivocally recognizing that high rates of maternal mortality constitute violations of the human rights of women, including the right to life. While the statement instead used the phrase 'could constitute violations of human rights', this was a solid step forward – a large set of governments were ready to recognize that maternal mortality could very well be a violation of rights. They were already suggesting that more attention needed to be paid to multiple forms of discrimination – a key human rights violation that leads to maternal mortality. They were also suggesting a role for the Council in addressing this and indicating that more could be done within existing international accountability mechanisms to address the human rights dimensions of maternal mortality and morbidity. The achievements of this joint statement in these key ways furthered the goals that the civil society coalition has set

16 New Zealand on behalf of Albania, Argentina, Armenia, Australia, Austria, Azerbaijan, Belgium, Bhutan, Bolivia, Bosnia and Herzegovina, Brazil, Bulgaria, Burkina Faso, Burundi, Canada, Chile, Colombia, Congo, Costa Rica, Cote D'Ivoire, Croatia, Cuba, Cyprus, Czech Republic, Denmark, Dominican Republic, Djibouti, Ecuador, El Salvador, Estonia, Finland, Former Yugoslav Republic of Macedonia, France, Gabon, Germany, Greece, Guatemala, Guyana, Honduras, Hungary, Iceland, Ireland, Italy, Japan, Latvia, Liechtenstein, Lithuania, Luxembourg, Maldives, Malta, Mauritius, Mexico, Moldova, Monaco, Montenegro, Mozambique, Nepal, Netherlands, Nicaragua, Norway, Panama, Peru, Poland, Portugal, Republic of Korea, Romania, Rwanda, Serbia, Singapore, Slovakia, Slovenia, Spain, Sri Lanka, Sweden, Switzerland, Thailand, Timor Leste, Turkey, Ukraine, United Kingdom, Uruguay, Venezuela; Joint statement to the Human Rights Council, 10th Sess., Item 3: General Debate, 16 March 2009. Available at http://portal.ohchr.org/portal/page/portal/HRCExtranet.

out in pursuing this work at the Council. The problem was that the joint statement did not represent a majority of UN member states, but a selection of them, which fell short of the desired commitment for the 'community of nations' as a whole to shift their perspective on this issue towards seeing it as a matter of human rights. The statement, however, served the useful purpose of building momentum for the Council to adopt a resolution on this topic. In this sense, the joint statement was a 'test balloon' to gauge the temperature of delegations at the Council to determine if there was sufficient support for a resolution to be brought forward. The overwhelming success of the joint statement indicated that there was.

8.7 Making history: the landmark June 2009 Human Rights Council on maternal mortality and morbidity

On 17 June 2009 the Human Rights Council adopted resolution 11/8 entitled 'Preventable maternal mortality and morbidity and human rights'. It was a unanimous decision of the Council with no vote called by any of its members but instead consensus among governments from all regions of the world. A very solid number, 69 governments, co-sponsored the resolution.[17] This resolution was a major milestone, being the first international intergovernmental recognition that maternal mortality and morbidity is a human rights issue. This was the huge paradigm shift that civil society organizations had been working towards – an international body made up of governments articulated the problem of maternal mortality and morbidity as a human rights problem. Indeed, the Human Rights Council stated it:

> Recognizes that most instances of maternal mortality and morbidity are preventable, and that preventable maternal mortality and morbidity is a health, development and human rights challenge that also requires the effective promotion and protection of the human rights of women and girls, in particular their rights to life, to be equal in dignity, to education, to be free to seek, receive and impart information, to enjoy the benefits of scientific progress, to freedom from discrimination, and to enjoy the

17 Main sponsors: Colombia and New Zealand. Co-sponsors joining before tabling: Australia, Austria, Belgium, Bolivia, Brazil, Canada, Chile, Republic of the Congo, Croatia, Cyprus, Czech Republic, Dominican Republic, Ecuador, Estonia, Finland, France, Germany, Greece, Guatemala, Honduras, Ireland, Israel, Italy, Liechtenstein, Lithuania, Luxembourg, Maldives, Mali, Malta, Mexico, Monaco, Netherlands, Nicaragua, Norway, Panama, Peru, Poland, Portugal, Romania, Rwanda, Slovenia, Spain, Sri Lanka, Sweden, Switzerland, Thailand, Turkey, Ukraine, United Kingdom of Great Britain and Northern Ireland, United States of America and Uruguay. Co-sponsors joining after tabling: Andorra, Cameroon, Costa Rica, Cuba, Equatorial Guinea, Hungary, Iceland, Jordan, Latvia, Mauritius, Morocco, Senegal, Serbia, Singapore, Slovakia and South Africa.

> highest attainable standard of physical and mental health, including sexual and reproductive health.[18]

While the Council did not use the term 'violation', as the negotiations had this paragraph taking a more affirmative framing, the Council was using human rights language and clearly identifying maternal mortality and morbidity as a human rights issue. In fact, in achievement of another goal of the civil society coalition working to advance this work, it named a range of specific human rights that the issue is linked with, including the rights to life, equality and non-discrimination.

With the Council taking up this issue in this resolution, it was actively discharging its mandate to promote and protect all human rights. The Council has a mandate to ensure that governments observe international human rights standards and also a role to encourage states to undertake certain courses of action to further the implementation of human rights. Governments are accountable to the Council as a political or intergovernmental body charged with human rights as its mandate. And the Council was very clear in its dictates in this resolution: that states must renew their political will and commitment and redouble their efforts to implement human rights obligations with respect to maternal mortality and morbidity. Through the Council's acknowledgement of maternal mortality and morbidity as a human rights issue, governments were implicitly acknowledging their responsibility under international human rights law to prevent maternal deaths and disability and their accountability for this generally and, specifically, to the Council. In this way, the landmark resolution was a major addition to the international accountability landscape. Perhaps this is even more so as the Council resolution reaffirmed the work of the treaty bodies and special procedures to address the human rights dimensions of maternal mortality and morbidity, which was an important intergovernmental endorsement of the critical work of these important accountability bodies.

In addition to this paradigm shift, the implicit acknowledgement by governments that they are accountable, the recognition of the work of international expert bodies and mechanisms, and recognition of the specific human rights that the issue implicates, the Council resolution had another key feature. It requested the High Commissioner for Human Rights to prepare a study of the human rights dimensions of maternal mortality and morbidity, including how the Council could add value through a human rights perspective to existing efforts and recommended options for better addressing the human rights dimensions of the issue. This study would prove to be a key development in enhancing understanding of how key human rights principles can be applied to maternal mortality and morbidity and of what the Council can do to deepen knowledge and accountability in this area.

18 *Preventable maternal mortality and morbidity and human rights*, UN Human Rights Council res. 11/8, UN Doc. A/HRC/RES/11/8, 17 June 2009, at para. 2.

8.8 Resistance to acknowledging and addressing maternal mortality as a human rights issue

In pursuing advocacy to advance international accountability for maternal mortality and morbidity, there was a great deal of resistance, unsurprisingly from governments themselves. This resistance was visible in both discussions of the joint statement from March 2009 and in the negotiations of the June 2009 Council resolution. It was a resistance to this paradigm shift that civil society and a number of states were encouraging – moving the issue out of the health and development boxes into one in which it was seen as a human rights issue with clear human rights components.

In this respect, a number of delegations were altogether resistant. One of these delegations stated that the joint statement and draft resolution represented an attempt to shift the blame for maternal mortality onto developing countries by calling it a 'human rights issue', whereas the problem really reflected a failure of development assistance. These delegations objected to the framing of maternal mortality and morbidity as a human rights issue and to the Council addressing it, suggesting that this issue belonged in other intergovernmental venues such as the UN Commission on Population and Development and the World Health Assembly.

Other delegations could recognize the human rights components of maternal mortality and morbidity but were concerned about recognizing maternal mortality as a clear human rights violation. This reflected a fear over what would follow with respect to their accountability in domestic, regional and international judicial or quasi-judicial bodies from the explicit recognition of a violation of human rights by the Council.

In developing the joint statement in March 2009, the main authors of the statement held an open informal to discuss openly a draft of the statement – a rare thing to see at the Council for a joint statement – to encourage dialogue and additional delegations to add their support to it. A joint intergovernmental statement and a resolution, where consensus of the members of the body representing the community of nations is desired, are very different outcomes, with the former requiring only brief negotiation. In the end, those governments wanting to endorse the joint statement were able to do so and those uncomfortable with its content were not required to join with the other governments making the statement. For the Council resolution – which would implicate all governments when adopted, thus 'raising the stakes' – coming to a consensus resolution required significant negotiation. These negotiations were intense.

In the beginning of the negotiations of the resolution, the resistance that a number of governments had been expressing in discussions of the joint statement manifested in a few significant ways. For example, as its opening position, the Pakistan delegation proposed to delete all references to human rights within the text. This position was fundamentally supported by the delegations of Indonesia and Azerbaijan. Pakistan participated actively throughout the negotiations with a view to advancing its interests and positions and, in fact, a day or two prior to when the resolution was due to be tabled, Pakistan threatened to bring written amendments to the resolution. This would have been a very bold manoeuvre and was a sure sign of its fundamental opposition to the resolution and what it was going to achieve.

There was also fear among a number of delegations that acknowledging maternal mortality within a human rights framework, given that unsafe abortion is a major cause of maternal deaths and morbidity, would strengthen arguments that governments have an obligation to remove criminal laws prohibiting abortion and to provide safe services. The result of this was a concerted attempt to remove all references to 'sexual and reproductive health' from the resolution. This effort was led by the Holy See along with Pakistan, Egypt and Indonesia.

There was also some initial polarization that occurred within the negotiations as delegations became aware of the positions of other delegations with whom they are often aligned. For instance, Egypt's position was initially more moderate than Pakistan's – it wanted to see the words 'under certain circumstances' added to the provision in the draft text, 'the high global rate of preventable maternal mortality and morbidity . . . could constitute a violation of human rights'.[19] However, as negotiations proceeded, its position became more in line with the positions that Pakistan was voicing in the negotiation room. In a similar way, China and South Africa were initially using the language of health and development, including further elements on international cooperation and assistance, but without seeking to delete human rights references. However, once again, as negotiations were proceeding, these two delegations began to reinforce Pakistan's positions to remove human rights references.

Given this strong and somewhat organized resistance to the resolution and to framing maternal mortality and morbidity as a matter of human rights, a key question to reflect on is: How was it that the resolution negotiations were so successful in producing a strong outcome?

While it is always difficult to pinpoint in negotiations what dynamics and what factors lead to individual decisions by delegations to acquiesce to consensus on an issue, there is often a range of possible factors behind these decisions and which together help to buffer these regressive positions.

First, the initial text was strong, which allowed for negotiation room. In addition, the co-sponsors (other than the chairs, Colombia and New Zealand) took strong positions not only in support of the draft text, but also by putting forth stronger proposals – for example, trying to add language on access to sexual and reproductive health services. Their positions made any concession actually much larger. It also allowed for the chairs of the negotiations to act

19 This was a formulation in the initial draft resolution, which was based on the March 2009 joint statement. That provision was subsequently reformulated to be more affirmative as described and quoted in the preceding section.

as facilitators seeking compromise between these various positions rather than needing to defend their text themselves. These co-sponsors, including the delegations of Luxembourg (on behalf of the European Union), Chile, Norway, the United States and Mexico, were an engaged and knowledgeable group. In defending the text, they were able to speak articulately and authoritatively in the negotiations on two things: the reality of maternal mortality and morbidity and how these issues are reflected in various legal texts. For example, when there was opposition to a reference to 'sexual and reproductive health' within the text, the co-sponsors were able to identify various key references to this term within previously agreed resolutions and statements and to explain why promoting sexual and reproductive health was important to maternal health. This helped silence the opposition to this reference.

There was also a group of co-sponsoring delegations that played the role of intermediaries between the co-sponsors and the strongest opponents. These were the delegations of Jordan, the Maldives, Mauritius and Singapore. As developing countries,[20] they played an important role in reaching out to other countries as bridge builders and compromise finders. In the negotiations, they helped to keep the tone positive and constructive, by raising numerous compromise proposals, thus showing that there was a middle ground and areas of compromise, keeping discussion focused and moving towards consensus. They were also able to help break down bloc dynamics by showing that typically strong regional blocs, such as the Organization of the Islamic Conference and the African Group, did not have a unified position and that all delegations were speaking from their individual perspective. In all, these delegations helped co-sponsors show that there was commitment to the resolution while trying to accommodate the viewpoints of other delegations.

The main co-sponsors who led the resolution and co-chaired the negotiations played an important role in achieving a strong result. New Zealand and Colombia at that time were both non-members of the Council and so did not have to vote on any 'hot-button' political issue that arose at the Council, thus buffering them from fallout over other negotiations. The two countries were also a palatable combination of a developing and an industrialized country – that is, the leads were more acceptable than two industrialized country leads would have been. As negotiators, the representatives showed a high level of transparency throughout the process. They were very clear as to what they were trying to achieve with the resolution, why they were bringing it before the Council, and that they wanted consensus on the resolution. They held regular bilateral negotiations with all participating delegations and ensured that all views were being heard. They made a demonstrable effort to accommodate perspectives, while making it clear that they were not going to lose the main thrust and essential points of the resolution. The negotiators,

20 Except for Singapore.

both Geneva-based diplomats, were well respected among other diplomats and had personal charisma that helped the resolution to be seen by other delegations as a more personal resolution of the negotiators themselves.

Last, the effect of civil society engagement on impacting the outcome of the negotiations on resolution was just as important as their engagement was to the development and advancement of the overall work on maternal mortality and morbidity at the Human Rights Council. Those who were part of the civil society coalition who were in Geneva for the negotiations, including ACPD and its SRI partners, the Center for Reproductive Rights and the Youth Coalition for Sexual and Reproductive Rights, had already formed or were able to form strong relationships with delegates. In this regard, these actors were able to advocate for states to strongly support key elements of the text and were able to provide advice on policy and strategy to the co-sponsors. They were also able to dialogue with some of the delegations that were opposed to the key elements of the resolution. The broader civil society coalition continued to support these advocacy activities by providing advice via email. Moreover, the coalition was able to generate attention from civil society organizations in countries to put pressure on their governments to co-sponsor the resolution or to drop their opposition to key elements of the resolution. This was extremely effective. For example, the International Planned Parenthood Federation was able to engage their in-country member associations to advocate with their governments to co-sponsor the resolution. In a splendid and important display of advocacy, a number of civil society organizations in Pakistan came together to engage government ministers and the media in support of the Human Rights Council resolution. In particular, they obtained statements of support for the resolution from a few ministers and succeeded in having multiple newspaper articles published specifically on the Pakistani delegation's opposition to the resolution.[21] This in-country organizing can only be one of the major reasons why Pakistan ultimately settled for small changes to the text, dropping its strong opposition, not carrying through with any written amendments, and ultimately joining consensus on a strong text. Such advocacy was also responsible for South Africa dropping its objections and, in fact, joining as a co-sponsor of the resolution.

The conglomeration of these factors led ultimately to the Human Rights Council's adoption of a strong resolution on maternal mortality and morbidity and human rights. This document is a milestone on the road towards enhanced international accountability for maternal mortality and morbidity; it indicates a fundamental shift in the perspective of governments towards seeing this as a human rights issue. While resistance to advancing work on maternal mortality at the Council did not disappear after this first resolution, objection

21 See World Population Foundation – Pakistan, Case study on advocacy initiative in Pakistan to support the preventable maternal mortality and morbidity and human rights resolution at the UN Human Rights Council, June 2009. Available at www.wpfpak.org/images/media/MMR_ Case_Study.pdf.

to the human rights framing of the issue has virtually disappeared with the subsequent work that has been done by the Council and the Office of the High Commissioner for Human Rights (OHCHR) in examining in further detail the human rights dimensions of the issue.

8.9 June 2010 – study by the Office of the High Commissioner for Human Rights

In June 2010 the OHCHR released its first study on the human rights dimensions of maternal mortality and morbidity. This document represented a sound first foray into the area. It was a study that furthered understanding of:

- the ways in which human rights violations result in maternal mortality and morbidity
- the ways that maternal mortality and morbidity in itself can constitute a human rights violation
- the elements of a human rights-based approach in the context of maternal mortality and morbidity.

In doing this, the study captured and summarized important developments made by the UN human rights treaty bodies through their examination of what states parties' obligations under international human rights treaties are. The more novel contribution that the study makes, however, is in looking at how state obligations in the area of maternal mortality and morbidity, including procedural obligations, are underpinned by seven human rights principles: accountability, participation, transparency, empowerment, sustainability, international cooperation, and non-discrimination. After defining how these various principles operate in this context, the OHCHR commented in the study that giving effect to these principles is the core of a human rights-based approach to eliminating preventable maternal mortality and morbidity.

In fact, the OHCHR went on in the study to identify that states were in need of guidance on how exactly to operationalize these principles within their programmes and policies to reduce maternal mortality and morbidity. What specific steps can and should be taken to implement or adopt a human rights-based approach to eliminating preventable maternal mortality and morbidity? To the OHCHR, answering that question for states was key and a clear gap in the human rights framework. It was a barrier to accountability that steps to implement a human rights-based approach to maternal mortality and morbidity were ill understood and ill explained. In the conclusions of the study, the OHCHR stated that:

> [W]hat is missing is the operationalization of a human rights-based approach to maternal mortality and morbidity. That is, many questions remain unanswered, such as: What are specific steps that can be taken to implement/adopt a human rights-based approach to eliminating

> preventable maternal mortality and morbidity? How can states ensure that constructive accountability mechanisms developed are consistent with human rights principles? What is the range of constructive accountability mechanisms that can be used to ensure effective reduction of maternal mortality and morbidity? What is needed to ensure that a constructive accountability mechanism is participatory, effective, and transparent?[22]

In identifying this gap in understanding what a human rights-based approach entails and in particularly identifying accountability, including constructive accountability, for maternal mortality and morbidity as an area in which greater understanding could be achieved, the OHCHR's conclusions were perfectly aligned with and furthered civil society's goals in working with the Council on this issue.

In fact, the development of an operational framework that would give policy guidance to states on concrete measures they can take to ensure that their policies and programmes related to maternal mortality and morbidity are grounded in a human rights-based approach was identified by the OHCHR as a necessary next step. And it was suggested that the Council lead the process by mandating a group of experts to develop this operational framework. The OHCHR also identified the implementation and monitoring of such an operational framework as not only necessary but also an area where there was a vacuum with no clear lead within the UN system. Once again, it was suggested that the Council could play an important role in the monitoring and implementation of this operational framework.

These two clear gaps in accountability at the international level identified by the OHCHR's study and the next step – developing an operational framework – pointed to in the study were clearly very constructive contributions that the Council could make to the global effort to eliminate maternal mortality and morbidity through its mandate to promote and protect human rights. This next step also represented a goal that the civil society coalition had set out. Working towards this goal was a major focus in moving work at the Council forward in relation to maternal mortality and morbidity.

8.10 Implementing the conclusions of the OHCHR study: September 2010–September 2011

The first study of the OHCHR was presented by the High Commissioner for Human Rights in the June 2010 session of the Council. This was directly followed by an expert panel and intergovernmental debate on the study in the same meeting. The tone of this debate was very positive, with very few

22 Report of the Office of the United Nations High Commissioner for Human Rights on preventable maternal mortality and morbidity and human rights, UN Human Rights Council, 14th Sess., Items 2 and 3, UN Doc. A/HRC/14/39, 16 April 2010, at para. 61.

'spoiler' statements. In fact, there was another joint statement delivered, this time by a massive 108 governments. This group of states welcomed the study of the OHCHR and urged the High Commissioner to transmit the study to New York as an important contribution to the Review Summit of the Millennium Development Goals. Such a contribution to the Summit would encourage the injection of a human rights perspective within the intergovernmental deliberations at the Summit.

Following the debate on the OHCHR study, a second resolution was brought forward at the September 2010 session of the Council. This second Council resolution was intended to be a resolution that helped build support for the Council's work on maternal mortality and that introduced Burkina Faso as the third lead co-sponsor that would also be co-chairing the negotiations. Much of its content was simply an amalgam of paragraphs from the 2009 resolution and the draft outcome document of the MDG Review Summit that was being negotiated in New York at the same time. The resolution called for an analytical compilation of good and effective practices in adopting a human rights-based approach to eliminating maternal mortality and morbidity, and invited states and other stakeholders to share such practices. At the time it was felt that a next step in the direction of operationalizing a human rights-based approach could involve the collection of good practices from states and other actors as to address maternal mortality and morbidity from a human rights perspective. It was believed that if states were contributing something positive about their national practices, there would be greater buy-in and support for expert work to develop an operational framework on implementing a human rights-based approach. In fact, it was felt that the compilation of good or effective practices could be directly fed into an expert consultation that would look at the operational aspects of a human rights-based approach to maternal mortality and morbidity in greater detail.

Despite this 'easier' content, the negotiations were not as easy as expected. In fact, there was much controversy about the provision welcoming the OHCHR study on the human rights dimensions of maternal mortality and morbidity. As the OHCHR study contained references to 'unsafe abortion' and to treaty body recommendations on safe abortion, many governments were opposed to any reference to the OHCHR study within the resolution. The co-sponsors, however, remained resolved to retain the reference. In a surprising twist, when the resolution was to be adopted, the opponents of this reference made a motion to defer action on the draft resolution until a later time. The motion was soundly defeated, but the exchange signalled just how resistance to work on maternal mortality at the Human Rights Council had changed – it was no longer about the human rights framing of the issue but it was more about broader reproductive health and rights aspects. The resolution was adopted by consensus with over 100 co-sponsors.

The OHCHR analytical compilation of good and effective practices achieved the goal of generating contributions from governments as to what they felt they are doing well nationally in the area of maternal mortality and morbidity. However, it was clear from the report that efforts to adopt a human rights-based approach to programmes and policies related to maternal mortality and morbidity are patchy and piecemeal. All the practices presented in the compilation could more fully integrate a human rights-based approach.

With governments having contributed their good and effective practices and the clear need for guidance for governments on the issue, the stage was set for the adoption of the third Human Rights Council resolution on maternal mortality and morbidity and human rights at the September 2011 session. In that resolution, the Council requested the OHCHR to convene an expert group to develop a technical guidance that operationalizes the implementation of a human rights-based approach to policies and programmes related to maternal mortality and morbidity. The resolution was adopted by consensus with over 100 co-sponsors.

With this resolution adopted, the civil society coalition will see the achievement in the near future of its goal of having the Council lead the way in ensuring states receive greater policy guidance on the steps they need to take to implement a human rights-based approach to maternal mortality and morbidity.

8.11 Looking ahead: operational guidance and the work of the independent Expert Review Group (iERG)

This progression of developments at the Human Rights Council has seen the achievement of a range of goals that a coalition of civil society actors had set out in order to see greater attention paid to the human rights dimensions of maternal mortality and morbidity. However, the last goal – the establishment, under the aegis of the Human Rights Council, of an international accountability mechanism that would hold states accountable in relation to maternal mortality and morbidity and would monitor the implementation of an operational framework on using a human right-based approach – has yet to be achieved. In this respect, it is important to look at other UN system developments in relation to maternal mortality and morbidity. Happening almost in parallel with the Council's work in this area have been efforts led by the UN Secretary-General to address women's and children's health. At the MDG Review Summit in September 2010, the Secretary-General launched his '*Global strategy* on women's and children's health', which aims to rescue MDGs 4 and 5 (respectively, on child and maternal health) as the two MDGs that are the furthest from realization.[23] It identifies key actions to be taken and

23 Reproduced in Part II of this volume.

has led to much needed financial commitment. As a follow-up to this, the Commission on Information and Accountability on Women's and Children's Health was launched in December 2010 to improve global reporting, oversight and accountability in these areas. In its final report, *Keeping promises, measuring results*, the Commission made 10 key recommendations to improve accountability for resources and results relating to reproductive, maternal, newborn and child health. Many of these relate to improving systems to better track resource expenditures at the national level. However, recommendations on improving national level accountability and transparency for results and resources are also included in the report. Significantly, in its final recommendation, the Commission established the independent Expert Review Group (iERG) to monitor the implementation of the Commission's recommendations. The iERG is composed of seven independent experts of a diverse range of expertise and experience who are charged with monitoring and assessing progress until 2015 in implementing the Secretary-General's *Global strategy* and the Commission's recommendations.

In terms of its structure, the iERG sounds similar to the mechanism that civil society organizations had envisaged the Human Rights Council creating, albeit with a larger mandate that includes newborn and child health in addition to reproductive and maternal health. One could fairly ask: Looking at its mandate, does the iERG have the potential to serve as the international accountability body that was envisaged? While the mandate of the iERG is fairly well defined, there are elements that are broadly formulated and lend themselves well to integrating a human rights perspective. Three such specific functions of the iERG are:

1 to track the implementation of the Commission's recommendations, which include recommendations to enhance national level accountability and transparency
2 to identify obstacles to implementing both the Commission's recommendations and the *Global strategy*
3 to make recommendations to improve the effectiveness of the accountability framework.

Under any of these three functions, the iERG could examine failures to give full effect to human rights-based approaches to maternal health and could recommend actions to remedy these that are in line with human rights standards and approaches. The final report of the Commission integrates human rights considerations in a piecemeal fashion and there are numerous key gaps in the Commission's recommendations from a human rights perspective.[24] However, there is ample scope for the iERG to ensure that

24 Joint letter by Action Canada for Population and Development, Amnesty International, Center for Economic and Social Rights, Human Rights Watch, International Planned

human rights standards and approaches are central to its work and to constructively assess whether governments and other stakeholders are fully integrating human rights principles into their programmes and policies related to maternal health.

Within the first year of the iERG's work, the operational guidance developed by independent experts convened as a result of the September 2011 Council resolution will be finalized and released. It will lay out specific steps that states and other stakeholders need to take in order to better implement a human rights-based approach to policies and programmes related to maternal mortality and morbidity. After this, the iERG will need to integrate this knowledge meaningfully into its work. Doing this would enhance international accountability for maternal mortality and morbidity, would encourage the growth and strengthening of national accountability mechanisms, and would further the work of civil society organizations active at the Human Rights Council to ensure that the human rights dimensions of maternal mortality and morbidity are fully understood and addressed by governments and all stakeholders.

Parenthood Federation and Ipas to United Nations Secretary-General, 27 May 2011. Available at www.who.int/pmnch/ media/membernews/2011_20110613_csoresponseto report_CIAWCH.pdf.

9 Postscript: towards ending preventable maternal deaths

Dr Flavia Bustreo
Assistant Director-General, World Health Organization

This book begins to explain the important synergies between health, human rights and accountability. It owes much to the important leadership that Paul Hunt has shown in the efforts to make these links explicitly understood by the public health community. The international roundtable convened in 2010, and which was the basis for this book, came at an important moment. For the first time in 20 years we began to see the overall number of maternal deaths in the world decline; as I wrote then, we began to have 'hope, at last'.[1]

Our most recent estimates published in 2012 indicate this hope was justified as the number of maternal deaths, during the decades from 1990 to 2010, declined from around 543,000 to 287,000 – almost halving the global total.[2] The rate of decline has accelerated in the past decade due to significant increases in the political commitment of many governments and intergovernmental organizations, as well as the valuable efforts of civil society, to women's and children's health. Collaborative global partnerships, such as the Partnership for Maternal, Newborn and Child Health, aimed at delivering effective interventions at scale in countries, played an especially important role.[3]

Back in 2005, when we worked on the first – and groundbreaking – WHO report on maternal mortality and child mortality, we focused on 'Making every mother and every child count' as a clear recognition that maternal mortality was an important measure of both women's health and of a health system's strength in general.[4]

It has not been a smoothly paved road. The challenge of measuring maternal mortality, for example, has been a critical preoccupation for the public health community because so few countries had a valid registration system able to

1 M.C. Hogan, K.J. Foreman, M. Naghavi, et al., Maternal mortality for 181 countries, 1980–2008: a systematic analysis of progress towards Millennium Development Goal 5, *The Lancet* 375, 2010, 1609–1623.
2 WHO, UNICEF, UNFPA, and World Bank, *Trends in maternal mortality: 1990 to 2010*, 2012.
3 F. Bustreo, J. Requejo, M. Seoane and M. Merialdi, *Making women and children count through partnership*, Global Health Diplomacy, 2012.
4 WHO World Health Report, *Make every mother and child count*, Geneva: WHO, 2005.

capture vital events. Consequently, we had to rely on a collection of methods to estimate maternal deaths and to use proxy indicators, such as skilled birth attendance or emergency obstetric care.[5] Dr Chan, WHO Director-General, has noted that we have focused on measuring, convinced that 'what gets measured gets done'.

Many chapters in this book highlight the important work done by the public health community to reduce maternal deaths, but perhaps it is the relevance of the work of the UN Human Right Council that deserves the greatest emphasis, which owes much to the work of the first UN Special Rapporteur on the right to the highest attainable standard of health, including his report on maternal mortality in India.[6] When the principal human right body in the United Nations system recognized that preventable maternal mortality was a violation of a fundamental right for women, I realized that this was a historical turning point. Several human rights treaties already recognized this implicitly, but the resolutions in 2009 and thereafter were the most explicit and direct call for concrete steps to be taken by governments and by the Office of the High Commissioner for Human Rights to redress this situation.

The Commission on Information and Accountability for Women's and Children's Health builds on the work of the WHO's report mentioned earlier and that of the Human Rights Council. The Commission's first recommendation is that: ' [By] 2015, all countries have taken significant steps to establish a system for registration of births, deaths and causes of death, and have well-functioning health information systems that combine data from facilities, administrative sources and surveys' (see Part II of this volume). Raphael Lozano and his colleagues recently concluded that countries' ability to count every mother and every child is still very weak; instead, we rely on estimates from the UN and academic institutions.[7] Progress in implementing the Commission's recommendations is therefore crucial, since reliable information is a condition *sine qua non* for ensuring accountability and progress on improving maternal and child health in every country. As we have seen, the Commission also recommended the establishment of an independent expert review group (iERG) to report regularly from 2012 to 2015 to the UN Secretary-General on how promises are kept and results measured. The first expert review group report was published in September 2012.

A critical concern and special emphasis of the Commission's recommendations is on maternal death surveillance and response. This concept evolved

5 C. Abouzar and T. Wardlaw, Maternal mortality at the end of a decade: signs of progress?, *WHO Bullettin* 79(6), 2001, 561–573.

6 Human Rights Council, Report of the Special Rapporteur on the right of everyone to the highest attainable standard of health, mission to India, UN Doc. A/HRC/14/20/Add.2, 15 April 2010.

7 R. Lozano, H. Wang, K.J. Foreman, et al., Progress towards Millennium Development Goals 4 and 5 on maternal and child mortality: an updated systematic analysis, *The Lancet*, 2011. Available at 20.DOI:10.1016/S0140-6736(11)61337–8.

from the idea of just a surveillance system reporting cases, to the development of an integrated and adequate response system. Such a system should build on the rights of women to healthcare and also feed into countries' reviews of progress. Most importantly, the Commission encourages action to improve women's health, including links to judicial and other forms of review and redress when rights have been violated.

For us at WHO, the important link between human rights, accountability and maternal deaths is indeed the common call for the improvement of maternal mortality measurement and most importantly 'the response' to preventing maternal deaths.

As maternal deaths continue to decline around the world, we must examine best practices concerning successful efforts to eradicate diseases. The effort to eradicate polio is an instructive precedent, where a strong network of surveillance has been coupled with a strong network that makes this information available to both the policymakers responsible for the public health response and to the community activists, who can use a legislative framework to advocate on behalf of affected populations. In India, the polio eradication programme has achieved the goal of ending polio cases since 2011. At the same time, there are a very large number of community workers who are trained to recognize and report paralysis of a leg. These same community workers could recognize maternal deaths and they could be trained to provide timely responses to events causing maternal mortality. In fact, in some states of India, the polio social mobilization network has already begun using community workers to encourage pregnant mothers to go for antenatal care and to deliver their children in hospitals.[8]

By continuing to work on both stronger measurement of maternal mortality and stronger accountability, grounded on the human rights principles and frameworks, and through learning from successful interventions and adopting intensive maternal deaths surveillance and response, I am convinced that the public health and human right communities together can ensure an end to preventable maternal deaths.

8 India polio communication update, Volume 2, June 2012.

Part II

Additional resource material on maternal mortality, human rights and accountability using extracts from key documents

10 Human rights, constructive accountability and maternal mortality in the Dominican Republic: a commentary[1]

L.P. Freedman

Introduction

Human rights norms could be readily used to characterize and categorize the chilling scenes of humiliation, neglect and abuse described by Miller, et al. in their report on institutional births and maternal mortality in the Dominican Republic. Laboring women have a right to be treated with basic human dignity, to get the quality of care that enables them to give birth safely, and that offers their children the best chance at a healthy start in life.

But can human rights be mobilized to do anything to change this situation? Amid grim accounts of conditions in public sector facilities, the report describes a process that gives reason for hope: here we see the early stages of a process that, whether explicitly and consciously or not, uses many of the techniques of a rights-based approach to reducing maternal mortality.

At the heart of rights-based approaches lies a notion of accountability. All too often, accountability is used to mean simply blame and punishment. Here, I use the phrase 'constructive accountability' to make clear that a rights-based approach to maternal mortality reduction is not primarily about enacting a system to find fault and pronounce punishment; rather, it is about developing a dynamic of entitlement and obligation between people and their government and within the complex system of relationships that form the wider health system, public and private. It is about building health systems that function for the benefit of people.

A classic approach to human rights reporting uses the human rights that have been enacted into law—for example, rights to life and to health; to healthcare and to non-discrimination—as standards against which to judge treatment of pregnant and laboring women in the health system. Important as that assessment is, to actually change conditions so that the public health system respects, protects and fulfills human rights, we ultimately need to use the impetus provided by human rights law to move beyond the legal realm

1 L.P. Freedman, Human rights, constructive accountability and maternal mortality in the Dominican Republic: a commentary, *International Journal of Gynaecology and Obstetrics* 82, 2003, 111–114. Footnotes omitted.

into the realm of good, evidence-based, rights-conscious medical and public health practice.

Miller, et al. do not, of course, give full details of the political and technical-scientific process by which the Dominican government came to pass the new regulations codifying the norms shown there in Table 2, but they appear to have been formulated based on a view that high-quality delivery services are an essential element of women's human rights. Constructive accountability—and the progressive realization of human rights—begins with putting such norms into place. From there, we can highlight important dimensions of the constructive accountability process demonstrated by the report in Miller, et al.

Using norms in a continuous feedback process

The 'norms for attention to women in labor and delivery' and 'norms for managing obstetric emergencies' are dated 2001. The assessment explicitly linking the team's observations to the standards set by the new norms was apparently conducted within months of their enactment. Dissemination of the assessment report led to a more careful review of specific maternal deaths, which, in turn, identified some individual physicians whose behavior and practices were egregious enough to justify sanctioning and loss of licensing. Of course, individual punishment (and knowledge that professional standards will be enforced) has an appropriate place in a constructive accountability system. The important point here is that individual sanctioning has not been used to scapegoat a doctor, pacify the public, and cover up wider, deeper problems. Instead, it has become one element in trying to implement an ongoing process of systemic change.

Indeed, a new dynamic of entitlement and obligation will require change on all sides. Providers in the health system clearly need to change their views of themselves, acknowledging that their fundamental obligation in law and in accordance with professional standards is to deliver quality care to patients. But that dynamic will only develop when patients—the people the system is meant to serve—are confident in their entitlement and have effective mechanisms to assert it. Some patients in maternity hospitals clearly found their treatment to be deeply humiliating: "The nurses and cleaners are animals with clothes on." But the longer *Report of the strategic assessment*, published by the Ministry of Health (SESPAS), USAID and the Population Council in February 2002, also hinted at just how complex the problem of changing expectations and developing a sense of entitlement can often be. After a description of brutal delivery practices at a referral-level hospital, which included roughly hustling the newborn away from the mother with hardly a word, the authors describe their interviews of four newly postpartum women sitting in wheelchairs outside the nursery (one still not having seen her child or received any report of the baby's condition):

> We asked each of them how they felt about their experiences; all replied that they were quite satisfied: "This is the best place to have a baby."

> Some had traveled long distances to have their baby in this "special place."

Human rights education meant to develop people's understanding of their entitlements and confidence in their right to assert them is one of the objectives that women's groups and civil society groups often assume for their work. But such change also needs to be supported by practices in the facility. For example, posting a patients' bill of rights and similar techniques are used by facilities in many parts of the world, from clinics in India to the teaching hospital at Columbia University in New York City. Providing a mechanism to enforce those rights is also an essential obligation of government.

But such specific steps to introduce and strengthen a dynamic of obligation and entitlement need not come only by fiat from above. The description by Miller, et al. of one well-performing facility makes clear that good management practices at that level can make an enormous difference as well. Criterion-based audits and a monitoring group that includes community members are among the tools useful for establishing ongoing constructive accountability mechanisms at the facility level

Participation of government and other stakeholders; transparency of results

In striking contrast to most human rights reports, Miller, et al. is co-authored by officials from SESPAS, the government department responsible for the hospitals it evaluates. The willingness of the Dominican government to bring these issues to light, including in an international medical journal, as it takes steps to address them, must be acknowledged with real appreciation. Rights-based change requires constructive relationships between government, health professionals, and civil society. In the political and economic dynamics of today's world, donors and lenders, who sometimes use their economic power and leverage to influence—even distort—these relationships, also need to be sensitive to and supportive of the dynamics of rights-based change.

Initial reports of the strategic assessment were disseminated in workshops that included representatives of governmental and non-governmental groups, which together helped prioritize problems and then nominated members for the assessment team. It would be naive to assume that these relationships among NGOs, government and professional bodies are without tension and moments of disappointment, even anger. But the commitment to an ongoing public, transparent process of assessment, change and reassessment is critical.

Reflecting on structural as well as individual problems

Miller, et al. make clear that the individual behavior of health providers is deeply embedded in a system that does not support them with appropriate training, supervision, assignment of tasks or salary. The analysis of rights violations and accountability lapses as being both individual and structural is a crucial prerequisite for making changes that will have lasting impact.

The analysis of the imbalance between overwhelmed referral facilities and the underused, understaffed primary facilities exposes a complex of structural deficiencies intertwined with individual preferences (no doubt complicated in their origin) that will require long-term commitment to correct.

Going forward

The very publication of the article by Miller, et al. in this volume is an important part of the constructive accountability process. Of course, the analysis can go deeper. There are unanswered questions: who are the women who have suffered such substandard care and borne the brunt of unacceptably high maternal mortality in the Dominican Republic? Is inequity in the health system falling along critical social fault lines, so that it needs also to be addressed as an issue of discrimination as well? What role have donors played? What role have health sector reform policies played? What needs to be done at the local level in each facility and at the structural level in the system as a whole to ensure that the norms are followed?

The process of strategic assessment and follow-up described in Miller, et al. is the beginning. The seriousness with which the government appears to be taking the issue is an important start. Now all actors have a role in ensuring that this process moves forward, that the facts elicited in assessments lead to appropriate measures for the progressive realization of the right to life and to health for the people of the Dominican Republic. Many of us will watch the process, hoping that the Dominican Republic will become the next success story for reducing maternal mortality—and that it will use a transparent, participatory, rights-based approach to do so.

11 Accountability and the right to the highest attainable standard of health[1]

Helen Potts

Introduction

. . . Accountability is a distinctive, complex and central feature of human rights. In the context of human rights, accountability is concerned with the requirement of the state to fully comply with its obligations under the international and regional human rights treaties to which it is a party. Concrete cases of individuals and groups seeking government accountability show that the real challenge is to convert this legal commitment into specific measures of implementation. Despite the critical importance of the role of accountability, little work has been done to explore its meaning and content in the context of the right to health. As a result, accountability is often seriously misunderstood. Sometimes, for example, accountability is misunderstood to mean only 'naming and shaming', or blame and punishment.

As a concept it is not new to the health sector. Sometimes it is understood simply in terms of financial accountability: a device to check that health funds are being spent as they should be. At other times it relates to the performance of the health sector: demonstrating and accounting for performance in light of agreed indicators. It is also understood in a political sense: the presence of institutions, procedures, and mechanisms to ensure that the government delivers on its electoral promises, represents citizens' interests, and responds to societal needs and concerns. It has also been described in terms of a 'short route to accountability', where it is understood as increasing the power of civil society to demand better services from private provision.

Right to health accountability is also concerned with these categories. However, right to health accountability is much broader. Accountability in the context of the right to health is the process that provides individuals and communities with an opportunity to understand how government (and its agents) has discharged its right to health obligations. Equally, it provides government (and its agents) with the opportunity to explain what it has done and why. Where mistakes have been made, accountability requires redress. It

1 Helen Potts, *Accountability and the right to the highest attainable standard of health*, Human Rights Centre, University of Essex, 2008. Footnotes omitted.

is a process that helps to identify what works, so it can be repeated, and what does not, so it can be revised. . . .

In the context of the right to health, there are many different types of accountability mechanism, including judicial procedures, national human rights institutions, health commissioners, democratically elected local health councils, public hearings, patients' committees, impact assessments, and so on. A sector as complex and important as the health sector requires a range of effective, transparent, accessible, independent accountability mechanisms. The media and civil society organizations also have a crucial role to play.

Monitoring and evaluation have been features of health planning for some time. What benefits will be gained by the incorporation of right to health accountability into the day-to-day work of health policymakers? Put simply, the incorporation of the accountability process into the day-to-day work of health policymakers will directly support the development and implementation of better quality health policy, improve health outcomes and also assist government to progressively realize the right to health. The chapter is an introduction to accountability rather than a detailed toolkit. It is designed to be used as a starting point for health policymakers to develop greater understanding of the area. . . .

Accountability

A. What is accountability?

Accountability is the process that requires government to show, explain and justify how it has discharged its obligations regarding the right to the highest attainable standard of health. This process also provides rights holders with an opportunity to understand how government has discharged its right to health obligations. As part of the process, if it is revealed that there has been a failure on the part of government or its agents to fulfil the obligations contained in the right to the highest attainable standard of health, rights holders are entitled to effective remedies to redress this failure.

Accountability is both prospective and retrospective. Viewing it as a prospective process draws attention to its potential to improve performance: to identify what works, so it can be repeated, and what does not, so it can be revised. Viewing it as a retrospective process draws attention to the remedies that should be available when there has been failure on the part of government to fulfill its obligations. As both a prospective and retrospective process, it necessarily includes the monitoring of conduct, performance, and outcomes. It is also continuous (see Figure 1) and commences with the government ensuring the incorporation and implementation of accountability processes into all health policy.

The accountability process requires the incorporation of monitoring into all aspects of policy development and implementation. This monitoring is conducted on a continuous basis by government. It can also be conducted by

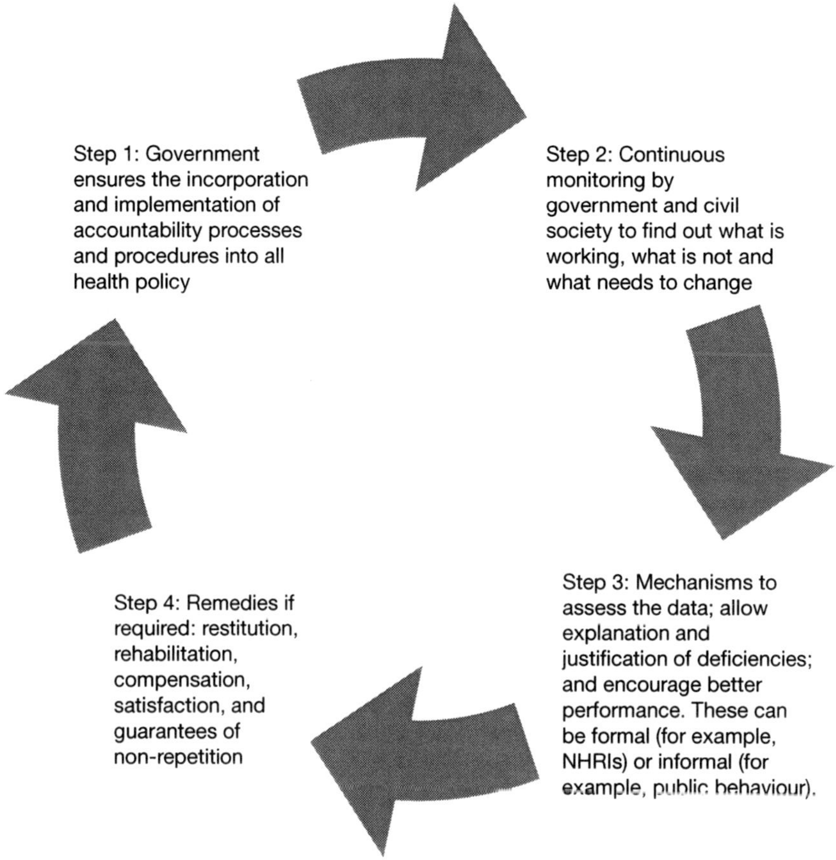

Figure 1 The accountability process

civil society, either collaboratively with government or independently. The accountability process also requires the presence of accessible accountability mechanisms to provide a forum for explanation and justification. This explanation and justification can take place in a variety of settings and need not be confined to formal settings such as the courts or national human rights institutions. Other settings include democratically elected health councils, public hearings, and national or local public meetings. The media also have a crucial role to play.

In addition, remedies for the non-fulfillment of right to health obligations are to be available. Remedies (see later) in the context of the right to health are broad, as they include the modification of monitoring processes, human rights training, and organizational improvements concerning planning, budgeting and policy formulation, in addition to judicial remedies such as compensation. Present in each of these elements—monitoring, mechanisms and remedies—is participation. While the form of participation will vary between the elements and also within them (e.g. judicial accountability mechanisms versus social accountability mechanisms), it is an essential element of the accountability process. Hence, an effective accountability process is comprised of the following essential elements: monitoring, mechanisms, remedies and participation. . . .

C. Monitoring in accountability

. . . Meaningful accountability is not possible without monitoring. Progressively realizing the right to health requires that policies and practice be brought into line with right to health standards. Monitoring therefore must be able to indicate what is working, what is not working, what has been omitted, and what changes need to be made.

Monitoring plays a dual role in relation to accountability:

a) It provides, on an ongoing basis, the information that government needs to determine what areas should be focussed on in order to reach its targets for the realization of the right to health.
b) It provides rights holders with the information they need to claim their rights and to hold the government and its agents to account when obligations have not been fulfilled.

Health policymakers use a very large number of health indicators relevant to health policy effectiveness and national and international reporting. However, these health indicators do not usually capture all that right to health monitoring demands. For example, right to health monitoring would also require indicators on the participation of individuals and groups in the development, implementation and review of health policy, as well as indicators on the protection of the right to seek, receive and impart information on the right to health. Ways to address this important deficiency in health indicators can be found elsewhere, for example, in the 2006 report of the Special Rapporteur on the right to health, to the Human Rights Council.

As rights holders are entitled to obtain information and as government has an obligation to release all relevant material, the results of monitoring must be made public. When the findings are released they are an important tool for accountability. There are multiple avenues available to government for the release of this information. For example, in many countries there is an institution at the national level that prepares, on a periodic basis, reports on the health status of a population. Right to health monitoring information could be included in these reports. In addition, many countries have a national human rights plan. The information gained from monitoring could also be released in the annual report to parliament on the implementation of the national human rights plan. This monitoring information could also be made available at the regional and international levels.

Government has an obligation to monitor its activity. In addition, government activity must also be monitored by civil society. Too much dependency on government monitoring could result in unquestioningly accepting the data that are offered. Accordingly, as part of the right to seek, receive, and impart information, civil society organizations should perform a monitoring role. This monitoring role can be undertaken independently or in cooperation with the government and its agents. . . .

D. Accountability mechanisms

. . . An accountability mechanism is the procedure through which government is answerable for its acts or omissions in relation to right to health obligations. The procedure provides rights holders with an opportunity to obtain information on government action, and to ask for explanations. It also provides government with an opportunity to explain its actions. In the absence of accessible and effective accountability mechanisms, the right to health will be largely meaningless to rights holders.

There are five broad types of accountability mechanism:

1 judicial (e.g. judicial review of executive acts and omissions, constitutional redress, statutory interpretation and public interest litigation)
2 quasi-judicial (e.g. national human rights institutions, regional and international human rights treaty bodies)
3 administrative (e.g. human rights impact assessment)
4 political (e.g. parliamentary committee review of budgetary allocations and the use of public funds, democratically elected health councils and healthcare commissions)
5 social (e.g. the involvement of civil society (independent or collaborative with government) in budget monitoring, health centre monitoring, public hearings, and social audits).

These different types of accountability mechanism can be found at national, regional, and international levels. Some mechanisms can be described as 'specific' and others as 'general' accountability mechanisms. Specific accountability mechanisms, such as national human rights institutions, have been developed specifically to address human rights accountability. General accountability mechanisms, while not developed for the purposes of human rights accountability, do have the capacity to address accountability in the context of the right to health (e.g. democratically elected health councils). . . .

E. Effective remedies

Governments have an obligation to ensure that:

- There are adequate legal or other appropriate remedies available to any rights holder claiming that his or her right to health has been violated.

- These remedies take one or more of the following forms: restitution; rehabilitation; compensation; satisfaction; and guarantees of non-repetition.
- The right to a remedy for a violation of the right to health includes the right to access national, regional (if applicable) and international procedures for protection.
- The procedures to obtain a remedy for violation of the right to health are known by all rights holders.

Remedies to redress violations of the right to health are key to ensuring that human rights have meaning. Remedies may take any one or more of the forms mentioned in the following.

Restitution

Restitution involves the re-establishment of a situation that existed prior to the violation of the right to health. For example, if legislation or policy has been introduced to limit access to healthcare services by particular groups, restitution would involve amendment of the legislation or reversal of the policy.

Compensation

Compensation should be provided for any economically assessable damage resulting from a violation of human rights. The state has an obligation to take all necessary measures to safeguard persons within its jurisdiction from infringements of the right to health by third parties. Such infringements include illness and injury caused through the non-regulation of privately controlled health services, and illness and injury caused through the non-provision of health services that are allowed by law. Economically assessable damage includes the following:

- physical or mental harm, including pain, suffering and emotional distress
- loss of opportunity, for example, education
- costs required for medicines and medical services
- material damages and loss of earnings, including future economic loss
- costs required for legal or expert assistance. . . .

Rehabilitation

Rehabilitation includes medical and psychological care as well as legal and social services. As rehabilitation includes provision of social services, this remedy could include the provision of services such as water and basic sanitation. . . .

Satisfaction and guarantees of non-repetition

These two remedies include:

- full and public disclosure of the truth
- an apology, including public acknowledgement of the facts and acceptance of responsibility
- an official declaration or a judicial decision
- judicial or administrative sanctions against the persons responsible for the violations
- inclusion of right to health training for government and health workers
- conducting and strengthening, on a priority and continued basis, right to health training to all sectors of society, in particular to government ministers and their department staff and members of other political parties
- legislation
- monitoring and enforcement mechanisms
- organizational improvements in the ministry concerning planning, budgeting, policy formulation
- renewed commitment to or reaffirmation of the original obligation, accompanied by an action plan including benchmarks and dates for achievement.

The first three remedies focus on the rights holder and are concerned with redressing the impact of the violation of the individual or group rights holder. The last two remedies, satisfaction, and guarantees of non-repetition, are particularly important in ensuring the introduction of systematic accountability processes in the long term. . . .

E. Participation in accountability

Accountability establishes a dialogue between the government and rights holders. It engages them in discussion. Hence, participation is present throughout the process of accountability. The methods of participation (for example, social audits, public hearings and legal representation in judicial mechanisms) will vary with the context.

Conclusion

. . . For a variety of reasons, it is not possible to provide a simple checklist of what needs to be in place to ensure accountability. However, there are some preconditions for effective accountability, such as:

- a strong commitment and long-term vision on the part of government that the right to health should be incorporated into the day-to-day work of health policymakers

- the presence of a national health plan that incorporates the right to health
- institutional mechanisms to ensure effective participation in the development, implementation and review of the national health plan
- the establishment of effective institutional arrangements for civil society and the government to work together
- the establishment of effective monitoring systems
- access to, and implementation of, the decisions of accountability mechanisms that are relevant to health policy
- the development of ongoing right to health training for health policymakers at all levels.

12 Toward transformative accountability: applying a rights-based approach to fulfill maternal health obligations[1]

Alicia Ely Yamin

Introduction

. . . Initiatives calling for rights-based approaches to maternal mortality and morbidity (MMM) all emphasize accountability, which has been lacking in the MDGs process. For example, the OHCHR publication relating to the MDGs process overall, *Claiming the millennium development goals: a human rights approach*, explains "the *raison d'être* of the rights-based approach is accountability." The UN Special Rapporteur on the right to health underscored the importance of accountability in human rights approaches to maternal mortality. Further, non-governmental organizations (NGOs) also explicitly focus on the centrality of developing effective.

Accountability in a human rights-approach to maternal health relates to obligations to "respect, protect and fulfill" a wide array of civil and political rights, as well as economic and social rights, and goes far beyond the health sector. Not only is maternal mortality fundamentally linked to women's social and economic status in society, but gender inequality and violations of women's sexual and reproductive rights constitute grave injustices even when they are not directly related to women's deaths or morbidity. A comprehensive rights-based accountability framework with respect to MMM requires the explication of these multiple obligations relating to all relevant rights. . . .

Accountability in the context of fulfilling the right to health: beyond individual cases and sanctions

In general, the concept of accountability refers to holding actors responsible for their actions in light of standards of behavior and performance. In a human rights framework, those standards are derived from both so-called "hard" and "soft" law sources, including, *inter alia*, binding international treaty norms

1 Alicia Ely Yamin, Toward transformative accountability: applying a human rights-based approach to fulfill maternal health obligations, *SUR International Journal on Human Rights* 7(12), 2010, 96–121. Footnotes omitted.

and statements from quasi-judicial international bodies relating to the adjudication of pertinent cases, as well as authoritative interpretations of relevant norms by treaty bodies, statements by UN Special Rapporteur on the right to the highest attainable standard of health, and international conference declarations and programs of action. They are also informed by domestic constitutional frameworks, legislation and regulations. However, fostering accountability in practice requires more than setting out norms in the abstract and establishing enforcement mechanisms. It requires a dynamic process of clarifying legal standards for actors at various levels, from health service providers to policymakers, and engaging with those actors with respect to the implications for their roles and responsibilities.

In a human rights framework, accountability combines elements of responsiveness, answerability and redress. Moreover, accountability is necessarily relational—i.e., there can be no human rights accountability without specifying "to whom?"—and therefore it is closely linked to the effective participation of people affected by health policies and programs. In the context of reforming health systems to meet maternal health needs, accountability entails financial, administrative, regulatory, political, and institutional dimensions, as well as legal. As Amnesty International's 2010 report states, accountability "allows us to look ahead" as well as back. An effective framework of accountability serves as the basis for promoting systemic and institutional changes that create conditions under which women can enjoy their rights to maternal health, and not just for punishing identified lapses in performance.

Indeed, the traditional model of human rights advocacy, which seeks to identify a violation, a violator, and a remedy is poorly suited to advancing accountability for improvement of maternal health. This is true for both practical and conceptual reasons. In practice, many health systems in which patients face abuses are extremely punitive with respect to frontline healthcare workers as well. For example, it is routine in many countries for health professionals who are associated with a maternal death to be summarily dismissed, without any procedure to discern whether they were, in fact, responsible for the death. These often unwritten policies are ostensibly intended to promote "accountability" and quality care in obstetric cases; they have the opposite effect. They create perverse incentives for health professionals to avoid dealing with obstetric emergencies, both as individuals and as institutions.

This does not mean a license for impunity. As Lynn Freedman writes: "Of course, individual punishment (and knowledge that professional standards will be enforced) has an appropriate place in a constructive accountability system. The important point here is that individual sanctioning has not been used to scapegoat a doctor, pacify the public, and cover up wider, deeper problems." When an individual provider could have done nothing to save a woman placing blame on him or her not only distorts incentives; it also diverts attention from the systemic problems that resulted in the woman's death. For example, the health center may lack the necessary supplies or drugs, or transportation. As Leslie London argues: "[F]rontline health workers are frequently unable to provide adequate access to care because of systemic factors outside their control and because of management systems that disempower them from acting independently and effectively." Focussing on individual health practitioners' conduct divorced from context in such a situation, as London writes: "frequently makes little headway and gives a human rights approach a bad name."

"Maternal death audits" and "reviews," whereby individual deaths of women are investigated with the aim of promoting reflection on institutional and systemic failures as well as individual failures, have been advanced by some as a means to promote "human rights-based accountability". Such reviews are done in myriad ways and therefore it is difficult to generalize. However, in general, as Human Rights Watch notes in its report on India, these reviews have a place in a broader accountability system, provided that they meet the following criteria:

1 they are conducted under strict confidentiality
2 they provide for due process
3 the scope of the investigation extends beyond the facility.

When these conditions cannot be guaranteed there is a serious risk of backlash against human rights-based approaches by those health workers we most need as allies. Additionally—and critically—these reviews should be used to complement, rather than substitute for, the continuous use of process indicators that evaluate how the health system is functioning, e.g., to measure the use and availability of emergency obstetric care.

The model of identifying a violation, a violator, and a remedy is conceptually inadequate as well. That is, it implicitly assumes that there is an equilibrium that is broken by the violation; an investigation can then be launched to determine culpability and provide redress to return the situation to equilibrium. This paradigm was developed to address violations of civil rights, such as abuses in police custody, where human rights advocates assumed (often incorrectly) that exposing and denouncing abuses could lead to punishment of perpetrators and deterrence of future harms. If this is often an invalid assumption with regard to civil rights abuses, it can be counterproductive with respect to fostering accountability with respect to fulfilling the right to maternal health.

In situations of high maternal mortality, we are confronting dysfunctional health systems where deaths may be attributable neither to negligence nor to lack of oversight at the facility level, but to the lack of available blood, supplies, transport, communications and the like—which all call for systemic changes. Thus, grievance redressal mechanisms that do not go beyond the facility level are likely to be ineffective, and, in turn, to foster even more disillusionment with unresponsive and poorly functioning health systems.

True deterrence—which as Amnesty International's 2010 report notes is a principal goal of—requires transforming the underlying, untenable situation that gives rise to widespread MMM, not restoring a prior equilibrium. . . .

A circle of accountability

A comprehensive accountability framework for fulfilling the right to maternal health at the national level shapes the initial design of policies and programs to address maternal mortality, their implementation and evaluation, and the remedies provided in the event of violations. . . .

National plan of action: the importance of public justification and participation to rights-based accountability

Although the right to health is subject to progressive realization and cannot be realized from one day to the next, states parties to relevant treaties undertake some immediate obligations, including the development of a national strategy and plan of action in respect of their public health goals. The UN Committee on Economic, Social and Cultural Rights (ESC Rights Committee) establishes the creation of a national public health strategy and plan of action, which is evidence based and sets out deliberate targets, as one of a set of basic or core obligations that all states undertake as parties to the ICESCR. Addressing maternal and reproductive health is an obligation of comparable priority and there is no country in the world in which a national plan of action should not include attention to maternal health.

All such plans of action should be based on a robust situational analysis regarding sexual, reproductive, and maternal health in the country, as well as the best evidence of what interventions are required to address maternal morbidity and mortality. The four pillars of reducing maternal mortality are now well understood: skilled birth attendance, access to emergency obstetric care (EmOC), a functioning referral network, together with family planning. Therefore, every national plan of action on maternal health must prioritize these four pillars in the context of strengthening the overall health system, as the "appropriate" measures to be adopting pursuant to international law, although legislative and programming measures will vary contextually based on the situational analysis. In keeping with international law, a national plan of action should also include a broad range of services related to sexual and reproductive health, which are aimed at enabling women to exercise agency with respect to their bodies, and, in turn, their lives.

Under international law, the process of devising a national plan must be transparent and participatory, and its implementation must be subject to periodic evaluation, which is also public. If maternal health is a matter of rights, the women who use health services are not objects of governmental charity or targets of a development policy designed elsewhere; they and their families are agents who have a role to play in the definition of programs and policies that structure the possibilities for their well-being. Therefore, participation cannot be hollow consultation; it must be linked to the policy decisions taken by a government (often in conjunction with a donor or multilateral institution). For example, the public is entitled not only to know whether health facilities are being required to provide for traditional birthing positions and other culturally appropriate care; civil society should be entitled to influence the definition of what constitutes culturally appropriate care.

Requiring policy decisions that affect people's rights, including women's rights to maternal health, to be justified and subjecting those justifications to public scrutiny is fundamental to accountability, and goes well beyond curbing patently arbitrary policies. There will always be questions that arise in the interpretation of a situational analysis or design of a national plan that are not technical in nature, but reflect profound value judgments. . . .

The Rawlsian ethicist, Norman Daniels, proposes "accountability for reasonableness," to ensure the justness of processes to set priorities in health. To meet the standards of accountability for reasonableness, which is broadly consistent with human rights concerns, the process of devising a plan of action and setting priorities must:

1 be subject to public justification
2 be reasonably related to the end of reducing maternal mortality and promoting maternal health
3 be enforceable
4 afford some form of appeal in certain circumstances, such as the evident neglect of a minority population.

Budgetary analysis: tracing expenditure and allocation as fundamental to accountability

Plans of action can be suffused with rights-based principles but progress toward fulfilling the right to maternal health requires expenditure. Budgets often offer the best evidence of whether governments are actually making maternal health a priority. Therefore, demanding transparency and accountability in budgets is a key to transforming health systems to meet women's needs. . . .

At times the budgetary issue is whether a state is devoting the "maximum extent of its available resources" to the right to health and to efforts to address maternal mortality in particular, in accordance with international human rights obligations. In *The missing link: applied budget work as a tool to hold governments accountable for maternal mortality commitments*, the International Initiative on Maternal Mortality and Human Rights (IIMMHR) draws on examples from Mexico, Tanzania and India to "underscore that the lack of real progress in reducing maternal mortality is unquestionably linked to the failure of governments to make maternal health a budgetary priority."

However, it is sometimes the case that substantial resources exist and may even be going into the health sector, but results are poor due to a wide ranging series of factors. These factors include: lack of capacity to absorb resources, ineffective investment of funds, weak financial management, poor procurement practices, limited oversight, and poor district-level management in decentralized healthcare systems. It is essential to go beyond the design of budgets to pinpoint accountability gaps in terms of allocation and implementation, in order to design targeted strategies, whether for corruption or for ineffective investment.

Among the most valuable information that budgetary allocation reveals from a human rights perspective relates to, "understanding *who* among the population is prioritized" which, in turn, "allows us to demonstrate whether the government is fulfilling its obligation of nondiscrimination." . . .

Requiring governments to publicly justify their budgetary allocations as well as the policies that lead to insufficient available resources to spend on social policies, including maternal health, constitutes an important step in fostering systemic accountability. So does providing the public with the tools and information necessary to assess whether expenditures have been effective.

In order to open budgets, the promulgation of freedom of information laws is crucial. However, generating a culture of participation, accountability and transparency at all levels of government is necessary to make budgets more responsive to people's, and in particular women's, needs. In order to assure such a culture, capacity building for civil society organizations in budget monitoring is essential. Moreover, donor states should be held to the commitments they have made in keeping with the Paris Principles and the Accra Agenda for Action to ensure transparency with respect to the way monies they provide or facilitate are spent, and similar requirements should be made of private donors.

Monitoring: the critical role of indicators in measuring progress and establishing priorities

Holding governments accountable for fulfilling the right to maternal health under international legal obligations requires monitoring "progressive realization." Human rights advocacy groups are expert at assessing the adequacy of policy measures states are taking, as well as determining when they are adopting legislation or policies that indicate retrogression, such as restrictions on contraception availability or draconian abortion bans. It is critical to identify such laws and policies, which constitute social determinants of MMM.

However, for both governments and advocacy groups, evaluating whether a state is making adequate progress on improving maternal health requires applying appropriate quantitative indicators. For example, as we are concerned with disparities as much as aggregate progress from a human rights perspective, it would be helpful to have disaggregated maternal mortality ratios (MMRs)—the indicator for whether states will achieve MDG 5(a). However, MMRs alone are inadequate as they rely on data that are generally difficult to collect and interpret, for both statistical and practical reasons. Moreover, MMRs alone do not tell us what the priorities are in terms of addressing MMM.

Therefore, in order for governments to measure their own progress—as well as for advocacy groups to hold them accountable for progressive realization—we need process indicators that: (1) can be measured continuously, so as to permit an assessment of the performance of a given administration; (2) are objective, and comparable across time and countries and/or sub-regions of countries; and (3) relate to the programmatic interventions that we know to be linked to reducing maternal deaths.

For example, data on met need for contraception and skilled birth attendance are critical, as are indicators such as access to antiretroviral medications, especially in regions where there is a deadly synergy between the HIV epidemic and MMM. All of these indicators should be disaggregated by income quintile, race/ethnicity and region.

Indicators that measure the availability, distribution, and use of emergency obstetric care (EmOC indicators) are also not only crucial, but can be being directly linked to requirements under international law that governments make the appropriate care available, accessible, acceptable and of adequate quality (the so-called AAAQ framework). A 2009 handbook sets out these updated EmOC indicators, which were devised by the WHO, Unicef, and UNFPA, in conjunction with the Averting Maternal Death and Disability program at Columbia University (AMDD). Importantly, the EmOC indicators can be monitored at both district and national level, as monitoring at a level "where there is power to effectuate change" is the key to transforming health systems.

Further, in the face of multifactorial causes underpinning high maternal mortality, the EmOC indicators can prove extremely useful to governments in setting priorities and, insofar as these are made publicly available, to advocates in holding governments accountable for adopting the appropriate priorities. . . .

The selection and application of indicators is a far from technical issue; dignity includes access to blood and sutures and we need a way to measure that access if accountability is to be meaningful. By linking the government responsibility for AAAQ, with the evidence we find regarding specific obstacles to women getting the necessary care, we can see that maternal deaths are the foreseeable result of systematic failures with respect to policy, programming, and budgeting decisions, in addition to social and cultural factors. Thus, to the extent this information is made publicly available, donors, advocates, and governments need no longer discuss abstract accountability for realizing the right to maternal health. Rather, it becomes possible to identify very concrete ways in which ministries of health can operationalize their legal obligations to fulfill the right to maternal health.

It is a substantial positive step toward accountability that Countdown to 2015 now includes an indicator on the availability of EmOC facilities in its global tracking. However, such tracking requires needs assessments and ongoing measurements of EmOC facilities, which have not been done in all countries, including many with high levels of maternal mortality. Although the EmOC indicators have been applied in approximately 50 countries, they have not always been used at the national level or on a continuing basis. A major step toward accountability would be to institute the continuous gathering and use of these data in health systems around the world, including both public and private facilities, and to ensure that the information is widely accessible.

Governments bear the primary responsibility under international law for selecting and using appropriate indicators, as well as for providing the public with transparent access to information regarding their measurement and implications. However, as donors and international agencies often drive the use of indicators, this is an area in which they can play an especially important role, through bilateral health assistance as well as the MDGs process. For its part, the HRC could promote meaningful accountability by having states report on the availability of EmOC facilities, if not all the EmOC indicators, as part of universal periodic review, and encouraging states that have not done so to adopt the EmOC indicators. UN treaty-monitoring bodies could take similar measures to emphasize the importance of monitoring the use and availability of EmOC in addition to family planning, skilled birth attendance, and other areas, in meeting maternal health-related obligations under relevant human rights treaties.

Fostering "constructive accountability" at the facility level

National- and district-level initiatives are crucial but the importance of regular monitoring and evaluation, and initiatives taken at the facility level should not be overlooked to increase transparency, responsiveness, and participation in the health system, which are all crucial to a human rights-based approach to accountability. Changes as simple as requiring that prices for any services or medications be posted clearly, and not subject to negotiation, or that staff wear nametags so patients can identify them by name can shift attitudes and relationships between providers and patients markedly. . . .

Facility-based accountability initiatives should be implemented in such a way as to be respectful of the staff's rights, as well as the rights of patients. Not only should health workers not be scapegoated for institutional failures, they should also not be subject to unreasonable demands. For example, no single staff member can be expected to work "24/7" so that there is always coverage; neither can they be expected to dip into their own salaries to pay for medicines or supplies for women experiencing obstetric emergencies. On the contrary, frontline health workers can be encouraged to participate in resolving the accountability deficits in their facilities by creating incentives for both the reporting and addressing of issues. Personal and institutional leadership has proven instrumental in implementing rights-based approaches to accountability at the facility level.

However, the users of health facilities, whether private or public, also need to be able to file grievances when they face mistreatment, discrimination, or inadequate care. Grievance redressal mechanisms must be accessible to all users and family members, including illiterate persons who cannot file written complaints. Moreover, in order to be effective they must permit addressing systemic issues that go beyond the facility.

Further, community participation in oversight of the facility should go beyond grievance redressal. In Peru, for example, the local committees for administration in health (CLAS) facilities involve local community members in managing councils that engage in planning, financial auditing and oversight of the facilities, along with the professional staff. Similar schemes exist in other countries, and are sometimes coupled with community-based human rights education. Such schemes should be studied to discern best practices in making facilities accountable to local communities for maternal and other healthcare, and for enabling local community members, and women in particular, to appropriate their sense of being rights holders demanding legal and social entitlements. The objective is to establish what Lynn Freedman refers to as "constructive accountability"—a new dynamic of entitlement and obligation. Implemented effectively, facility-based accountability can foster fundamental changes in attitudes among both community members as well as health staff about their rights and responsibilities, and the role of the health system.

Remedies: the role of courts and quasi-judicial bodies as integral to transforming health systems

Monitoring alone is insufficient to produce human rights-based accountability. Fundamental to the force of rights is their binding legal nature. Judicial and quasi-judicial remedies therefore have a key role to play in at least four areas related to the right to health, and to maternal, sexual, and reproductive health in particular: implementation of existing laws and policies; reform of policies and budgets that fail to take reasonable account of health rights; removal of legal restrictions on care; and challenges to systemic violations of women's maternal and reproductive health rights in practice.

First, remedies should be available to ensure accountability for the implementation of existing laws and policies. It is, unfortunately, all too common for legislation and policies relating to reproductive and sexual health not to be implemented through adequate regulations. For example, in the case of *Paulina Ramirez v. Mexico*, the Center for Reproductive Rights together with the Spanish body Reproductive Choice Information Group (GIRE) brought a petition to the IACHR in 2002 involving the failure of the government to enact adequate regulations relating to the access to abortion in rape cases, which was provided for under law. The case was settled with the Mexican government through an amicable resolution procedure, whereby the government agreed not only to compensate the named petitioner but also to issue a decree regulating guidelines for access to abortion for rape victims. Moreover, the process of litigation and the surrounding mobilization on the issue played an important role in changing the public debate around abortion in Mexico and leading to the eventual liberalization of the abortion law in Mexico City. . . .

Second, remedies can achieve reforms of policies and budgets that do not adequately protect health rights. In the now well-known *Treatment Action Campaign* case (*Minister of Health v. Treatment Action Campaign*, 2002), the South African Constitutional Court found the restriction of Nevirapine treatment for prevention of mother-to-child transmission (PMTCT) to 18 pilot sites to be unreasonable in light of its constitutional obligations relating to the right to health. The Court not only ordered the extension of PMTCT to the whole country, but also called for a national plan of action with regard to PMTCT and established itself as guardian of the implementation of that plan of action.

The Colombian Constitutional Court has held that reducing the national budget for the subsidized health insurance scheme, which provides coverage to the poor, was inconsistent with the government's obligations relating to the right to health. The Court considered such budgetary reductions to constitute impermissible retrogression, especially as they would affect the most vulnerable sectors of Colombian society.

Third, remedies must be available to challenge legal barriers to care that are discriminatory or directly violate health rights. Abortion restrictions have produced substantial litigation of this type. For example, in a pair of important cases, the Colombian Constitutional Court declared unconstitutional the prohibition of therapeutic abortions as violating women's rights to health and life with dignity. The Court later mandated that all health institutions ensure access to providers who would perform such abortions, noting that conscientious objection was a right of individuals and not institutions. Importantly, the Court's ruling in this case as in others applies to both private and public providers. Indeed, judicial intervention has been important in setting out the scope of private actors' obligations with respect to providing care in a number of countries.

After Nicaragua revised its penal code in 2008 to include a total ban on abortion, even when a woman's life is at risk, a coalition of non-governmental organizations in Nicaragua and around the region brought a case to the IACHR (*Amelia*) challenging the provisions of the law as violating, *inter alia*, the rights to life and health. The IACHR issued precautionary measures in the case, ordering the Nicaraguan government to ensure that the petitioner had access to appropriate medical treatment for her condition. The case has been accompanied by mobilization around the issue, at both the national level and through Amnesty International at the international level.

Fourth, legal remedies are essential in cases where there are systemic violations of women's health rights in practice. For example, legal recourse proved a pivotal part of a larger strategy of accountability in Peru when between 1996 and 1998 an estimated 260,000 overwhelmingly indigenous women were sterilized without fully informed consent and under conditions in which their rights to health and lives were at risk. A coalition of Peruvian NGOs litigated the emblematic case of Maria Mamérita Mestanza Chávez (*Peru v. Maria Mamérita Mestanza Chávez*), in which a woman was involuntarily sterilized and later died as a result of the operation as emblematic of a pattern of violations of fundamental rights and discrimination against indigenous women in Peruvian society. After the case was dismissed in the Peruvian legal system, these NGOs successfully resolved a petition in the Inter-American system. . . .

In short, the use of remedies in these ways goes far beyond restitution of a pre-existing equilibrium or promises of non-repetition. Rather, judicial and quasi-judicial interventions can play important roles in a larger accountability strategy aimed at transforming discriminatory and exclusionary health systems and practices that bear on women's maternal and reproductive health and well-being.

In addition to judicial remedies, national human rights institutions (NHRIs) can sometimes promote systemic accountability for the progress of maternal health goals, as well as for violations of maternal health-related rights. Over the past decade in Peru, for example, the *Defensoría del Pueblo* (Human Rights Ombudsman's Office) has actively pursued monitoring and oversight of reproductive and maternal health rights. This has led, *inter alia*, to revised regulations and policies relating to issues ranging from informed consent to regulations regarding traditional birthing positions. Unfortunately, Peru is an exception. Given the current interest from donor states and foundations in NHRIs, it would be important to address systematically limitations on budgets, human resources, skill sets, and mandates that are currently preventing the majority of NHRIs from being effective accountability mechanisms in the realm of maternal health and other areas.

Donor accountability: promoting compliance with obligations of "international assistance and cooperation"

Many of the decisions that affect the scope of women's rights to maternal health in the global south are taken by governments in the north and in international organizations controlled by member states from the north. The ESC Rights Committee has been clear: "For the avoidance of any doubt, the Committee wishes to emphasize that it is particularly incumbent on States parties and other actors in a position to assist, to provide 'international assistance and cooperation, especially economic and technical' which enable developing countries to fulfill their core and other obligations [including their core obligations relating to maternal and reproductive health]."

Nevertheless, the contours of such obligations are not clear and international declarations regarding obligations of international assistance and cooperation remain extraordinarily weak. The Paris Principles on aid effectiveness, for example, emphasize "harmonization" and "alignment," without binding commitments based on rights. The Accra Agenda for Action is somewhat stronger than the Paris Principles, calling for assistance to be carried out "in ways consistent with their agreed international commitments on gender equality, human rights, disability and environmental sustainability." However, this wording is not followed by the elaboration of specific obligations of support.

Moreover, unlike the other MDGs, MDG 8, which calls for actions from donor countries, sets no targets. In general "the global partnership for development" envisioned in MDG 8 has not materialized around maternal and reproductive health, and basic health systems improvements. Meaningful inclusion of human rights in the MDGs, and into development practice more broadly, demands that targets and corresponding indicators be established through which to hold donor states accountable, as well as national governments in the global south. Those indicators should relate not merely to increasing sustained support for child and maternal health (MDGs 4 and 5, respectively) and health systems more broadly, but also to changes in a wide array of other policies that affect the possibilities of women to enjoy their rights to maternal health.

But such indicators alone are insufficient. Promoting accountability of donor states and international financial institutions requires concerted efforts to raise the costs of noncompliance with both obligations to refrain from policies and actions that undermine the right to health and to provide affirmative economic, as well as technical, assistance. Those costs can be financial, political and social. For example, the HIV/AIDS movement has been particularly effective in shifting the cost–benefit calculus of international actors, including donor states and transnational corporations, as well as governments regarding policies and funding relating to access to antiretrovirals and HIV/AIDS generally. It is still unclear whether increasing engagement by human rights NGOs, including Amnesty International's important global campaign on maternal mortality, will lead to mobilizing a sustained international movement on maternal health that could exert substantial pressure on donor states. Such pressure would relate to refraining from doing harm, as well as to economic and technical assistance. An obvious example with respect to the obligation to "do no harm"—to refrain from actions that undermine maternal health—relates to the recruitment of healthcare workers from countries in the global south that are facing dire shortages of healthcare personnel to meet their right to health obligations. As a policy briefing on MDG 5 from realizing rights states: "Donor countries must ensure policy coherence in this respect. Moreover, not addressing health worker migration undermines donor credibility—why build up health systems in developing countries just to take away precious human resources from them? Policy coherence on this is critically important." In May 2010 the World Health Assembly unanimously adopted a global code of practice on the international recruitment of health personnel. The code calls for voluntary commitments to adopt responsible recruitment policies, but its existence now provides a framework that may encourage cooperation as well as potentially be used to raise the political costs of noncompliance for any individual country that fails to adopt and abide by such commitments.

Second, donor governments must increase economic assistance, as well as technical support. MDG 5 has been the most underfunded MDG and, not surprisingly, has shown very uneven progress. Although a 2010 study in *the Lancet* shows some promising evidence of improvement, it remains clear that enormous increases in global health funding over the last decade have not translated into the necessary investments in basic health services and reproductive health. Even the most optimistic picture presents great disparities in progress, and global levels of maternal mortality are far higher than that required to achieve the 75% overall reduction since 1990 levels called for under the MDGs.

Although most maternal and newborn care is funded domestically, many poor countries are simply not in a position to provide the necessary services to save women's lives. For example, in late 2009 donor agreements made possible the establishment of a free care policy for pregnant and lactating women and infants in Sierra Leone, where Amnesty International had documented that user fees posed one of the greatest barriers to access to care.

Overall, however, while the MDGs have coincided with marked increases in global health funding, this has been largely around HIV/AIDS. Whereas from 1990 to 1998 12% of all donor funding (12% of DAC) was allocated to HIV/AIDS and STI control, over the 1999 to 2004 period, this percentage had risen to 25% (24% DAC) in 2007. In contrast, family planning decreased over the same period from 10% to 6% (14% to 6% DAC), and reproductive healthcare donor funding showed slight dips from 8% to 6% total donors (7% to 6% DAC). ODA for maternal, newborn and child health accounted for only 31% of all ODA for health in 2007.

The issue is not cutting up the ODA pie differently; the issue is increasing the pie. A 2009 UN report concludes: "Without political will and a firm commitment to population, reproductive health, and gender issues, it is unlikely that the goals and targets of the International Conference on Population and Development and the Millennium Summit will be met."

A number of authors have argued that the consensus on the need to address the global HIV/AIDS pandemic—because in part the financial, political and social costs of not doing so would be too high for countries in the north, as well as those in the south—has been more important in increasing funding than the targets set out in MDG 6. Moreover, the creation of the Global Fund to Fight AIDS, Tuberculosis and Malaria (Global Fund) and the United States President's Emergency Plan for AIDS Relief created important institutional mechanisms through which to establish donor state commitments. The March 2010 UN Secretary-General's Report on the MDGs states that, in light of the need to improve the quality, predictability, and durability of aid, in addition to the quantity: "Pooling of donor resources into multi-donor funds has proved time and again to be a fruitful approach, with great successes, for example, in the control of several infectious diseases."

In this regard, a number of authors argue that the Global Fund's mandate might be expanded to include maternal and child health, or health systems broadly. Such proposals go significantly beyond integrating maternal and reproductive health into HIV/AIDS programs, which is feasible under the current mandate.

The Global Fund, which was established in 2002, is a far from perfect mechanism. Criticisms regarding sustainability, inefficiency, and lack of transparency have plagued it, resources have not been allocated equitably among HIV/AIDS, tuberculosis and malaria, and interventions have at times undermined rather than strengthened health systems. Moreover, the creation of a mechanism cannot stand alone; constant pressure from the HIV/AIDS movement in different countries has played an important role in sustaining financial commitments to the Global Fund.

Nevertheless, expansion and adaptation of the Global Fund presents the possibility of engaging donor states in long-term commitments to maternal health and health systems more broadly. The framework established through the Global Fund critically does not assume that addressing critical health needs be done in a "sustainable" way—i.e., that aid is for a time certain and efforts should be directed at making poor governments fend for themselves despite a lack of financial, material and human resources and a global architecture that stacks the odds against them. Instead, there is an assumption of some international responsibility and a concomitant ongoing international commitment for funding activities to address HIV, TB and malaria. There desperately needs to be a similar global commitment for investing in health systems, and maternal health in particular. Expanding and adapting the Global Fund, or creating a similar mechanism, would demonstrate serious donor commitment as well as potentially raise the political and social costs of erratic suspensions of aid for health systems in the long term.

Conclusions

. . . I have argued here that promoting transformative accountability with respect to fulfilling the right to maternal health requires more than decrying the scandalous injustice of those deaths, and more than demanding that states act consistently with their international legal obligations. It requires translating the powerful normative discourse of human rights into operational guidance and concrete tools for development practitioners, health planners, and service providers, as well as the users of health systems. Transformations of health systems are unlikely to occur with punitive approaches that lead to, intentionally or otherwise, a focus on individual sanctions. They are far more likely to occur by putting into place measures that promote systemic and institutional changes, which in turn foster different relations between providers and users of health services.

National governments should be held accountable for decisions from the initial situation analysis and design of plan of action regarding maternal health to budgeting, monitoring, and evaluation, and the provision of remedies. At every stage, transparency, access to information and meaningful public participation are crucial to rights-based accountability. Additionally, donor governments need to be held responsible for policy coherence and increased financial assistance for health systems and maternal health, which will require innovating mechanisms as well as political and social mobilization to raise the economic, political and social costs of noncompliance.

Further, there is an important relationship between international bodies and mechanisms and national ones in terms of promoting accountability. UN treaty-monitoring bodies and special procedures, together with the Human Rights Council and other regional bodies such as the IACHR and the African Commission, have key roles to play in ensuring that laws and policies are consistent with governments' human rights obligations, that adequate progress is being made consistent with appropriate indicators on a nondiscriminatory basis; that sufficient resources are being allocated effectively; that efforts to reduce maternal mortality give special attention to marginalized populations; and that adequate mechanisms of redress exist at the national level.

A human rights approach to MMM calls for subverting a wide range of the "pathologies of power" that systematically marginalize women and their health needs. However, challenging the power structures that prevent women from having choices over their lives must include those in the health system that condemn women to needless suffering and death. As Paul Hunt and Gunilla Backman write: "In any society, an effective health system is a core institution, no less than a fair justice system or democratic political system . . . It is only through building and strengthening health systems that it will be possible to secure sustainable development, poverty reduction, economic prosperity, improved health for individuals and populations, as well as the right to the highest attainable standard of health." Improving health systems cannot be seen as a technocratic exercise; by bringing human rights to bear, transforming health systems can and should be understood as a means of constructing social citizenship for women in a society—and most critically for poor, rural and marginalized women. In a world in which women's reproduction is so heavily cathected, so intimately bound up with religious and cultural power, it is radical indeed to demand that health systems take women's suffering—and rights—seriously.

13 Human Rights Council Resolution 11/8: preventable maternal mortality and morbidity and human rights (2009)[1]

Reaffirming the Beijing Declaration and Platform for Action, the Programme of Action of the International Conference on Population and Development and their Review Conferences and the targets and commitments regarding the reduction of maternal mortality and universal access to reproductive health, including those contained in the 2000 Millennium Declaration (General Assembly Resolution 55/2) and the 2005 World Summit Outcome (General Assembly Resolution 60/1),

Reaffirming also the Millennium Development Goals, in particular the Goals on improving maternal health, promoting gender equality and empowering women, reducing child and infant mortality and the development of a global partnership, Recalling the obligations of States parties to the Convention on the Elimination of All Forms of Discrimination against Women, the Convention on the Rights of the Child, the Convention on the Rights of Persons with Disabilities, the International Convention on the Elimination of All Forms of Racial Discrimination, the International Covenant on Civil and Political Rights, the International Covenant on Economic, Social and Cultural Rights and the Convention on the Protection of the Rights of All Migrant Workers and their Families, Convinced that increased political will and commitment, cooperation and technical assistance at the international and national levels are urgently required to reduce the unacceptably high global rate of preventable maternal mortality and morbidity,

Recognizing the leading role of the World Health Organization in maternal health and the work under the annual World Health Assembly agenda item on the monitoring of the achievement of the health-related Millennium Development Goals,

Recognizing also that the unacceptably high global rate of preventable maternal mortality and morbidity is a health, development and human rights challenge, and that a human rights analysis of preventable maternal mortality

1 UN Human Rights Council, Resolution 11/8, Preventable maternal mortality and morbidity and human rights, UN Doc. A/HRC/RES/11/8, 11th Session, 17 June 2009. Footnotes omitted.

and morbidity and the integration of a human rights perspective in international and national responses to maternal mortality and morbidity could contribute positively to the common goal of reducing this rate, with a view to eliminating preventable maternal mortality and morbidity,

Welcoming the ongoing efforts of the United Nations human rights treaty bodies to highlight the human rights aspects of preventable maternal mortality and morbidity, including those of the Committee on the Elimination of Discrimination against Women, the Human Rights Committee, the Committee on the Rights of the Child, the Committee on Economic, Social and Cultural Rights, and of the special procedures, in particular those described in the report of the Special Rapporteur on the right of everyone to the enjoyment of the highest attainable standard of physical and mental health (A/61/338),

Recognizing that the Council has a constructive role to play in raising awareness of the human rights aspects of the unacceptably high global rate of maternal mortality and morbidity and in supporting, promoting and enhancing existing national and international efforts to reduce this rate,

Welcoming its initiative to hold an interactive dialogue at its eighth regular session on maternal mortality and the human rights of women, on 5 June 2008,

Recognizing that preventable maternal mortality and morbidity affects women and their families in all regions and cultures, and that it is exacerbated by factors such as poverty, gender inequality, age and multiple forms of discrimination, as well as factors such as lack of access to adequate health facilities and technology, and lack of infrastructure,

1. Expresses grave concern at the unacceptably high global rate of preventable maternal mortality and morbidity, noting in this regard that the World Health Organization has assessed that over 1,500 women and girls die every day as a result of preventable complications occurring before, during and after pregnancy and childbirth, and that, globally, maternal mortality is the leading cause of death among women and of girls of reproductive age;
2. Recognizes that most instances of maternal mortality and morbidity are preventable, and that preventable maternal mortality and morbidity is a health, development and human rights challenge that also requires the effective promotion and protection of the human rights of women and girls, in particular their rights to life, to be equal in dignity, to education, to be free to seek, receive and impart information, to enjoy the benefits of scientific progress, to freedom from discrimination, and to enjoy the highest attainable standard of physical and mental health, including sexual and reproductive health;
3. Requests all States to renew their political commitment to eliminating preventable maternal mortality and morbidity at the local, national,

regional and international levels, and to redouble their efforts to ensure the full and effective implementation of their human rights obligations, the Beijing Declaration and Platform for Action, the Programme of Action of the International Conference on Population and Development and their review conferences, and the Millennium Declaration and the Millennium Development Goals, in particular the Goals on improving maternal health and promoting gender equality and empowering women, including through the allocation of necessary domestic resources to health systems;

4. Also requests States to give renewed emphasis to maternal mortality and morbidity initiatives in their development partnerships and cooperation arrangements, including by honouring existing commitments and considering new commitments, and the exchange of effective practices and technical assistance to strengthen national capacities, as well as to integrate a human rights perspective into such initiatives, addressing the impact that discrimination against women has on maternal mortality and morbidity;
5. Encourages States and other relevant stakeholders, including national human rights institutions and non-governmental organizations, to give increased attention and resources to preventable maternal mortality and morbidity in their engagement with the United Nations human rights system, including with the human rights treaty bodies, the universal periodic review and special procedures;
6. Requests the Office of the United Nations High Commissioner for Human Rights to prepare a thematic study on preventable maternal mortality and morbidity and human rights, in consultation with States, the World Health Organization, the United Nations Population Fund, the United Nations Children's Fund, the World Bank and all other relevant stakeholders, and requests that the study include identification of the human rights dimensions of preventable maternal mortality and morbidity in the existing international legal framework; an overview of initiatives and activities within the United Nations system to address all causes of preventable maternal mortality and morbidity; identification of how the Council can add value to existing initiatives through a human rights analysis, including efforts to achieve the Millennium Development Goal on improving maternal health, and recommended options for better addressing the human rights dimension of preventable maternal mortality and morbidity throughout the United Nations system;
7. Decides to address the thematic study requested in paragraph 6 above within the programme of work of its fourteenth session, and to consider taking further possible action on preventable maternal mortality and morbidity and human rights at that session, and invites the Office of the High Commissioner, the World Health Organization, the United

Nations Population Fund and the Special Rapporteur on the right of everyone to the enjoyment of the highest attainable standard of physical and mental health to participate in an interactive dialogue on the study in the Council.

27th meeting
17 June 2009 [adopted without a vote]

14 Report of the Office of the United Nations High Commissioner for Human Rights on preventable maternal mortality and morbidity and human rights (2010)[1]

Human rights-based approach to maternal mortality and morbidity

. . . 32. The practical implications of the human rights values of dignity and nondiscrimination result in a set of working principles that form the basis of a human rights approach. The treaty bodies and United Nations experts have clarified the importance of seven such principles: accountability, participation, transparency, empowerment, sustainability, international cooperation and non-discrimination. These principles have particular application when examining a human rights-based approach to addressing maternal mortality and morbidity as discussed in this section.

Accountability

33. Accountability is at the core of the enjoyment of all human rights and has two main components: addressing past grievances and correcting systemic failure to prevent future harm. Accountability is sometimes narrowly understood to mean blame and punishment, whereas it is more accurately regarded as a process to determine what is working (so it can be repeated) and what is not (so it can be adjusted).

34. The Human Rights Committee has articulated State obligations regarding accountability in the context of the right to life, in the form of a State obligation to prevent, investigate or redress harm caused by acts of private persons or entities. In this connection, the Committee emphasized the need for administrative mechanisms to give effect to the obligation to investigate allegations of violations promptly, thoroughly, effectively and impartially.

1 UN Human Rights Council, Report of the Office of the United Nations High Commissioner for Human Rights on preventable maternal mortality and morbidity and human rights, UN Doc. A/HRC/14/39, 16 April 2010. Footnotes omitted.

35. CESCR has clarified that States must establish mechanisms and institutions that can that effectively address both the individual and the structural nature of harm caused by discrimination in the enjoyment of rights. It has also specified that strengthening independent human rights structures and the participation of human rights advocates is an important element in ensuring relevant to human rights can function properly. The Special Rapporteur on the right to health has defined accountability as "ensuring that health systems are improving, and the right to the highest attainable standard of health is being progressively realized, for all, including disadvantaged individuals, communities, and population".

36. Regular monitoring of the health system and the underlying physical and socio-economic determinants of health that affect women's health and ability to exercise their rights is a critical component of accountability. Without monitoring, systemic failures in reducing maternal mortality and morbidity cannot be corrected. When States adopt and implement a national public health strategy and plan of action, they should also develop "appropriate indicators to monitor progress made, and to highlight where policy adjustments may be needed". Monitoring helps States parties develop a better understanding of the "problems and shortcomings encountered" in realizing rights, providing them with the "framework within which more appropriate policies can be devised". Data based on appropriate indicators should be disaggregated on the basis of the prohibited grounds of discrimination to monitor the elimination of discrimination as well as to ensure that vulnerable communities are benefiting from health-care schemes.

37. As an accountability measure designed to reduce maternal mortality, the Special Rapporteur on the right to health has strongly recommended that all States introduce, as a matter of urgency, a comprehensive, effective registration system, as well as a system of maternal death audits, in order to find out why the deaths occurred. Such maternal death audits, the Special Rapporteur notes, should be a non-judicial review that goes beyond medical reasons to identify the social, economic and cultural reasons that led or contributed to the death.

38. The principle of accountability is closely linked to the right of victims to remedy including reparation. Effective access to remedies and reparation contributes to a constructive accountability framework by focusing on system failures and encouraging repair. The components of remedies and reparation were articulated through the Basic Principles and Guidelines on the Right to a Remedy and Reparation for Victims of Gross Violations of International Human Rights Law and Serious Violations of International Humanitarian Law approved by the General Assembly in 2005. . . .

15 Concise technical guidance on the application of a human rights-based approach to the implementation of policies and programs to reduce preventable maternal morbidity and mortality[1]

Office of the United Nations High Commissioner for Human Rights

Introduction

5. The primary purpose of the present report is to assist policymakers in improving women's health and rights by providing guidance on devising, implementing and monitoring policies and programs to reduce maternal mortality and morbidity, and fostering accountability in accordance with human rights standards. . . .

18. Accountability is not an afterthought in a rights-based approach, but fundamental to each stage of the process—from identifying accountability gaps in a situational analysis to ensuring appropriate monitoring mechanisms and remedies in a national plan, to allocating resources for these mechanisms and remedies, to ensuring feedback from the ground through to implementation in practice. Lessons learned through structures of accountability must inform the continual process of adjusting existing programs and future planning. . . .

19. The design, organization and coordination of the components of the health system should be guided by fundamental human rights principles, including non-discrimination/equality, transparency, participation and accountability. . . .

1 Human Rights Council, Technical guidance on the application of a human rights-based approach to the implementation of policies and programs to reduce preventable maternal morbidity and mortality: Report of the Office of the United Nations High Commissioner for Human Rights, UN Doc. A/HRC/21/22, 2 July 2012. Footnotes omitted.

23. Where the health system is decentralized, the national Government remains accountable for complying with human rights obligations, including those relating to sexual and reproductive health. . . .

V. Accountability

67. As has been stressed throughout the present report, accountability is central to every stage of a human rights-based approach. It requires not just transparency but meaningful participation by affected populations and civil society groups. Effective accountability also requires individuals, families and groups, including women from vulnerable or marginalized populations, to be aware of their entitlements with regard to sexual and reproductive health and are empowered to make claims grounded in them.

68. In the sections above, emphasis was put on the importance of assessing accountability gaps within and beyond the health sector in the situational analysis and addressing them through planning and budgeting, as well as regular, ground-up diagnostic exercises and follow-up, in order to ensure implementation in practice. Monitoring, the dimensions of review and oversight, and remedies are also critical elements of the circle of accountability, as is establishing donor accountability.

A. Monitoring

69. Monitoring in a human rights framework requires the use of indicators, not all of which are quantitative or relate to the health sector. A rights-based approach requires systematically tracking and evaluating:

a Changes in structural factors over time; this includes, but is not limited to, examining whether adopted laws explicitly recognize sexual and reproductive health rights; adopting a national plan; and modifying laws that discriminate against women, as well as institutions, such as creating a national human rights institution;
b Policy and budgetary efforts within and beyond the health sector. Policy efforts include, for example, costing, resourcing and implementation measures with regard to the national plan. Resources and expenditures relating to sexual and reproductive health should also be tracked, as should the capacity to relate spending to human rights goals and commitments, such as the elimination of financial barriers to care;
c Concrete results in terms of women's sexual and reproductive health, and maternal mortality and morbidity in particular; this includes outputs, outcomes and impact in health system categories, ranging from availability, accessibility, acceptability and quality (both through objective indicators, such as case fatality rates, and subjective measures of women's satisfaction) of health facilities, goods and services to ultimate effects, such as fertility and adolescent birth rates and maternal mortality ratios.

70. Effective monitoring requires functioning health information systems, civil registration systems and disaggregated data. The disaggregation of information on the basis of sex, age, urban/rural residence and ethnicity, as well as of education, wealth quintile and geographic region insofar as possible, is essential for ensuring non-discrimination and equity, and affording due protection to vulnerable and marginalized groups.

71. Quantitative indicators should facilitate the drawing of conclusions with regard to compliance with international obligations relating to sexual and reproductive health rights. In addition to disaggregation, as stated above, quantitative indicators should be (a) continuously or frequently measurable in order that the actions taken by an administration may be measured in a timely manner; (b) objective, to permit comparison across time and countries and/or subregions; (c) programmatically relevant, to enable priority setting and identification of accountability gaps; and, ideally, (d) subject to local audit to promote accountability to populations served. Not all maternal health indicators currently used at the national and international levels comply with such criteria; however, both Governments and development partners should foster accountability by ensuring that as many of the criteria as possible are met, including data objectivity (as in measures of skilled birth attendance).

72. Monitoring should facilitate the strengthening of the health system, including of the health information system. Emergency obstetric care is a core obligation under international law, and is the core maternal health intervention that depends most on a functioning, coordinated health system. Broader collection of information on the availability and use of emergency obstetric care, which depends on health facility survey data, can strengthen health information systems. Health information systems should also address biases in current demographic and health data, which may affect vulnerable and marginalized groups, such as by excluding floating and migrant populations and women who do not have live births.

73. Monitoring should encompass non-State actors, including, but not limited to, pharmaceutical, commodities and device manufacturers, insurance companies and private service providers.

B. Forms of review and oversight

74. Human rights accountability requires multiple forms of review and oversight, including:

a Administrative accountability with regard to sexual and reproductive health calls for internal rules and norms in health facilities and within the Ministry of Health, which set standards for conduct and make subordinates accountable to superiors, to be monitored by a person or committee with no conflicts of interest;

b Social accountability calls for civil society and public participation at all levels of decision-making regarding sexual and reproductive health, and throughout the project cycle. Community-based oversight of facility staff, finances and quality of care at facilities, such as "community scorecards", "community-based local administration" of health facilities and accompaniment of women by family and community members can all contribute to social accountability and should be implemented according to context;

c Political accountability calls for both national and subnational Governments to be able to justify to legislators the criteria used and decisions taken regarding sexual and reproductive health. For legislative oversight to be meaningful, the Executive should transparently share budget and planning documents, as well as results, and provide adequate time and information for meaningful deliberation by parliamentarians and local legislatures;

d National legal accountability includes the duty of the State to guarantee effective enjoyment of human rights, including the duty to provide effective legal remedies to victims. Legal remedies can be judicial and non-judicial, such as by through a national human rights institution;

c International accountability calls for the systematic integration of information on efforts to prevent and reduce maternal mortality and morbidity into reports submitted to international human rights mechanisms, including regional human rights bodies, treaty-monitoring bodies and for the universal periodic review of the Human Rights Council, together with implementation of recommendations thereof.

75. A human rights-based approach depends on fostering accountability of multiple actors and at various levels, within and beyond the health sector, including, but not limited to:

a Professional accountability. Although frontline health workers must not be treated as scapegoats for institutional failures, effective standards should be in place to ensure quality of care, and sanctions by professional associations, medical councils and/or licensing bodies should be applied in the event of proven negligence, abuse or malpractice, irrespective of whether providers are tenured;

b Institutional accountability. Accountability at the facility level requires continuous oversight and regular follow-up with regard to any gaps identified. Complaint procedures should be instituted in all facilities for health system users, including appeal procedures for decisions by institutional management or ethics committees denying access to any form of sexual and reproductive health care. Furthermore, internal ombudsperson procedures should be instituted for review of health workers' complaints in each facility, with possibility for appeal;

c Health system accountability. In addition to continuous systemic monitoring and regular diagnostics of obstacles, reviews of all maternal deaths should be conducted routinely in order that lessons may be learned at all levels of the health system—from individuals' behavior and practices to national policies, and along the continuum of care from home to hospital. Maternal death reviews should be conducted in the spirit of shared responsibility rather than attributing blame, and to inform actions to prevent future maternal deaths;

d Private actor accountability. Corporate enterprises and other non-State actors have a responsibility to respect women's sexual and reproductive health rights, which means that they should act with "due diligence" or appropriate care to avoid interfering with such human rights. In turn, appropriate laws, policies, regulations and guidelines should be established and enforced by the State with regard to such infringements;

e Donor accountability. Donors have obligations of international assistance and cooperation with regard to sexual and reproductive health rights, including both financial and non-financial obligations, as described below.

C. Remedies

76. Remedies are essential to give effect to rights. They may take the form of restitution, compensation, satisfaction or guarantees of non-repetition. Remedies may be administrative, but appeal to judicial review from administrative proceedings will often be appropriate. Remedies may also be provided through a national human rights institution. In all cases, remedies should be accessible, affordable, timely and effective, which will require adequate funding, capacity and mandates.

77. Judicial remedies have a key role to play in relation to sexual and reproductive health rights, including:

a Ensuring the implementation of existing laws and policies;

b Reforming laws, policies and budgets that do not adequately protect sexual and reproductive health rights;

c Challenging discriminatory barriers to sexual and reproductive health care and;

d Providing redress for violations of sexual and reproductive health rights in practice.

78. National human rights institutions should also promote accountability with regard to sexual and reproductive health rights by, inter alia, investigating violations of women's sexual and reproductive health rights; monitoring implementation of legislation, performance of selected institutions, court judgments and recommendations made by international human rights bodies;

and organizing public hearings and education campaigns about maternal mortality and morbidity and human rights.

79. To ensure the effective use of remedies, the State must systematically raise awareness about the applicability of claims relating to women's sexual and reproductive health rights among lawyers, judges and the public, and provide adequate funding for accountability mechanisms.

80. Systems of effective recourse depend on parliamentarians supporting improved accountability for violations of women's sexual and reproductive health rights, including by addressing physical, economic and other barriers to recourse systems, especially for vulnerable or marginal groups; lack of timely relief; lack of awareness of remedies; inadequacy of existing causes of action to secure redress; and deficiencies in funding, mandate, independence or competencies of national human rights institutions. . . .

16 Global strategy for women's and children's health[1]

United Nations Secretary-General Ban Ki-moon

Introduction

With just five years left to achieve the Millennium Development Goals (MDGs), global leaders must intensify their efforts to improve women's and children's health. The world has failed to invest enough in the health of women, adolescent girls, newborns, infants, and children. As a result, millions of preventable deaths occur each year, and we have made less progress on MDG 5, improving maternal health, than any other. . . .

Now is the time for all partners to join forces in a concerted effort. This means scaling up and prioritizing a package of high-impact interventions, strengthening health systems, and integrating efforts across diseases and sectors such as health, education, water, sanitation, and nutrition. It also means promoting human rights, gender equality and poverty reduction. All actors should work to optimize current investments. All are account-able for their commitments and need to raise the additional, predictable funding required to deliver basic health services and meet the health-related MDGs. . . .

Focusing on the most vulnerable

This strategy focusses on the time when women and children are most vulnerable. For pregnant women and newborns alike, the greatest risk of death comes during childbirth and in the first few hours and days afterwards. Adolescents are also vulnerable, and we must make sure they're given control over their life choices, including their fertility.

This requires a focus on the most vulnerable and hardest-to-reach women and children: the poorest, those living with HIV/AIDS, orphans, indigenous populations, and those living furthest from health services. . . .

1 United Nations Secretary-General, *Global strategy for women's and children's health: the partnership for maternal, newborn and child health*, 2010. Footnotes omitted.

Building on our health and human rights commitments

The *Global Strategy* builds on commitments made by countries and partners at several events: the Program of Action agreed at the International Conference on Population and Development; the Beijing Declaration and Platform for Action agreed at the Fourth World Conference on Women; the ECOSOC Ministerial Review on Global Health; UNGA side session, "Healthy Women, Healthy Children: Investing in Our Common Future"; and the 54th session of the Commission on the Status of Women. It also builds on regional commitments and efforts, such as the Maputo Plan of Action, the Campaign on Accelerated Reduction of Maternal Mortality in Africa (CARMMA), and the African Union Summit Declaration 2010 for Actions on Maternal, Newborn and Child Health.

Women's and children's health is recognized as a fundamental human right in treaties such as the International Covenant on Economic, Social and Cultural Rights (CESCR), the Convention on the Elimination of All Forms of Discrimination against Women (CEDAW), and the Convention on the Rights of the Child (CRC). The Human Rights Council also recently adopted a specific resolution on maternal mortality.

Investing in the health of women and children makes good sense

Women and children play a crucial role in development. Investing more in women's and children's health is not only the right thing to do; it also builds stable, peaceful and productive societies. Increasing investment has many benefits. . . . It helps women and children realize their fundamental human rights. People are entitled to the highest attainable standard of health. This fundamental principle of development and human rights is affirmed by many countries in a range of international and regional human rights treaties. . .

Holding ourselves accountable

Accountability is essential. It ensures that all partners deliver on their commitments, demonstrates how actions and investment translate into tangible results and better long-term outcomes, and tells us what works, what needs to be improved and what requires more attention. Key principles include:

- a focus on national leadership and ownership of results
- strengthening countries' capacity to monitor and evaluate
- reducing the reporting burden by aligning efforts with the systems countries use to monitor and evaluate their national health strategies
- strengthening and harmonizing existing international mechanisms to track progress on all commitments made (see Figure 3)

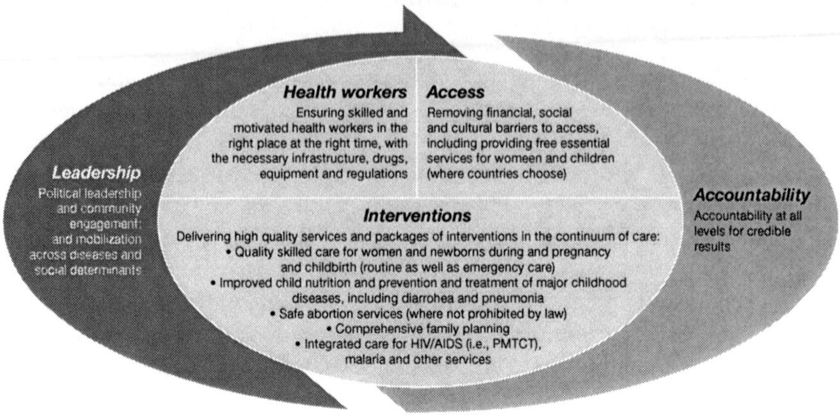

Figure 1 The global consensus for maternal, newborn and child health

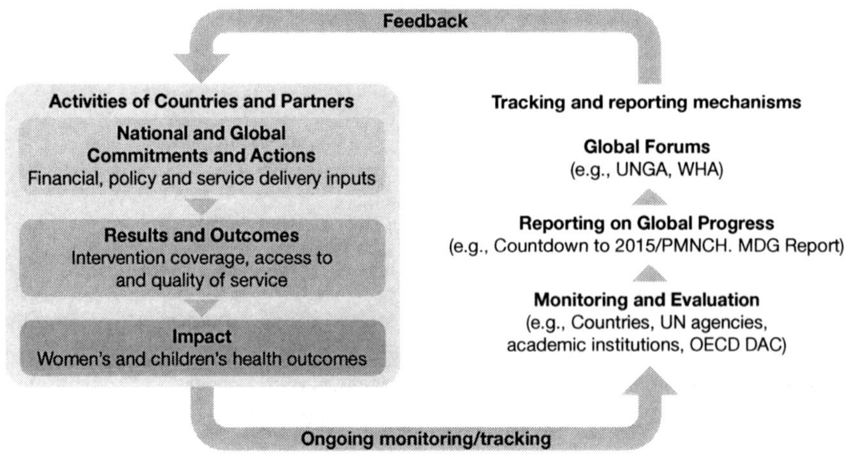

Figure 3 Approach to tracking progress

National leadership and ownership are the foundation of accountability. Most monitoring, evaluating, and reporting takes place, or at least starts, at the country level, and partners at all levels should strive to make countries accountable for the success of their national health strategies. Strong community-based efforts should hold governments and other organizations accountable for delivering on their commitments and ensure all money is used in a transparent manner. India's National Rural Health Mission, for example, has a community-based performance-monitoring mechanism to ensure that services reach their targets and that communities participate in delivery.

Strengthening national capacities also requires harmonized investment in monitoring and evaluation systems, to improve the availability and quality of data. This must support countries' efforts to strengthen their health information systems in line with the "Call for Action on Health Information". Priority investments will vary from country to country, and might include filling gaps in essential data (on births, maternal and child deaths, health status, and intervention coverage), tracking resources and expenditure more effectively, and enhancing the analysis of data quality. The availability of essential data is critical so that health workers are equipped with the information they need to make decisions.

Existing global mechanisms must also be used to support accountability efforts at the national and global levels. For example, a key objective of the Partnership for Maternal, Newborn & Child Health (PMNCH) is to track progress and commitments on MDGs 4 and 5. Several mechanisms are being explored to track donors' financial commitments and disbursements, such as the OECD-DAC's peer-reviewed assessments of aid policies and implementation, and the Countdown to 2015 Report. Further mechanisms are being explored to report on the work of civil society organizations, and to contribute to country-level initiatives, such as promotion of National Health Accounts to track health expenditures, and the United Nations initiative to develop a "unified costing tool".

Reducing the reporting burden on countries will contribute to more timely, effective and efficient monitoring, evaluation and reporting. It is important to accelerate efforts to develop an agreed set of core health indicators, reducing the overall number of indicators countries report on while ensuring that key information, such as on efforts to address gender equality and deliver services to vulnerable communities, is collected. This will also encourage regular and accurate national reports, which will assess and track performance and progress. These should result in fewer requests by donors and multilateral institutions for separate reports.

To ensure that stakeholders are held accountable for their commitment and progress is sustained, the implementation of commitments made as part of this *Global strategy* should be tracked every two years, in line with standard international practice. This will build upon the principles outlined in this document while ensuring existing country-level and global monitoring and reporting initiatives are coordinated and complement the development of high-quality, comparable reporting.

Current initiatives and mechanisms—such as the MDG reports, Countdown to 2015, the International Health Partnership+ Initiative, analysis and research conducted by academic and international institutions, and other related processes—will inform the development of the biennial report. The UN Secretary-General requests that the World Health Organization chair a process to determine the most effective international institutional arrangements for global reporting, oversight and accountability on women's and children's health, including through the UN system. . .

17 A review of global accountability mechanisms for women's and children's health[1]

The Partnership for Maternal, Newborn & Child Health

Executive summary

The United Nations Secretary-General's *Global strategy* for women's and children's health, launched in September 2010, generated significant financial, policy, and service delivery commitments. The following stakeholders all made commitments: governments, multilateral organizations, non-governmental organizations, donors, foundations, healthcare professional associations, academic institutions, and the private sector. The *Global strategy* sets out the key areas where action is urgently required to improve the health of women and children worldwide. One of these areas is "improved monitoring and evaluation to ensure the accountability of all actors for results." This report reviews accountability arrangements with respect to all the stakeholders that made commitments to the *Global strategy*, focussing on mechanisms for *monitoring, review and remedy or action*, which are the three key steps for accountability.

The *Global strategy* requests the World Health Organization (WHO) to: "Chair a process to determine the most effective international institutional arrangements for global reporting, oversight and accountability on women's and children's health." In December 2010 the Secretary-General established a Commission on Information and Accountability for Women's and Children's Health. In May 2011 at the World Health Assembly, the Commission will propose an accountability framework and an action plan for "global reporting, oversight and accountability on women's and children's health. It will create a system to track whether donations for women's and children's health are made on time, resources are spent wisely and transparently, and whether the desired results are achieved."

In the Delhi Declaration of 2010, adopted by the Partnership for Maternal, Newborn & Child Health (PMNCH) in November 2010, partners agreed to

1 The Partnership for Maternal, Newborn & Child Health, *A review of global accountability mechanisms for women's and children's health*, PMNCH: Geneva, 2011. Footnotes omitted.

collaborate with WHO to speedily implement the Secretary-General's request. Further, partners affirmed that the PMNCH, based on its multi-stakeholder constituency "is an active participant to track commitments and results and thus ensure mutual accountability." As a complement to the Commission's work to set up an accountability framework and action plan, PMNCH will develop a 2011 progress report on all stakeholders' commitments to the *Global strategy*. PMNCH undertook this review of global accountability mechanisms to inform its engagement with the Commission's work and the development of the 2011 progress report on *Global strategy* commitments.

This review of the global accountability landscape for women's and children's health is not comprehensive, but rather focusses on illustrative examples of accountability mechanisms at the global level. It would be valuable to undertake similar reviews of regional and national accountability mechanisms. Coordination between global accountability arrangements for commitments made in response to the *Global strategy* and regional and national monitoring and accountability procedures, as well as other global procedures, is important to coordinate action and enhance accountability of stakeholders for results at all levels.

This review also includes examples of accountability arrangements in the fields of international health, development, and human rights more generally. The decision to broaden the focus of the report was made because there are limited examples of global accountability procedures focussing specifically on women's and children's health. The examples referred to in this report are illustrative precedents of a variety of options, which may be considered in the process of developing accountability for stakeholders with commitments arising from the *Global strategy*.

The review confirms that while monitoring is central to accountability, it is not the same thing as accountability. It provides definitions of key accountability principles and terms, such as monitoring; review, including independent and non-independent review, peer review; remedy and mutual accountability.

Key findings and recommendations include the following:

- Monitoring. Currently, a large amount of data on states and women's and children's health is collected and evaluated. However, there are significant data gaps. Vital registration and health information systems in countries need to be strengthened to generate accurate data on women's and children's health. Data are also very limited on activities of non-state stakeholders—including multilateral organizations, non-governmental organizations, donors, foundations, healthcare professional associations, academic institutions and the private sector—working in the area of women's and children's health. Arrangements are urgently needed to develop monitoring for general and specific commitments of *all* stakeholders under the *Global strategy*.

The Commission for Information and Accountability for Women's and Children's Health will propose an accountability framework and action plan to address these overarching issues. The PMNCH progress report on commitments to the *Global strategy* will help address specific gaps through voluntary, structured reporting from multiple constituencies.

- Review. Few global review processes focus on accountability for women's and children's health, and none is well placed to provide accountability for all the different stakeholders that made commitments made to the *Global strategy*. A body that performs an independent review function is urgently needed to: consider an agreed core set of quantitative and qualitative data from all stakeholders; commend good practices; signal where there is room for improvement; and make constructive, practical, remedial recommendations.
- Remedy or action. The independent review body should present the observations and recommendations to a body or bodies that represent the different stakeholders. These include the United Nations general assembly and other bodies such as non-governmental organization coalitions, healthcare professional associations, and private sector forums. Stakeholders should then take the required remedial actions so that results can be achieved at all levels. Technical and financial assistance will be required to strengthen health information systems and to help implement and monitor the activities of the multiple stakeholders that made financial, policy and service delivery commitments to the *Global strategy*.

In short, monitoring and independent review mechanisms should feed into a cyclical processes that facilitates remedial actions and ensures stakeholders' individual and mutual accountability to achieve results at all levels for women's and children's health. . . .

Definitions of selected key terms and concepts (Figure 1)

Accountability

Accountability involves identifying the commitments and duties of stakeholders and making stakeholders answerable for their performance. There are three main components of accountability:

1 Monitoring, which involves finding out what is happening where, and to whom. If stakeholders are to be held accountable, it is vital to monitor and evaluate quantitative and qualitative data. Monitoring is a precondition for reviewing whether what is happening is consistent with previously agreed commitments. Although critically important, monitoring is not accountability.

2 Review, which refers to a process that assesses whether or not pledges, promises and commitments have been kept, and whether duties have been discharged. Review can be independent or non-independent (see below).

3 Remedy or action, which is a critical, but often neglected, component of accountability. A remedy is a measure or measures to put things right, as far as possible, when they have not gone as promised or planned. The process is sometimes referred to as *redress*. International review bodies may make practical, constructive, remedial recommendations, not only for the stakeholder under review, but also for other bodies that might be able to assist the stakeholder, such as a donor or an agency providing technical assistance.

Independent review

An independent review body is composed of individuals, often experts in their field, who serve in their independent capacity, i.e., they do not take instructions from those nominating or appointing them, or from any other person or organization, and they exercise their professional, autonomous judgment. While the members of an independent review body are usually nominated or appointed by particular stakeholders, once appointed they serve in an independent capacity.

Non-independent review

Non-independent review bodies are mechanisms whose members are also representatives or delegates of a stakeholder and who serve in this capacity.

Peer review

Peer review is a form of reciprocal evaluation among like stakeholders; for example, states. Peer review can, and often does, involve participation by other stakeholders, including civil society.

Mutual accountability

Mutual accountability means that different stakeholders are accountable to each other. The principle is enshrined in international development commitments. It is one of the central principles of the Paris Principles on aid effectiveness (2005), an international agreement to which over 100 ministers, heads of agencies, and other senior officials committed their countries and organizations, as well as the Accra Agenda for Action (2008), which builds on commitments in the Paris Principles. In these contexts, mutual accountability refers to accountability between partner countries and donors in respect of the use of development resources. The *Global strategy* for women's and children's health has a focus on multi-stakeholder accountability. For mutual accountability, arrangements would need to allow for the accountability of all stakeholders to one another.

18 Working Group on Accountability for Results: final paper[1]

Commission on Information and Accountability for Women's and Children's Health

Introduction

6. The accountability framework we have used is based on three separate but related activities. First, monitoring. Monitoring means acquiring data to find out what is happening, where, and to whom. Monitoring alone, however, is not accountability. A second crucial activity is analysis and review: have pledges, promises, and commitments, general and specific, been kept by countries, donors, and non-state actors? In other words, did we deliver? The third element of accountability is remedy (or action): what needs to be done to put things right or maintain and accelerate progress? This cyclical process of monitoring, review, and action publicly recognizes success, draws attention to good practice, identifies shortcomings, and recommends what needs to be done. Our framework applies at both country and global levels, and includes important human rights principles, including equality and non-discrimination, transparency, and participation.

Actions at country level

7. Accountability begins with national sovereignty and the responsibility of a government to its people and to the global community. Two national functions are critical if proper reporting and oversight of commitments and pledges on women's and children's health are to take place. First, a sound health information system to collect and report health data. Second, a national deliberative mechanism to review these data, measure progress for country decision makers, hold those decision makers accountable to their people and to the global community, hold the global community accountable to countries, and devise remedies for remaining predicaments and barriers. . . .

1 Working Group on Accountability for Results, Final paper, *Commission on Information and Accountability for Women's and Children's Health*, May 2011. Footnotes omitted.

Country-level accountability arrangements

16. As we have noted, monitoring alone is not accountability. There has to be an institutional mechanism to review emerging information about women's and children's health, to identify successes and continuing obstacles to progress, and to recommend what needs to be done. The challenge for countries is to make women's and children's health a high-level national political priority, not only an objective of the Ministry of Health. The commitment of heads of state must be translated into accountability frameworks that reflect this national leadership. Evidence submitted by WHO to this Commission shows that country arrangements for accountability are at least modest, at worst weak. In addition to high-level political engagement, country-based accountability arrangements need an independent, autonomous element to review whether or not national and global stakeholders are keeping their commitments. In some countries, this task may be given to an existing institution—e.g., an ombudsperson or a national human rights body.

17. While all countries will need national arrangements on monitoring, review, and action for women's and children's health, these arrangements will, as noted earlier, depend on national and local contexts. Whatever arrangements are devised, they must be transparent, inclusive, accessible, and effective. They must complement, not duplicate, existing systems that are generating valuable information. And they must address the discrimination, exclusion, and barriers women and children face in accessing health services. There are several models countries might adopt. As one example, some countries may wish to establish national health commissions for women's and children's health. These commissions would be chaired by an independent, prominent, and respected thought leader representing the interests of women's and children's health, be accountable (and report) to national parliaments, be inclusive of all relevant government departments (including ministries of finance to ensure accountability for resources), and engage non-governmental actors.

18. The essential idea behind a national health commission would be to elevate the health system (for women and children) to the level of a "core social institution", akin, for example, to the justice system. We envisage that national health commissions would convene annual or biannual meetings of all stakeholders to address national progress against country health plans and international goals, as well as subnational inequities and predicaments. The commissions—and these annual or biannual meetings—should be informed by the views of a national level independent person or body—e.g., an ombudsperson with expertise in women's and children's health. They would recommend remedies and actions that might extend to restriction, compensation, and guarantees of non-repetition. Most importantly, they would provide a means for accountability to citizens and health care users.

19. Why create a national health commission? The most common existing review mechanism for women's and children's health is the annual health

sector review. Annual Ministry of Health reports describe progress across a range of health performance measures. Results are discussed and the findings incorporated into succeeding national health plans. However, these health sector reviews often suffer from several weaknesses—too many indicators and targets, major data gaps, limited analytic capacity, weak political traction, and lack of engagement of key actors (e.g., civil society). The Countdown to 2015 process has tried to promote country action through national Countdown conferences (e.g., in Senegal and Zambia). But this mechanism has not been reproduced in a systematic or effective way across all high-burden countries.

20. The benefits of a broader national accountability mechanism for women's and children's health would be multiple: country ownership, fully aligned with national health plans; a means to reduce fragmented and duplicated monitoring arrangements imposed on countries by donors and agencies; incentives to create demand for better information and to build stronger institutions for data collection, analysis, reporting, and dissemination; intersectorality; and the opportunity to engage civil society organizations in a national dialogue. National health commissions would be empowering institutions, enabling citizens to participate in a process to track and trace progress in women's and children's health alongside other dimensions of the health sector. The functions of a national health commission would include:

- coordinating a national accountability system
- reporting national and subnational progress on outcomes and coverage
- curating knowledge and best practice from health programs
- policy development, implementation, and review
- creating grievance redress bodies, nationally and subnationally
- resource mobilization, allocation, and tracking
- building partnerships among stakeholders
- strengthening political leadership
- advocacy and mobilization
- identifying research priorities.

21. The review process led by a national health commission would also link to the third element in our accountability framework—namely, remedy or action. The results of the commission's work would be included in subsequent national plans, together with commitments over budgets, timelines, and further accountability measures, all led by the highest levels of political authority, including national parliaments.

22. Our concept of a national health commission comes partly from studying the way countries have responded to the UN General Assembly Special Session (UNGASS) on AIDS, held in 2001. Without question, UNGASS mobilized countries in an unprecedented way to address AIDS. We see an exceptional opportunity to build on the success of UNGASS on behalf of women and children. Part of the UNGASS response was the creation of national AIDS commissions as multisectoral coordinating entities to lead and

monitor the national response to AIDS. They have facilitated country mobilization around one national strategy, one national authority, and one national monitoring system. They are inclusive of civil society. And they have embedded high-level political commitment into the AIDS response.

23. National AIDS commissions are not perfect. The advice taken by the Working Group has been that unless a national health commission was given greater and more formal legal authority, it could not fully achieve the objectives we are proposing for it. In particular, the formal relationship between a national health commission and the Ministry of Health would have to be carefully managed to avoid "distracting power-struggle issues". That said, national AIDS commissions "have been able to catalyse and spearhead strong leadership and advocacy in support of the national AIDS policy and action frameworks, and to provide effective multisectoral coordination, especially among non-governmental actors and development partners". One might even envisage national AIDS commissions being legally strengthened and their remits extended to broader health issues, including women's and children's health. The UNGASS+10 review in 2011 might provide such an opportunity for integration.

24. We recommend that, building on existing efforts, countries, together with the financial and technical assistance of partners, urgently put in place independent, transparent, inclusive, and effective national arrangements of monitoring, review, and action for women's and children's health. The data generated by such a process would provide the basis for the country's submission to the Secretary-General's Independent Review Group (see paragraph 39). This Review Group should give its own constructive feedback, taking account of local contexts.

Monitoring of progress

. . . 30. We strongly believe that equity must be an essential component of any national and global accountability mechanism. Disaggregation of data is essential to understand where and how to direct future programmatic efforts. Equity can be measured in several ways—for example, by disaggregating data for wealth, gender, age, urban/rural residence, country region, and ethnicity (or a suitable proxy measure of ethnicity, such as region or language). Future surveys should collect disaggregated data to enable an equity-focused approach to accountability.

31. A further neglected aspect of monitoring is the quality of care that women and children receive. Quality measures are essential complements to tracking uptake or coverage. By quality, we mean whether care is effective, safe, and the experience positive for the user. Substandard care undermines progress towards achieving mortality reduction goals, especially among the poorest women and children. It is a waste of scarce health resources and violates the right to the highest attainable standard of health. But data on quality of care are mostly lacking—a political as well as a technical failure.

Several possible measures are currently being evaluated, such as timely access to emergency Caesarean section and the availability of essential drugs. We urge the Commission to emphasize the importance of measuring quality in delivering the Secretary-General's *Global strategy* and to task accountability mechanisms at country and global levels to include quality in their appraisals of progress towards women's and children's health.

32. Accountability does not rest only with the 74 countries we have highlighted in this report. There must also be high-quality monitoring, independent review, and action for all actors working to improve women's and children's health—including donors and non-state actors. As the *Global strategy* makes clear: "In line with the principles of the Paris Declaration, the Accra Agenda for Action, and the Monterrey Consensus, all partners must work together" on country-led health plans; a comprehensive, integrated package of essential interventions and services; integrated care; health systems strengthening; and health workforce capacity building.

33. After reviewing considerable evidence and experience about indicators and their monitoring, we recommend that for the purpose of holding national and international communities accountable for progress, the Commission adopt two groups of indicators on women's and children's health. The first group on health status represents the ultimate goal. This is a key indicator group aimed mainly at political accountability. However, some of these health status measures, such as the maternal mortality ratio, are relatively insensitive to change and therefore do not show progress over short time intervals. The estimates we have today, for example, represent the cumulative effect of policies going back over many years. A second group of coverage indicators, reflecting the continuum of care, is a more sensitive and timely set of measures, pointing to almost real-time changes in the conditions for women's and children's health. . . .

Global reporting, oversight, and accountability

38. Accountability begins in countries. But there also needs to be some mechanism to ensure reliable arrangements for global reporting, oversight, and accountability. Accountability extends to state and non-state actors for the health policies and programs they design and implement, and the extent to which their laws, policies, and programs meet human rights standards. The commitments and responsibilities of all parties must be identified and each held accountable for their performance. Currently, accountability mechanisms for the MDGs are weak. There is disturbing "accountability gap" in the global architecture around women's and children's health.

39. We recommend that a Secretary-General's independent review group on women's and children's health be established to provide a regular, independent, and transparent process for ensuring commitments made by all partners—to results and resources—are being delivered, and to identify practical measures that need to be taken to achieve those commitments.

40. An independent review group, agreed by all partners, but separate from any single partner organization, would meet the urgent need for a legitimate, objective, and credible mechanism for global oversight of the Secretary-General's *Global strategy*. We do not believe that existing mechanisms or networks fill this widely accepted accountability gap for women's and children's health. There are many examples of independent UN and non-UN associated expert review groups for the Commission to consider. We believe that establishing such a group would add substantial global momentum to improving women's and children's health. A fuller discussion of what an independent review group would do is provided in an appendix to this report.

41. We envisage that the independent review group would periodically examine performance data on results and resources from all partners (including recipient and donor countries, the private sector, civil society, philanthropic organizations, and professional groups), identify examples of good practice, pinpoint obstacles to progress, raise concerns, recommend actions, and provide an overall assessment of progress. The core task of the group would be to ask whether partners had kept their promises and to identify practical measures that need to be taken. The group would undertake its work in public through submission of results from national review mechanisms, reports from partners and interested parties (including academic and research communities), discussions with those parties and partners, field visits, and publication of a concluding report. The independent review group and country review arrangements would work closely together. The group's findings would feed directly into a country process to translate recommendations into actions, which may include a request that financial and/or technical assistance be provided. The goal would be to create a process that is open, transparent, responsive, and efficient. It would not add another layer of bureaucracy to policymaking. On the contrary, it would provide an effective means to deliver the Secretary-General's *Global strategy*.

42. Who would sit on the independent review group? From looking at examples of other expert review mechanisms across the UN, we believe that a small team of 15 to 20 widely respected practitioner, academic, civil society, and policy experts would provide the necessary capacity. They would be nominated by partners to serve independently, and they would be led by an individual of international stature. Their final selection would be made by the Secretary-General after wide consultation. Once approved, they would exercise their professional judgments without taking instructions from any organization or partner. The advantages of such a group, by contrast with several other independent review procedures in the UN, would be its specific focus on women's and children's health and the high level of independent expertise it could bring to bear on the issues under its review.

43. Who would the independent review group report to? Given that the *Global strategy* is an initiative of the UN Secretary-General, we suggest the independent review group report to the Secretary-General.

44. We also note that the independent review group we propose would need to be adequately resourced for its work to be effective, trusted, and transparent. The operations of the group would require administrative and technical support, perhaps based within the Secretary-General's office, or perhaps linked to the Partnership for Maternal, Newborn, & Child Health.

45. Earlier, we recommended that part of the monitoring framework at national and global levels should focus on a small number of indicators for maximum political and policy impact. In the near absence of country health information systems, some of these data are mainly derived from estimates. Currently, there are multiple sources of these estimates—from the UN, academic institutions, and civil society, among others. The debates that follow from these complementary estimation initiatives can be valuable. They sharpen understanding about what is known and uncertain, and they give welcome public attention to women's and children's health (promoting greater demand for better health information systems). Strong, open scientific debate must be part of any robust accountability process. Efforts to harmonize estimates into a single number or to choose only one source of data on which to base these indicators would stifle debate and reduce the quality of the accountability process.

46. We recommend that the Commission emphasizes the paramount importance of bringing the best available science to bear on global monitoring processes. Assessments of country progress should be based on a scientific, not a political, process—that is, on peer-reviewed scientific evidence rather than on data whose publication depends on endorsement by any one concerned party. The independent review group should be free to use the best available evidence to reach its recommendations. The group should explicitly report the source of the data it has used and explain how and why those data have been selected.

47. That said, debate and disagreement can sometimes impede clarity for decision makers about what action they should take. We have also proposed that part of the necessary accountability framework should include a broader list of indicators. We have recommended that one of the most reliable sources of indicators is the Countdown to 2015 initiative. The Countdown was created as an independent technical process focused on monitoring all stakeholders in women's and children's health—donors, the UN, and other non-state actors, as well as countries.

48. We recommend that the Commission endorses the work of the Countdown to 2015 process as a critical input to national reviews and the independent review group, and finds ways to strengthen, sustain, and broaden its independent work as a critical, although not exclusive, part of global oversight and monitoring for women's and children's health. . . .

Appendix

Our report recommends that a Secretary-General's independent review group (IRG) on women's and children's health be established (paragraphs 38–48).

This Appendix does not repeat these earlier paragraphs but develops options for commissioners to consider under that recommendation. It does not offer a blueprint. If our recommendation is accepted, consultations will be needed to further develop and refine these proposals (e.g., see para. 30 below).

Our working group has considered several possible structures for an IRG. For example, one might envisage a high-level, more political group that meets for a short period once a year—reviewing reports prepared by other bodies, consulting, and issuing a statement that assesses the overall progress of the Secretary-General's *Global strategy*. Several members of our working group favored such a mechanism. The advantage, they argued, of a high-level group would be that it attracts visibility and attention.

We have also considered a more substantive version of an IRG. This option is based on the idea of a robust, genuine, unstaged review of commitments arising from the *Global strategy*—holding accountable countries, donors, and non-state actors. It is this option that is now developed further.

In summary, one could envisage a small and agile IRG that meets for about four weeks each year, supported by a small secretariat. We anticipate that such an IRG would divide into working groups that meet, and conduct reviews, in the regions. The IRG would draw extensively from the data and information already provided by existing initiatives on women's and children's health, such as the Countdown. Indeed, the IRG would complement and reinforce these existing initiatives by providing an independent review of the commitments made by all stakeholders in relation to the Secretary-General's *Global strategy*. The core task of the IRG would be to ask whether stakeholders have kept their promises and to identify practical measures that need to be taken in order to do so. The IRG would help all stakeholders to implement the *Global strategy*.

An independent review body is composed of experts in their field. They exercise their professional, autonomous judgment. Although nominated or appointed by relevant stakeholders, once appointed they serve in their independent capacity. Independent review deepens the actual and perceived impartiality, credibility, legitimacy, integrity, and authority of the accountability process.

While there are many critically important global initiatives on women's and children's health, none provides an independent review of all stakeholders' commitments and responsibilities. This is the "accountability gap" that is widely recognized among observers of women's and children's health, and which has, at least in part, resulted in slower than hoped for progress in improving maternal, newborn, and child survival. It is this gap that our recommendation aims to fill.

Existing UN independent review bodies

Independent review is commonplace within the UN "family". These UN review bodies are not the same—each reflects its distinctive context and objectives. The IRG has to reflect the unique challenges raised by the Secretary-General's *Global strategy*. By way of illustration, however, here are examples of existing UN independent review bodies.

World Bank Inspection Panel. Established in 1993, the Panel comprises three members who are appointed by the Bank's executive board for non-renewable periods of five years. Panel members are selected on the basis of a range of criteria, including their integrity and independence from Bank management. The panel investigates Bank-financed projects to determine whether or not the Bank has complied with its numerous operational policies and directives, such as those on the financial terms and conditions of loans, disbursement policies, gender and development, and social and environmental safeguards.

Independent Evaluation Office (IEO) of the International Monetary Fund. The IEO was established in 2001 to conduct independent and objective evaluations of Fund policies and activities. The Office is independent from management and operates at arm's length from the Fund's board of executive directors. It consists of a Director and 11 other staff. As the Director's terms of reference put it: "Actions taken by the Director will be taken on the basis of his or her independent judgment."

International Labor Organization Committee of Experts on the Application of Conventions and Recommendations. This Committee comprises 20 eminent independent experts appointed by the ILO governing body for three-year terms. Once appointed, the experts serve in their personal capacity. The Committee considers information from states, and elsewhere, on the implementation of ILO conventions, and reports annually to the (non-independent) International Labor Conference Committee on the Application of Standards, comprising government, employer, and worker delegates.

The Joint ILO-UNESCO Committee of Experts on the Application of the Recommendations concerning Teaching Personnel (CEART). CEART comprises 12 appointed members, who act in their independent capacity. The ILO and UNESCO appoint six members each for renewable terms of six years. CEART reviews reports on the application of the ILO-UNESCO Recommendation concerning the Status of Teachers (1966), makes findings, and issues recommendations.

International Health Regulations (IHR) Review Committee. The IHR Review Committee consists of around 30 members selected from the roster of experts for the IHR or other WHO expert committees. The Committee's duties include carrying out an independent review of the global response to the H1N1 pandemic. The Committee considers the global response of states, WHO, and pharmaceutical companies.

Independent Monitoring Board (IMB) for the Global Polio Eradication Initiative. Meeting for the first time in December 2010, the IMB was established at the request of the WHO executive board and the World Health Assembly to check on the implementation and impact of the new Global Polio Eradication Initiative Strategic Plan (2010–2012) against major milestones and indicators, and to advise countries and partner agencies on corrective actions. It reports to the heads of the partner agencies, WHO, Rotary International, the US centers for disease control and prevention, UNICEF, and the Gates Foundation. Despite its name, IMB appears to have both monitoring and review functions. With nine members, the IMB has agreed to meet on a quarterly basis.

United Nations Human Rights Treaty Bodies. These groups of independent experts are appointed to review states' implementation of international treaties covering a wide range of civil, political, economic, social, and cultural human rights. Today, there are eight independent treaty bodies (e.g., Committee on the Rights of the Child) reviewing eight human rights treaties (e.g., Convention on the Rights of the Child, ratified by 193 countries.) Treaty bodies range in membership from 18 to 23 independent experts. The first human rights treaty body was established 40 years ago.

Outline of an IRG process

Our report recommends a particular focus on the 74 countries where 98% of maternal and child deaths take place—the combined group of nations covered in the Countdown to 2015 report and those identified in the *Global strategy* as the lowest income countries (para. 34). However, the *Global strategy* emphasizes the role of all stakeholders. Consequently, the IRG will review the role of all major stakeholders—donors, implementing country governments, multilateral agencies, civil society, and the private sector—in relation to the 74 countries. In a particular country, the group would ask if all major stakeholders are keeping their general and specific commitments under the *Global strategy* and it would also recommend practical measures for further action. In short, while the starting point would be the commitments of the national government, the IRG would also review the commitments of other major stakeholders in the country, including donors.

The IRG's secretariat would collect existing data and information from, for example, official sources of national governments; Countdown reports, including country profiles; national MDG reports; annual flagship reports of UN agencies; UNICEF's child mortality website; the WHO Making Pregnancy Safer website; the Institute for Health Metrics and Evaluation; IHP+; World Health Statistics; OECD reports; among others.

Where the country has one, the IRG secretariat would liaise and collaborate closely with the national monitoring or accountability mechanism for women's and children's health, with a view to drawing from its data and information. In this way, highly engaged and strong local accountability bodies or mechanisms will secure much of the work that needs to be completed before the IRG meets. Accountability will be a permanent, not an episodic, concern.

The IRG would have access to a synthesis report prepared by the secretariat, as well as the original data sources. In some cases, the IRG might commission a particular report to assist with its work.

The IRG would invite key stakeholders to report briefly on their implementation of the general commitments arising from the *Global strategy* and, if any were made, their specific *Global strategy* commitments. We envisage stakeholders will often be able to draw extensively from existing reports, e.g., Countdown or OECD.

The IRG would prepare a short, public report on each country review. This report would summarize:

- the achievements and good practices of key stakeholders
- the main obstacles confronting implementation of the *Global strategy*
- the IRG's main concerns
- constructive, practical, remedial recommendations for further action by key stakeholders
- an assessment of the degree to which key stakeholders are meeting their general and specific commitments arising from the *Global strategy*.

As emphasized in our final report (paras 45–47), the IRG should use the best available evidence to inform all its work and explicitly explain the source of the data it has used and how and why those data have been selected.

The IRG is not an implementing agency. Its recommendations would be considered, and action taken, by national and international stakeholders and partners working in close collaboration. Where the country has one, the IRG will present its report to the national-level monitoring or accountability body for women's and children's health.

This process would be repeated every two years. Thus, two years later the IRG would check, and discuss with key parties, what steps have been taken to implement the IRG's earlier recommendations. If stakeholders, without adequate explanation, have not taken appropriate steps, this will be recorded in the IRG's public reports.

In special cases, one or two IRG members might visit a country to obtain firsthand experience of challenges and progress, as well as to promote and discuss implementation of the IRG's recommendations.

IRG working groups in the regions

We envisage the IRG would have approximately 15 to 20 members and we propose it divides into working groups. The IRG would determine the number and composition of its working groups. For illustrative purposes, we assume it may establish three to four working groups of five members each. Each year the IRG would also meet in plenary for at least one week to review its working methods, ensure consistency between working groups, adopt its annual report, and so on.

Our final report gives particular attention to stakeholders in 74 countries. For the most part, the IRG would review key stakeholders in those countries. However, the IRG might also wish to separately review some international stakeholders. For example, it might wish to review a donor's overall contribution to the *Global strategy*. Thus, we are assuming that, in a two-year cycle, the IRG would wish to conduct approximately 100 reviews—i.e., 74 country and 26 other reviews—about 50 reviews a year.

Reviews must use modern information technology as much as possible. However, we strongly recommend that a review does not become a technocratic exercise. As outlined above, we recommend the process includes discussion between the IRG, key stakeholders and others. While reviews will vary in length, we envisage that a country review will take about one day.

We would recommend that most country reviews take place in the regions.

Conclusions

Our final report signals how the IRG members might be selected and appointed (para. 42) and recommends that the IRG reports to the Secretary-General (para. 43). We would only add that, in addition to presenting its report to the Secretary-General/General Assembly, the IRG might also be required to report to suitable multi-stakeholder bodies—e.g., the Partnership on Maternal, Newborn, & Child Health. In this way, the IRG provides a critically important independent review element in multi-stakeholder mutual accountability processes.

Our final report also raises the question of where the IRG's administrative and technical support might be based (para. 44). As our final report notes, one possibility is the Secretary-General's Office. We recognize that there may [be] other options.

19 Keeping promises, measuring results[1]

Commission on Information and Accountability for Women's and Children's Health

1. Introduction

. . . All stakeholders agree on the importance of having a new, robust accountability framework to ensure that available resources and results are identified, recognized, reviewed and reported on in order to more rapidly improve women's and children's health.

Accountability is essential. It contributes to ensuring that all partners honor their commitments, demonstrates how actions and investment translate into tangible results and better long-term outcomes, and tells us what works and what needs to be improved. The Secretary-General, therefore, asked the Director-General of the World Health Organization (WHO) to coordinate a process to determine the most effective international institutional arrangements for global reporting, oversight and accountability on women's and children's health. . . .

In this, our final report, we fulfill all of our objectives. We have proposed a framework that places accountability soundly where it belongs: at the country level, with the active engagement of national governments, parliaments, communities and civil society. We also make strong links between country-level and global mechanisms and holding donors accountable. Ten recommendations have been agreed by all commissioners. They focus on ambitious, but practical actions that can be taken by all countries and all development partners, including civil society, private foundations, and the corporate sector. . . .

2. The accountability framework

The foundations of the accountability framework (Figure 1) are built on the fundamental human right of every woman and child to the highest attainable standard of health and on the critical importance of achieving equity in health and gender equality. Women's and children's health is recognized as a fundamental human right in such treaties as the International Covenant on

1 World Health Organization, *Keeping promises, measuring results*, Commission on Information and Accountability for Women's and Children's Health, 2011.

Economic, Social and Cultural Rights; the Convention on the Elimination of All Forms of Discrimination against Women; and the Convention on the Rights of the Child. The Human Rights Council also recently adopted a specific resolution on maternal mortality. The goal of the framework is to ensure that the most off-track Millennium Development Goals, for maternal and child health, are met by 2015. . . .

The urgent need for collective action is clear.

In addition, the framework embraces the *Global strategy*'s key accountability principles:

- focus on national leadership and ownership of results
- strengthen countries' capacity to monitor and evaluate
- reduce the reporting burden by aligning efforts with the systems countries use to monitor and evaluate their national health strategies
- strengthen and harmonize existing international mechanisms to track progress on all commitments made.

Accountability begins with national sovereignty and the responsibility of a government to its people and to the global community. However, all partners are accountable for the promises they make and the health policies and programs they design and implement.

National accountability mechanisms are more likely to be effective if they are selected by countries, rather than directed from outside, and fit their

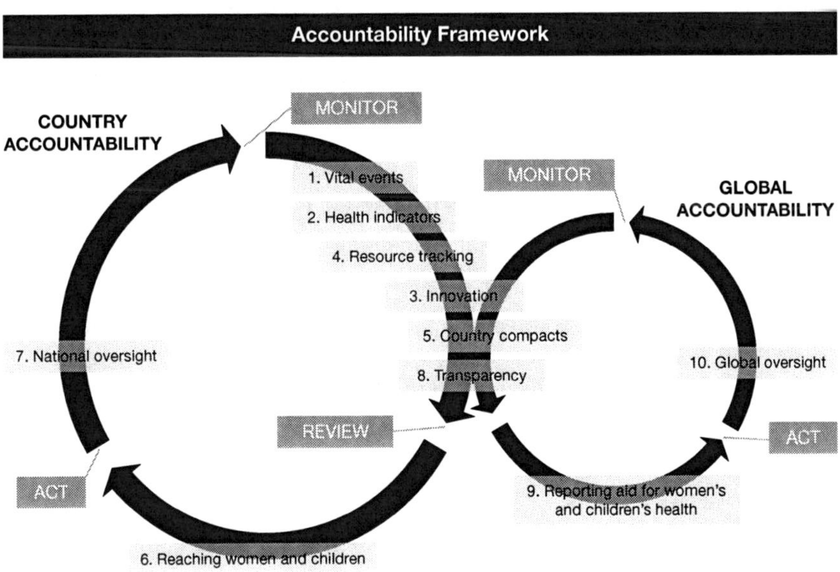

Figure 1 The accountability framework for women's and children's health

specific circumstances. The accountability framework assumes that mechanisms will be nationally or locally selected, with strong legitimacy and high-level political leadership, and be effective, transparent and inclusive of policy, technical, academic, professional, and civil society constituencies.

The accountability framework covers national and global levels and comprises three interconnected processes—monitor, review, and act—aimed at learning and continuous improvement. It links accountability for resources to results, i.e., the outputs, outcomes and impacts they produce.

Monitor means providing critical and valid information on what is happening, where and to whom (results) and how much is spent, where, on what, and on whom (resources).

Review means analyzing data to determine whether reproductive, maternal, newborn, and child health has improved, and whether pledges, promises and commitments have been kept by countries, donors and non-state actors. This is a learning process that involves recognizing success, drawing attention to good practice, identifying shortcomings and, as required, recommending remedial actions.

Act means using the information and evidence that emerge from the review process and doing what has been identified as necessary to accelerate progress towards improving health outcomes, meeting commitments, and reallocating resources for maximum health benefit. This includes more support for and wider adoption of policies and programs that are having a positive impact, and taking action to address what is not working, remedying problems with data, weak practices and any mismatch between actual resources and promises. It also includes learning from best practices and experience to enhance the effectiveness of efforts to improve women's and children's health.

Most countries already have some sort of monitor-review-act system in place, and these should be built on and strengthened. In most countries, the focus must be on strengthening and aligning such accountability mechanisms. In several countries, these systems are extensive and include subnational review processes as an integral part of national reviews, broad stakeholder participation and consultation, and involvement beyond the health sector. Figure 19.2 highlights elements of the monitor-review-act accountability framework in Ghana, Rwanda, and the United Republic of Tanzania.

While the immediate scope of the Commission relates to women's and children's health, the framework is relevant to health more broadly and, thus, could serve as a catalyst for strengthened accountability within national health systems and across the whole global health community.

3. Holding all stakeholders accountable: 10 recommendations

The commission is making 10 specific, measurable, attainable and time-bound recommendations for implementing the accountability framework, and which highlight the urgent actions needed to overcome the impediments

Ghana, Rwanda and the United Republic of Tanzania have developed their own systems of monitoring, review and action, based on many years of experience with sector-wide approaches in health. In general, these approaches help to ensure that the health-sector strategy is linked with broader development goals and planning processes, notably national strategies for economic growth and poverty reduction. There is also a consistent link between reviews and resource allocation through medium-term expenditure frameworks and annual operational planning cycles, and there are subnational processes of review and action.

National **monitoring** of progress and performance as part of health-sector strategic plans focuses on a core set of indicators: 18 in Rwanda, 37 in Ghana and 40 in the United Republic of Tanzania. Reproductive, maternal, newborn and child-health indicators account for at least half of these core indicators; they are also core indicators in the monitoring component of overall development plans.

Data availability and quality have improved during the past decade, mostly because of more frequent health surveys. The monitoring inputs in annual reviews, however, are mostly based on facility and administrative sources, which are affected by persistent problems with the timely availability and quality of data. The completeness, timeliness and quality of the data are areas all three countries are looking to improve with the aid of Information and Communication Technologies (ICTs). In Rwanda, the facility and administrative reporting systems appear to be improving significantly as a result of developing an overall architecture, introducing ICTs, and using performance-based funding. Reliable and timely data on births and deaths and causes of death are lacking in all three countries. In general, more systematic investments are needed to improve the performance of the national health information system, ensuring that a reliable and transparent monitoring system is in place.

The **institutional mechanisms** to support critical elements of monitoring (including data generation, compilation and sharing, quality assessment, analysis and synthesis, and communication of results) need considerable strengthening in all three countries. These functions tend to be concentrated in the Ministry of Health, with limited capacity in staff manpower and skills. Involving key country institutions and independent assessment should be integral parts of the monitoring process. In Ghana, independent consultants from within and outside the country are contracted to prepare the annual review report. In the United Republic of Tanzania, the review is mostly prepared by the Ministry of Health and Social Welfare, with inputs from national institutions. In Rwanda, although no formal report synthesizes all monitoring data for the reviews, performance-based funding and the use of ICTs are leading to greater transparency and data access.

Health-sector **reviews** and planning summits are conducted on at least an annual basis, with broad stakeholder involvement. Reproductive, maternal, newborn and child-health reviews are embedded in the well-established processes. Development partner participation is prominent, but civil society's role is less clear. Monitoring and evaluation subcommittees of the health sector committee involve multiple stakeholders. Many but not all development partners have aligned themselves with these country-led monitoring and review platforms, which are also promoted as part of the International Health Partnership principles.

In the context of the *Global Strategy*, the three countries have made specific commitments that are a subset of existing country plans for reproductive, maternal,

Figure 2 The accountability framework in different countries *(Continued)*

newborn and child health. The *Global Strategy* is perceived as an opportunity to strengthen the implementation of national strategies to accelerate progress towards MDG 4 and particularly MDG 5.

Note: see www. http://www.everywomaneverychild.org/pages?pageid=14&subpage=69 for the report of the three country case studies.

Figure 2 (Continued)

to greater accountability. The recommendations seek better information for better results; better tracking of resources for women's and children's health; and stronger oversight of results and resources, nationally and globally. Progressive target dates acknowledge that countries' capacities vary and that they will move forward at different rates. How the recommendations can be achieved is detailed in the agenda for action that follows.

Better information for better results

1. Vital events: By 2015, all countries have taken significant steps to establish a system for registration of births, deaths and causes of death, and have well-functioning health information systems that combine data from facilities, administrative sources and surveys.

There can be no accountability without timely, reliable and accessible health information and data. Solid information at the country level is essential to measure and monitor results. A strong capacity in countries to collect data on the health of women and children is essential to determine where investments should be focused and whether progress is being made. Many countries do not have well-functioning, integrated health information systems that combine information from population-based sources, such as surveys, with facility and administrative data. Major efforts are required to move towards one sound country system that meets all data needs for women's and children's health; ICTs provide new opportunities to do so.

The inability to count births and deaths and identify causes of death has been called a "scandal of invisibility." Vital statistics from various sources provide information that benefits individuals, societies and decision makers. Solutions to these data gaps exist, but building civil registration systems to deliver accurate and reliable data demands long-term political commitment and investment. That kind of political will has been mostly lacking, resulting in the information base for improving women's and children's health being heavily dependent on surveys conducted several years apart. In many countries, these surveys have had significant inputs from outside agencies, such as the demographic and health surveys, and multiple indicator cluster surveys.

Countries most off-track for women's and children's health generally have the weakest civil registration systems. There is no single blueprint for collecting reliable vital statistics. Each country's challenges are unique, so solutions must be tailored to circumstances and needs. Investments must be channeled into data gathering, together with the human and institutional capacities to support such systems.

ICTs have great potential to help countries overcome persistent obstacles in developing birth and death registration systems and rapid reporting of vital events. Liberia, for example, is experimenting with using mobile phones to register births. Together with WHO and other partners, the Health Metrics Network is looking to revitalize the monitoring of vital events through innovative information technology solutions (MOVE IT for the MDGs), combined with a periodic report describing the state of the world's information systems for health.

2. Health indicators: By 2012, the same 11 indicators on reproductive, maternal and child health (see Box 2), disaggregated for gender and other equity considerations, are being used for the purpose of monitoring progress towards the goals of the *Global Strategy*.

The 11 indicators of women's and children's health should be reported for the lowest wealth quintile, gender, age, urban/rural residence, geographic location and ethnicity; and, where feasible and appropriate, for education, marital status, number of children and HIV status.

In addition, the Commission urges countries to monitor the quality of care that women and children—boys and girls alike—receive, especially in the poorest countries. Quality means safe and effective care that is a positive experience for the user. Subnational data should also be collected as they are especially important for a complete assessment of equity and the right to health of all women and children.

3. Innovation: By 2015, all countries have integrated the use of Information and Communication Technologies in their national health information systems and health infrastructure.

ICTs can help enormously to disseminate and share information on results and resources for women's and children's health. ICTs provide new possibilities to capture and process data, link information systems, increase the timeliness of information produced, and store data for institutional memory. Constructing patient records, collecting data remotely, and transmitting those data for central storage and analysis are a few examples of the practical benefits of ICT systems, which allow for clear and rapidly accessible audit trails of administrative and financial transactions. Combining internet and mobile communications also supports data collection directly from individuals and health facilities in remote and rural areas, and enables that data to be shared in a timely and equitable manner. . . . Improved storage and access at public

One set of indicators has been selected to monitor the status of women's and children's health:

- maternal mortality ratio (deaths per 100 000 live births);
- underfive child mortality, with the proportion of newborn deaths (deaths per 1000 live births);
- children under five who are stunted (percentage of children under five years of age whose height-for-age is below minus two standard deviations from the median of the WHO Child Growth Standards).

These three health status indicators are essential for monitoring MDGs. Stunting, a nutrition indicator, is important for understanding not only outcomes, but also determinants of maternal and child health. Nutrition is also a useful proxy indicator for development more broadly.

These indicators are relatively insensitive to change and do not show progress over short periods (in the absence of birth and death registration systems they can only be measured with substantive time lags). Therefore, more sensitive and timely data that can monitor almost real-time changes in a set of key interventions to improve women's and children's health are needed. This objective can be achieved by monitoring a tracer set of eight coverage indicators:

- met need for contraception; (proportion of women aged 15–49 years who are married or in union and who have met their need for family planning, i.e. who do not want any more children or want to wait at least two years before having a baby, and are using contraception);
- antenatal care coverage (percentage of women aged 15–49 with a live birth who received antenatal care by a skilled health provider at least four times during pregnancy);
- antiretroviral prophylaxis among HIV-positive pregnant women to prevent vertical transmission of HIV, and antiretroviral therapy for women who are treatment-eligible;
- skilled attendant* at birth (percentage of live births attended by skilled health personnel);
- postnatal care for mothers and babies (percentage of mothers and babies who received postnatal care visit within two days of childbirth);
- exclusive breastfeeding for six months (percentage of infants aged 0–5 months who are exclusively breastfed);
- three doses of the combined diphtheria, pertussis and tetanus vaccine (percentage of infants aged 12–23 months who received three doses of diphtheria/pertussis/tetanus vaccine);
- antibiotic treatment for pneumonia (percentage of children aged 0–59 months with suspected pneumonia receiving antibiotics).

These eight coverage indicators have been selected because they are strategic and significant: each one represents a part of the continuum of care and each one is connected with other dimensions of health and health systems. A measure of contraception is needed as a tracer for reproductive health. Antenatal care provides a measure of access to the health system and is critical to ensuring proper coverage of care to identify maternal risks and improve health outcomes for the mother and newborn. HIV-related indicators are included to emphasize the need to move towards a more holistic approach to health care, and to encourage further integration of health

Figure 3 The 11 indicators of maternal, newborn and child health *(Continued)*

services. Skilled birth attendance, postnatal care and breastfeeding are critical elements of the continuum of care. The recommended vaccine is delivered routinely and so helpfully measures a child's ongoing interaction with the health system. Finally, case management of childhood pneumonia is an indicator of access to treatment. Although a vaccine will have a long-term impact on pneumonia, case management will remain an important measure of success.

These 11 indicators have been selected from a combination of the 11 MDG indicators and the 39 indicators used by the Countdown to 2015 for Maternal, Newborn and Child Survival. The Commission endorses the use of both sets of indicators. However, although all countries monitor and report on a large number of health indicators, updates on health status indicators are often based on predictions and there are major gaps in the availability of recent data to assess progress. Therefore, the Commission has recommended a small subset of 11 core indicators to ensure the collection of consistent and timely data needed to hold governments and development partners accountable for progress in improving women's and children's health, without adding to countries' reporting requirements. Reducing the reporting burden – i.e. duplicative reporting requirements – is a priority for the Commission and low-income countries. Collecting better information will be easier if scarce resources in countries are allocated to do so; this approach includes having all partners focus their efforts and reporting requirements around these indicators.

*A skilled attendant is an accredited health professional —such as a midwife, doctor or nurse—who has been educated and trained to proficiency in the skills needed to manage normal (uncomplicated) pregnancies, childbirth and the immediate postnatal period, and in the identification, management and referral of complications in women and newborns. *Making pregnancy safer: the critical role of the skilled attendant: A joint statement by WHO, ICM and FIGO*. World Health Organization, 2004. http://whqlibdoc.who.int/publications/2004/9241591692.pdf

Figure 3 (*Continued*)

databases will enhance transparency. New methods and information will be more easily shared, and participation in the review process expanded. Social networking offers fresh opportunities for strengthening accountability mechanisms, while broadband technologies can accelerate connectivity between community, national, and global levels, and progress towards generating, synthesizing and sharing comprehensive health information for improving women's and children's health.

The use of e-health and m-health should be strategic, integrated, and support national health goals. In order to capitalize on the potential of ICTs, it will be critical to agree on standards and to ensure interoperability of systems. Health information systems must comply with these standards at all levels, including systems used to capture patient data at the point of care. Common terminologies and minimum data sets should be agreed on so that information can be collected consistently, easily shared and not misinterpreted. In addition, national policies on health data sharing should ensure that data protection, privacy and consent are managed consistently.

The potential applications for ICTs are as diverse as ICTs themselves, and must be employed at every opportunity for a more complete understanding of patient care, including patients' own understanding of the services to which they are entitled.

Better tracking of resources for women's and children's health

4. Resource tracking: By 2015, all 74 countries where 98% of maternal and child deaths take place are tracking and reporting, at a minimum, two aggregate resource indicators: (i) total health expenditure by financ- ing source, per capita; and (ii) total reproductive, maternal, newborn and child health expenditure by financing source, per capita.

Tracking resources is critical for transparency, credibility, and ensuring much needed funds are used for their intended purposes and reach those who need them most. Parliaments have an important role to play in holding governments accountable for such reporting The long-term objective is for governments to annually report on their total health expenditure from all financing sources (including the government, private entities such as firms and individual households and development partners) and for specific health priorities, such as maternal health, malaria, and HIV, or population groups (women and children, for example). To this end, countries, starting with those with the greatest burden of women's and children's mortality and morbidity, should receive development partner support to strengthen their capacity to track and report on these two aggregate resource indicators.

Monitoring expenditures on health, and more specifically on women's and children's health, is not done on a systematic basis. Many low-income countries do not have the capacity to routinely produce expenditure estimates. The Commission recognizes that countries are starting with different capacities to track resources and will need to progressively expand their reporting of health expenditures over time. If necessary, countries can start by annually tracking total government health expenditure and external assistance, and providing more detailed reporting on private sources as their capacity increases. All stakeholders will have a role to play in providing timely and accurate information to governments to enable a comprehensive understanding of available resources and their use.

Tracking expenditure on women's and children's health stretches the capacities of many countries. Rapid and simple estimation methods need to be further developed by WHO and the Organization for Economic Co-operation and Development for use by countries with limited capacity.

To enable countries to achieve this target, their capacity to track resources for health, organize data into established accounting frameworks, and analyze and use information in national policy and accountability processes needs to be strengthened. Capacity is lowest in low-income countries. Efforts to build this capacity should be made as part of longer term efforts to strengthen underlying public expenditure management systems.

5. Country compacts: By 2012, in order to facilitate resource tracking, "compacts" between country governments and all major development partners are in place that require reporting, based on a format to be agreed in each country, on externally funded expenditures and predictable commitments.

In most countries, agreements, or compacts, between governments and all major development partners can be integrated into existing mechanisms, such as joint financing arrangements, international health partnership compacts, memoranda of understanding, and codes of conduct. They are necessary to ensure all partners provide governments with their budget and expenditure reports in an agreed format, thereby reinforcing mutual accountability and giving a clear picture of external health financing and the linkages with national health priorities. Monitoring such agreements via scorecards will further help to ensure compliance.

As part of these agreements, all major development partners (including bilateral donors, private foundations, corporations, and nongovernmental organizations) operating within a country should be required to report annually and in a coordinated manner on both the volume and purpose (including reproductive, maternal, newborn, and child health) of their health expenditures. They should also provide predictable forward plans, based on a format to be agreed in each country, to the relevant government ministry. Regional and international organizations provide forums that can empower countries to take this step and encourage all development partners to participate.

Development partners should also report their development assistance for health against the aid effectiveness indicators developed through the Paris Principles and Accra Agenda for Action in order to demonstrate that their funding and programs for women's and children's health are aligned with country priorities, strategies and planning cycles. Resource flows should also be reviewed to understand the quality of the assistance provided, including how much reaches the country and can be programmed at the country level.

6. Reaching women and children: By 2015, all governments have the capacity to regularly review health spending (including spending on reproductive, maternal, newborn and child health) and to relate spending to commitments, human rights, gender and other equity goals and results.

This recommendation is for reviewing resource flows in countries. Initially, countries with less capacity might be able to review only annual government health expenditures. As capacity increases, all countries should make annual reviews of health spending from all financing sources.

First, countries should review spending against priorities budgeted in national (and, where appropriate, subnational) health plans. Ideally, this entails an annual analysis of total health expenditure and its distribution across priority diseases, such as HIV, and population groups (e.g., women and children).

Countries should also review country-level data on external resources that have been received for comparison with similar information provided by development partners to the creditor reporting system managed by the Organization for Economic Co-operation and Development. Connecting global-level information to national-level information is critical to understanding the amount and nature of external resources available for use at country level. To this end, all major providers of external resources should sign into the country compacts and consider reporting their assistance to the creditor reporting system.

Second, countries should review whether investments are equitably distributed and directed to communities of concern to improve the health of women and children. This entails disaggregating indicators by sex, socioeconomic status, and other demographic or geographic variables to reveal inequities in the financial burden and use of services among population groups. Such analyses can inform assessments of whether governments are meeting their commitments to ensuring the right to health.

Third, countries should compare overall public spending on health with results achieved and prioritize intervention investments according to effectiveness and the efficient use of available resources. This prioritization should be linked to the level of impact. Impact can be shown through modeling and measured directly. If direct measurements of impact are not feasible, proxy measures can be used. Proxy measures for results, such as three doses of the combined diphtheria, pertussis, and tetanus vaccine coverage, or assisted deliveries, can be used to make a general comparison of results achieved with money spent.

In many countries, parliaments have a mandate to perform these review functions. Efforts to strengthen the capacity of countries to direct resources to women and children should involve parliaments.

Better oversight of results and resources: nationally and globally

7. National oversight: By 2012, all countries have established national accountability mechanisms that are transparent, that are inclusive of all stakeholders, and that recommend remedial action, as required.

The timeframe of this recommendation is particularly ambitious because national arrangements are the anchor of our international institutional arrangements. Although the nature of these review mechanisms will vary from country to country, they should be transparent and inclusive, ensuring all key stakeholders, including civil society and communities, are well represented. They should consider independent reviews of data. It is also important that national reviews span subnational, district, and local levels.

Many countries already regularly review progress and performance in the health sector against country health plans and international goals. The involvement of higher political levels, such as a president's or a prime minister's office, generates better progress on reproductive, maternal, newborn and child health, and helps strengthen crucial political will.

One of several potential options to strengthen review mechanisms in countries is to establish a national commission for women's and children's health. Chaired by a head of state or government, accountable (and reporting) to parliament, inclusive of all relevant government departments, and engaging nongovernmental actors, such a body would operate in a similar manner to national AIDS commissions (see Figure 19.4).

Some countries engage a health ombudsperson to increase the independence of the review.

One essential function of a national review is to assess whether health gains and investments are equitably distributed. This entails disaggregating all data on the core indicators. The two sets of indicator to monitor resources flows should be disaggregated by sex, socioeconomic status, and other demographic or geographic variables to reveal health inequities, and inequities in the financial burden and use of services among population groups. Countries should also periodically review and analyze barriers in access to health services for women, especially young women.

The highest levels of political authority, including national parliaments, should act to ensure the results of the review inform subsequent national plans, together with commitments on budgets, timelines and further

In 2001, the United Nations General Assembly Special Session (UNGASS) on AIDS mobilized countries in an unprecedented way to address the epidemic. Part of the UNGASS response was to create national AIDS commissions as multisectoral coordinating entities to lead and monitor the response. They have facilitated country mobilization around one national strategy, one national authority and one national monitoring system. They engage civil society and have embedded high-level political commitment into the AIDS response.

Although national AIDS commissions are not perfect and do not have formal legal authority, they "have been able to catalyse and spearhead strong leadership and advocacy in support of the national AIDS policy and action frameworks, and to provide effective multisectoral coordination, especially among non-governmental actors and development partners". There may be exceptional opportunities for countries to build on and leverage the success of UNGASS on behalf of women and children.

Source: Morah E, Ihalainen M. National AIDS Commissions in Africa: performance and emerging challenges. *Development Policy Review* 2009, 27:185–214.

Figure 4 Learning from national AIDS commissions

accountability measures. It is especially important to invest in strengthening community-level accountability mechanisms. One example is scorecards used by communities to monitor health services.

8. Transparency: By 2013, all stakeholders are publicly sharing information on commitments, resources provided and results achieved annually, at both national and international levels.

Information flows between the producers and users of data (e.g., citizens, program implementers, development partners, academics, researchers, civil society, and the media) are insufficient. Databases should be made more user friendly to encourage wider use of the information.

Accountability requires that information on results and resources is readily accessible to anyone. Parliaments, which oversee the performance of governments, have a particularly important role in ensuring transparency and inclusiveness, and encouraging continued scrutiny, challenge and debate.

Information should flow freely in accordance with information-sharing principles established by the government. Governments and development partners, including private foundations and the corporate sector, should make information on health outcomes and resources spent on health available on a public domain website. Transparency in information can drive community, national, regional and global efforts to increase accountability and to assess relative country progress.

In this context, exercises such as the report being compiled by the Partnership on Maternal, Newborn & Child Health to track commitments made in response to the *Global strategy* should provide useful and easily accessible baseline data on the financial, policy and program commitments announced in September 2010. Going forward, all donors should identify the sources and the intermediaries of financial flows when reporting on commitments in order to avoid double-counting.

The greater availability of information will not only raise awareness of women's and children's health, but allow closer scrutiny of whether health improvements are equitable and whether funds are being used responsibly and equitably. Transparency will foster learning and continuous improvement, and more informed decision making by all partners.

Such transparency can enhance accountability and overall health system performance, but the capacity to act on such information must be strengthened. Users inside and outside government should be empowered with information on health determinants, equity issues and budgetary constraints, and through guidance on advocacy techniques to enhance their ability to seek changes in budgets or policies.

9. Reporting aid for women's and children's health: By 2012, development partners request the OECD-DAC to agree on how to improve the Creditor Reporting System so that it can capture, in a

timely manner, all reproductive, maternal, newborn and child health spending by development partners. In the interim, development partners and OECD implement a simple method for reporting such expenditure.

All major development partners, including emerging donors, private foundations and corporate donors, should provide to the global aid database (the creditor reporting system of the Organization for Economic Co-operation and Development) more timely, complete and consistent information on resources for health. Development partners reporting on financial resources devoted to women's and children's health can be a vital complement to countries reporting on their own health expenditures, and help ensure mutual accountability.

Expenditure by development partners on reproductive, maternal, newborn and child health cannot easily be identified from the creditor reporting system data, because these services overlap the current system of coding. The Development Assistance Committee of the Organization for Economic Co-operation and Development should urgently identify ways to improve the reporting system so that expenditure on reproductive, maternal, newborn, and child health can be better captured and in a timely fashion. In the interim, development partner expenditure on reproductive, maternal, newborn and child health can be estimated using methods developed by the G8 in consultation with the OECD.

10. Global oversight: Starting in 2012 and ending in 2015, an independent "Expert Review Group" is reporting regularly to the United Nations Secretary-General on the results and resources related to the *Global Strategy* and on progress in implementing this Commission's recommendations.

One of the Commission's objectives is to recommend international institutional arrangements for global reporting, oversight and accountability on women's and children's health. Several national and international interagency groups, technical organizations and academic institutions already perform extensive field work and publish regular reports that address many elements of global oversight. They monitor and review different aspects of women's and children's health and recommend action. This work should continue and be strengthened.

The purpose of global oversight is to assess progress in implementing the *global strategy* and the recommendations of the Commission in order to accelerate improvements in women's and children's health. The specific functions are to:

- track and ensure all stakeholders honor their commitments to the *Global strategy* and the Commission; including the US$ 40 billion of commitments made in September 2010, and to track implementation of the recommendations of the Commission

- assess progress towards greater transparency in the flow of resources and achieving results
- identify obstacles to implementing both the *Global strategy* and the Commission's recommendations
- identify good practice, including in policy and service delivery, accountability arrangements and value-for-money approaches
- make recommendations to improve the effectiveness of the accountability framework.

However, to provide a stronger accountability mechanism—and to ensure critical remedies and actions are taken—we propose an independent expert review group be established and operate until 2015. This time-limited group would draw extensively on existing data, reporting and assessments at country and global levels, in particular through national accountability frameworks, to avoid duplication, fragmentation and increasing transaction costs through a light process with high impact. The group would synthesize all available information and evidence, address discrepancies, and make its own analysis and recommendations in an annual report to the United Nations Secretary-General.

The key principles underpinning our proposed international institutional arrangements are: partnership, independence, transparency, credibility, and efficiency. Networks and partnerships, such as the Partnership on Maternal, Newborn & Child Health, should be used to their maximum potential to promote participation in the review process and in outreach about the Commission's report. The public should also have the opportunity to participate in the review process.

The group should comprise five to nine members, appointed by the United Nations Secretary-General, with at least half from low- and middle-income countries. There will be broad international representation and diversity of knowledge and experience in the field of women's and children's health. WHO will lead a transparent process to solicit nominations from all of the stakeholders supporting the *Global strategy*. Nominated individuals will be expected to exercise autonomous, professional judgment and serve in an independent capacity.

The members of the expert review group should be announced in September 2011, the first anniversary of the *Global strategy*'s launch. A small, well-resourced secretariat hosted by WHO should be established to collect data, help prepare reports, and provide general support to the group. . .

20 Realising sexual and reproductive health rights in Kenya: myth or reality? Report of the public inquiry into violations of sexual and reproductive health rights in Kenya[1]

Kenya National Commission on Human Rights

. . . 5.6 International human rights framework

. . . The right to accountability and redress affords everyone the right to effective, adequate, accessible and appropriate education and information on the legislative and judicial and other measures to redress sexual and reproductive rights. Sexual (and reproductive) rights have been identified as human rights and they include the right to equality and equal protection of the law, the right to life, liberty and to be free from torture and cruel inhuman treatment, the right to privacy, right to personal autonomy, the right to health and benefits of scientific progress and the right to education and information. The optional protocol to CEDAW reaffirms the determination of states parties that adopt the protocol to ensure the full and equal enjoyment by women of all human rights and fundamental freedoms and to take effective action to prevent violations of these rights and freedoms. The protocol introduces another level of accountability for state parties through the provision of complaints mechanism open to individual citizens and to public inquiry by the monitoring committee. However, Kenya has, to date, not ratified the optional protocol. Nevertheless, Kenya as a state party to CEDAW is obliged to ensure women enjoy all the rights provided. . . .

1 Kenya National Commission on Human Rights, *Realising sexual and reproductive health rights in Kenya: myth or reality? A report of the public inquiry into violations of sexual and reproductive health rights in Kenya*, May 2012. Footnotes omitted.

4.6.1. Conclusions

Evidence from the inquiry demonstrates that Kenya has failed to address the well-known factors and barriers that perpetuate high maternal mortality and morbidity. Factors such as poor quality of maternal health services, high cost of care, weak referral systems, inadequate capacity in terms of personnel and facilities to provide care, negligence and malpractices among health providers, sociocultural barriers among others have over time colluded to perpetuate maternal mortality and morbidity. Restrictive laws and lack of policies and programmes on safe abortion have also significantly contributed to the high maternal mortality and morbidity in Kenya. The inquiry concluded that women continue to die or suffer disability due to preventable causes.

These factors prevail against the backdrop of myriad international and regional human rights frameworks and commitments that Kenya is a party to and the national legal, policy and institutional frameworks that are aimed at enhancing maternal health.

From the foregoing therefore, the inquiry concludes that Kenya is still far from realising the maternal health rights as stipulated in international and regional human rights frameworks to which it is a party and in accordance with its domestic laws and policies.

The inquiry thus makes a number of recommendations to government and other stakeholders that are essential in working towards the realisation of maternal health rights in Kenya. . . .

4.6.2. Recommendations

1. Mitigating maternal mortality and morbidity

- The government must work towards implementing the Human Rights Council resolution on preventable maternal mortality by adopting a human rights-based approach to all interventions aimed at reducing maternal mortality and morbidity. This will empower people to participate in decision making and policy development. It will also strengthen the capacity of the duty bearers to give services and the rights holders to demand their rights and hold the duty bearers accountable.
- The Ministry of Health should work out a clear implementable strategy for the Constitutional provisions on the right to health including reproductive health and the underlying determinants. The strategy must seek to make the services available and accessible, of high-quality standards, affordable and culturally acceptable.
- Government and stakeholders should rethink the accountability mechanisms that seek to record deaths occurring from preventable causes with a view to make them effective. In which case, the strategy should seek to record these deaths as they occur and indicate their causes.

- The government must work out a strategy to address all the five known and identified sources of delays that eventually lead to maternal deaths:

  a time it takes to recognise that a woman is facing life-threatening health complications – this delay can be eliminated through educating the community on how to identify life-threatening signs in an individual that require emergency interventions
  b time it takes to make the decision to seek services – this can be eliminated through sensitising men and other persons that influence health-seeking behaviour at community level
  c time it takes to travel in search of the services – strengthening the referral system by improving the infrastructure, especially the transport system. This will require involvement of the decision makers (parliament and now county committees) to address poor infrastructure and allocate enough resources for transport in the health sector
  d time taken to receive the services on arrival at a health facility – this should entail the improvement of the capacity and effectiveness of healthcare professionals in giving services. This can be achieved through training, providing adequate equipment and supplies, and recruitment of adequate personnel
  e failure by the government and donors to affectively address the issues of maternal mortality – this would entail increased resourcing and prioritisation of maternal health issues. Noteworthy, with the establishment of devolved county governments, there are opportunities for the government to effectively address the problems relating to geographic access to maternal healthcare. In which case, the county governments need to devise innovative approaches to ensure the 'hard- to-reach' areas can access health services and that the vulnerable members of the society, such as disabled persons, are identified and provided with adequate maternal and child healthcare services. Further, the Community Health Strategy (2006) presents an opportunity for extending maternal health services to the grassroots (Level 1), but this requires establishment of robust and efficient referral mechanisms in order to ensure prompt access by Level 2 and 3 facilities. . . .

2. Strengthening health system . . .

- The government and other stakeholders should implement (where standards exist) ethical standards and guidelines that govern medical practice with a view to eliminate cases of mistreatment in health facilities and medical negligence and malpractice that often result in maternal morbidity and mortality. The codes of practice must incorporate the obligations of healthcare providers to the patient and also outline the rights of the patient. Clear penalties in cases where the provisions are not adhered to must be spelt out. The codes of practice and standards must be based on international human rights standards and the Kenyan Constitution 2010. . . .

- The government must make it mandatory that all health facilities establish complaint mechanisms. To facilitate this, government should issue guidelines on how these should be established. These are important in enabling clients forward their complaints to the relevant authorities for action in cases where they feel violated. Further, the government should compel all facilities to post information on patients' rights in visible settings in healthcare facilities along with information about how a patient can file a complaint. . .

21 The role of litigation in ensuring women's reproductive rights: an analysis of the Shanti Devi judgment in India[1]

Jameen Kaur

Introduction

The complete realization of a woman's reproductive rights is an "integral part of a modern woman's struggle to assert her dignity and worth as a human being." Feminist scholars have argued that "how reproduction is managed and controlled is inseparable from how women are managed and controlled." The struggle for reproductive self-determination has specific significance for women and girls in India, where a maternal death occurs every five minutes. According to government figures for 2007–2009, the maternal mortality ratio in India has dropped to 212 deaths per 100,000 live births from 254. Even so, this figure is still shockingly high in comparison to other middle-income countries. For example, the maternal mortality ratio is 45 in China, 56 in Sri Lanka, 16 in Chile, 45 in Cuba, 110 in Brazil, and 130 in Egypt. Factors that heighten women's and girls' risks of maternal death lie deeply rooted in the discrimination and inequality they suffer, which have a negative impact on their reproductive health and decision making, and security and sexuality, which, when combined, deny them their right to reproductive self-determination.

The three main clinical causes of maternal deaths in India are hemorrhage (38%), sepsis (11%) and complications of abortion (8%). According to the Indian Planning Commission, maternal deaths are largely attributed to the absence of skilled birth attendants at delivery, poor access to emergency obstetric care in case of complications, and no reliable referral system for women who experience complications. Unjustly, many more women and girls will suffer preventable injuries, infections and disabilities, often serious and lasting a lifetime, due to failures in maternal care. The disparities in who is at risk within India reflect the additional obstacles women and girls face due to their caste, religion, income, education levels and where they live. The report

1 *Reproductive Health Matters* 20 (39), 2012, 21–30. Footnotes omitted.

of the UN Special Rapporteur on the right to health's most recent mission (2010) to investigate maternal mortality in India observed:

> For a middle-income country of its stature and level of development, the rate of maternal deaths in India is shocking . . . Although the problem is not simply a matter of funding, public spending on health remains among the lowest in the world. There is a yawning gulf between India's commendable maternal mortality policies and their urgent, focused, sustained, systematic and effective implementation. For the most part, maternal mortality reduction is still not a priority in India.

This paper analyses the role litigation played in seeking redress for the violation of the reproductive rights of Shanti Devi, who died in childbirth, and some of the socioeconomic, cultural, political and legal factors that influence the power dynamics involved, from the level of the family to that of national and international institutions.

India's obligations to respect, protect, and fulfill women's reproductive rights . . .

National case law

Indian case law established the right to life, which encompasses the right to health and human dignity, in the landmark judgment in *Paschim Banga Khet Samity v. State of West Bengal*, in which the Supreme Court of India for the first time considered the right to emergency medical care as a fundamental right and directed that:

> [T]he primary duty of the Government is to secure the welfare of the people. . . . The Government discharges this obligation by running hospitals and health centres which provide medical care to the person seeking to avail those facilities. Article 21 imposes an obligation on the State to safeguard the right to life of every person . . . Failure on the part of a Government hospital to provide timely medical treatment to a person in need of such treatment results in violation of his right to life.

Further, in *Smt. Nilabati Behera v State of Orissa & Ors*, the Supreme Court of India acknowledged the right to compensation as a remedy of a violation:

> A claim in public law for compensation for contravention of human rights and fundamental freedoms, the protection of which is guaranteed in the Constitution, is an acknowledged remedy for enforcement and protection, of such rights. . . .

Shanti Devi's case

Shanti Devi's case was originally filed as an individual case (writ petition). However, in its claims for legal redress, the petition sought wider accountability for the lack of fulfillment of all women's reproductive rights—focussing specifically on the delivery of government obligations in Delhi and Haryana states. With this strategy, this case ensured that the Court took into account the constitutional and human rights obligations of central government.

The writ petition in Shanti Devi's case was taken forward by her brother-in-law, under a legal mechanism known as *public interest litigation*. The vision of public interest litigation was to create access to justice for the poor and marginalized sectors of Indian society, when their constitutional rights had been violated. It originated in the late 1970s through a series of decisions passed by the Supreme Court of India. Its key features are that it allows for the expansion of the interpretation of *locus standi*, the right of an individual to bring a proceeding to a court when she is not personally affected by the issue complained of, in cases involving constitutional rights violations if:

> [S]uch person or determinate class of persons is by reason of poverty, helplessness or disability or socially or economically disadvantaged position, unable to approach the Court for relief, any member of the public can maintain an application for an appropriate direction . . . seeking judicial redressal for the legal wrong or injury.

and to enable greater access to justice by establishing:

> [E]pistolary jurisdiction, setting that [the Court] would readily respond even to a letter addressed by such individual[s] acting pro bono publico [voluntarily in the greater public interest], and treat it as a formal writ petition [case] for [public interest litigation] purposes.

History of the case

Shanti Devi and her husband Kishan Mandal were from the state of Bihar (a low-performing state), of the marginalized scheduled caste community and landless. This profile placed Shanti at a higher risk of maternal death based on her caste, income, education level, and geographical location. In 2006 the couple migrated to the state of Haryana (a high-performing state) with their two sons, aged 6 and 11 years. They rented a room in a compound where they shared a toilet/wash cubicle with 30 other families. Kishan Mandal worked as a daily laborer earning Rs3500 (£40–45) per month, thus living below the poverty line.

In November 2008, while pregnant, Shanti Devi fell down the stairs of her compound and subsequently could no longer feel the baby moving. Kishan

Mandal first took his wife to a local traditional healer for medical assistance, who advised that the baby might be dead, and instructed them to go to the nearest government hospital in Faridabad, in Haryana. The staff there informed them that there was nothing they could do and instructed them to go to the Sanjay Gandhi government hospital in New Delhi, 55km away, saying free medical treatment would be provided because of their economic status. No further assistance was provided, despite Shanti's condition deteriorating. Kishan Mandal had to negotiate and hire an autorickshaw at a cost of Rs100 (£12–15), which further delayed Shanti Devi's access to emergency obstetric care. On arrival at Sanjay Gandhi hospital, medical staff advised that they could not surgically remove the dead fetus because there was no available bed in the intensive- care unit. After a period of waiting a bed was arranged for Shanti Devi at the privately run Saroj hospital, which was built in the heart of New Delhi on the agreement that it would reserve and earmark 10% of its operational beds and total treatment capacity for indigent patients, and treat them free of charge, under the Delhi Municipal Corporation Act (1957).

A doctor from Sanjay Gandhi had accompanied Shanti Devi, with a certified letter stating that she was a woman living below the poverty line and must be provided medical treatment free of cost. Once that doctor left, however, staff at Saroj hospital demanded Rs2.5–3 lakh (£3000) from Shanti Devi's family for treating her. Unable to pay such fees, the family brought Shanti Devi back to Sanjay Gandhi hospital. A bed in the intensive-care unit was eventually found by Sanjay Gandhi staff in another government-run hospital, Deen Dayal hospital, where the dead baby was finally removed. Shanti Devi was discharged in a weak condition.

Shanti Devi's brother-in-law, Laxmi Mandal, filed a writ petition in the Delhi High Court in December 2008. The case was argued pro bono by the Human Rights Law Network that as Shanti was still weak and in need of medical assistance, she must be immediately readmitted to hospital and given free medical treatment, and that the accused—namely, all the government and private hospitals involved, the state government and the Union of India—should be held accountable for violating her reproductive rights. Due to the Court's intervention, Shanti Devi was admitted to Deen Dayal hospital and discharged 18 days later. However, she was not provided, as per government obligations, with access to family planning counseling or a method of contraception, or any other essential follow-up care.

Within six months of her second discharge from hospital, and while the case was still being heard in the Delhi High Court regarding the delays in providing her with emergency obstetric care following her previous pregnancy, Shanti Devi again became pregnant, for the sixth time. That pregnancy was never registered with any government health workers or public health center. In her seventh month of pregnancy, she went into labor and delivered a baby girl prematurely at home without a skilled birth attendant or any medical assistance. Within the hour after delivery, she began hemorrhaging and died on 20 January 2010—a year after she was first discharged from Deen Dayal hospital.

The High Court's orders regarding Shanti Devi

. . . The case was first heard by the Delhi High Court in December 2008. The level of knowledge of the complex issues involved varied immensely between the three different judges who heard this case during its course. Importantly, it was the last judge, Justice Muralidhar, whose understanding of the issues was thorough, who was responsible for delivering the Court's final judgment on 4 June 2010. . . .

In fact, Shanti Devi did not receive any of the maternity services guaranteed under the National Rural Health Mission during any of her six pregnancies, whether antenatal check-ups, iron tablets (despite her being severely anemic) or family planning information. Further, Shanti Devi's obstetric history was not taken correctly in any of the hospitals she was sent to following her fall on the stairs; had this been done, it would have revealed that she was a high-risk case pregnancy.

The judgment in *Paschim Banga Khet Samity v. State of West Bengal* regarding the right to emergency medical care was used successfully in Shanti Devi's case to argue that she had had a right to emergency obstetric care. Shanti's death was not recorded or investigated as a maternal death until the Court asked for the audit to be done, despite the requirement by the government to record all births and deaths and investigate all maternal deaths. On reading the audit, the Court said: "What is clear in Shanti's case is that the maternal mortality was clearly avoidable."

Although Shanti Devi and her husband were scheduled caste migrants living below the poverty line (BPL), they did not have the relevant documentation to prove their status. This contributed to their being refused free treatment and benefit payments:

> The processes of obtaining a BPL card are often beyond the capacity of the poor, especially if they are also migrants and marginalized. . . .
>
> Instead of making it easier for poor persons to avail of the benefits, the efforts at present seem to be to insist upon documentation . . . This onerous burden . . . constitutes a major barrier to their availing of services. This is one reason why the coverage of these schemes has been poor in all these years. . . .
>
> . . . There is no assurance of "portability" of the schemes across the states. In the present case, Shanti Devi travelled from Bihar to Haryana and then to Delhi. In Haryana, she was clearly unable to access the public health services. At Delhi, she had to once again show that she had a BPL card, and on being unable to do so, she was denied access to medical facilities. For the migrant workers this can pose a serious problem. . . .

Lack of BPL documentation also acted as an obstacle to ensuring healthcare for Shanti's newborn baby, and again it was only because of the Court's intervention that the infant was provided with medical treatment at all. As the Court pointed out:

> It is said that the newborn . . . is currently being treated in . . . hospital . . . [but] there is every possibility of the said hospital turning out the baby girl since the father Kishan Mandal does not have a ration card in that State. . . .

Legal remedy in the form of compensation was awarded to Kishan Mandal. In addition, the Court safeguarded Kishan Mandal's entitlements, e.g., ration cards, cash entitlements under the JSY cash incentive scheme, the National Maternity Benefit Scheme maternity benefits, the National Family Benefit Scheme family benefit and benefits for the welfare of his three children.

Delhi High Court rulings on government policy and programs

The Court raised important concerns about the extent of implementation of government reproductive health programs, and the lack of accurate data:

> Statistics furnished by the state governments on the performance of the JSY show the number of institutional deliveries, but do not indicate what percentage of the total number of deliveries in the state they constitute. Only when such information is available and provided under the schemes, is the categorization of states as high-performing states and low performing states possible. The Central Government must insist on this kind of information for meaningful assessment of the working schemes.

The Union of India and the government of Delhi were told:

> There appear to be no operation[al] guidelines issued that can actually facilitate the accessing of free medical care by expectant mothers and the newly born babies belonging to the BPL category . . . The Union of India will have to come out with a set of instructions in coordination with GNCTD [National Capital Territory of Delhi] . . . to ensure that entitlement to free medical treatment to persons below the poverty line is not denied merely on account of them having to move away from their place of ordinary residence.

To support the investigation of all maternal deaths, the chief medical officer of Haryana state had issued a circular in May 2009 detailing how maternal death audits were to be implemented. But, when staff at the primary health center in Faridabad, Haryana, were interviewed, they advised that they did not have a system for auditing each maternal death. The center, which covers a population of 100,000, did not report a single maternal death during the period of April 2009 to March 2010. This reinforces findings by UN Special Rapporteur on the right to health in his 2010 mission to India that: "The majority of maternal deaths in India are not recorded."

While the Shanti Devi case was being heard, the director of the national rural health mission in Haryana issued directions that all maternal deaths would be audited in Haryana in future, and all relevant staff were to receive appropriate training for this. Following the final judgment, the Union of India ordered an implementation program that would ensure that all maternal deaths, both at the community level and/or at medical facilities, would be thoroughly audited in all states across India. The case also resulted in high-level discussions between state governments on the rights of economic migrants (personal communication, Human Rights Law Network advocates, June 2011).

The Court sought to ensure that the government was held accountable for its failure to meet its legal obligations to protect, respect and fulfill women's reproductive rights. . . .

Further litigation: opportunities and challenges

Shortly after the final judgment in Shanti Devi's case, the chief justice of the Delhi High Court took a *suo moto* decision to intervene and seek accountability in the case of a maternal death of a homeless woman in New Delhi. The ruling on that petition, referring to the Shanti Devi case, made a landmark order for land to be obtained from the National Capital Territory of Delhi to construct shelter homes and provide food and medical services for homeless pregnant and breastfeeding women and girls. . . .

Most recently, the case *Sandesh Bansal v. Union of India (PIL) W.P. 9061/2008*, whose final judgment was delivered in February 2012, also achieved accountability for the high levels of maternal deaths in the state of Madhya Pradesh, India. The Court ordered the immediate implementation of the national rural health mission with a focus on strengthening infrastructure, providing access to timely maternal health services, skilled personnel, effective referral and grievance redressal mechanisms. A time-bound plan for "strict and timely" implementation was ordered, consistent with national rural health mission requirements, with the Court setting specific directives. . . .

The maternal death audit in Shanti Devi's case provided insurmountable evidence of how her rights were violated. Such audits are also an "opportunity to look beyond the narrow medical cause of death and review social, economic, cultural, institutional, systemic and other factors." Health experts advise that "verbal autopsies . . . must never be used to provide the basis for litigation, management sanctions or blame." Instead, for them to be fully effective in ensuring systemic change within the health system, they must be promoted as confidential procedures and not as a tool to place blame or punishment, which would be counterproductive because individual health professionals would not participate openly and transparently for fear of sanctions. Justice Muralidhar did not seek to make individual practitioners scapegoats for Shanti Devi's death but remained focussed on the bigger picture—the conduct of the central and state governments and the functionality of the health system. Nevertheless, when a court orders a maternal death audit it does pose real risks and challenges for improving the delivery and accountability of maternity care.

Litigation is only one tool that can be used to seek accountability when human rights have been violated and/or denied. But as many activists understand, the larger picture, and the interactions and behaviors of various actors must also be engaged with. Political scientist Prof. Gloppen has written extensively on the use of litigation in holding governments accountable for the right to health: "Success in litigation can be evaluated from three different perspectives: success in Court; success in the material sense; and success in the social sense . . ."

In this regard, it is success in the social sense that is proving the most challenging to achieve. State governments in India have yet to issue instructions to ensure the portability of schemes and entitlements, particularly for economic migrants. Central government still needs to issue clarifications to state governments to ensure that all pregnant women living below poverty level are receiving the appropriate benefits and payments. Moreover, a committed government campaign is needed to raise awareness at all levels (grassroots to government administrators responsible for maternal healthcare implementation) that a homemaker should be considered a primary breadwinner for the purpose of receiving benefits.

One of the principal challenges that remains is people's lack of awareness of their human rights and entitlements to begin with. This is due to lack of government outreach programs informing communities of their rights and entitlements, and lack of accountability mechanisms within health programs, which are not transparent, monitored or functioning effectively. . . .

Extent of understanding of reproductive rights law by the judicial system

Reproductive rights is an area of law that has only recently gained development and recognition, one that requires:

> [A] multidisciplinary analysis drawing on sociolegal and political economy and policy analysis, medical and epidemiological knowledge, health, economics and health systems analysis as well as ethical analysis. . . .

In future cases, a clear strategy should be developed before deciding to move forward, assessing the risks and how the intended litigation complements and/or has an impact on the work of existing civil society groups already lobbying and being active on the issue. How will the issues identified in the case influence and engage with existing/planned government laws, policies and programs? And who will be responsible for delivering and monitoring the change on the ground? . . .

Conclusion

. . . This chapter has analyzed the influence of litigation in ensuring that Shanti Devi's death, which should have been avoidable, did not become yet another silent, unaccounted for maternal death. Whilst there is much still to be done to ensure that this landmark judgment is truly embedded within policy and practice in India, some steps towards institutional change have already been taken, and more must be fought for. . .

22 Human rights accountability for maternal death and failure to provide safe, legal abortion: the significance of two groundbreaking CEDAW decisions[1]

Eszter Kismödi, Judith Bueno de Mesquita, Ximena Andión Ibañez, Rajat Khosla and Lilian Sepúlveda

Introduction

In 2011 the Committee on the Elimination of Discrimination against Women (CEDAW Committee) issued two groundbreaking decisions: *Alyne da Silva Pimentel v. Brazil* and *L.C. v. Peru*. The cases involve two critical issues for women's sexual and reproductive rights: access to appropriate and quality maternal health services, and access to safe, legal abortion. . . .

. . . This article explores the global implications of these decisions, highlighting some of the international human rights procedures that may be used to hold states to account for their obligations if national accountability is absent or ineffective.

The facts of the two cases

Alyne da Silva Pimentel v. Brazil concerned a 28-year-old Brazilian woman of African descent. She had a five-year-old daughter and was six months' pregnant with her second child when she died in late 2002, following inadequate treatment at a local health center and the failure of the center to provide timely referral to emergency obstetric care. The health center was private but partly state financed, and was in one of Rio de Janeiro's poorest districts. Alyne was near the end of her second trimester of pregnancy when she went there, complaining of high-risk pregnancy symptoms, including severe abdominal pain, nausea, and vomiting. Staff at the health center misdiagnosed these symptoms and sent her home, delaying emergency medical care.

1 *Reproductive Health Matters* 20(39), 2012, 31–39. Footnotes omitted.

She went back to the health center two days later and was finally admitted. Doctors could no longer detect a fetal heartbeat, and therefore induced delivery. After the stillbirth, Alyne's nausea, vomiting, and abdominal pain persisted and worsened, and she became disoriented. She underwent surgery to remove portions of the placenta 14 hours after delivery. After the operation, her condition continued to worsen; she began severe hemorrhaging and vomiting blood. Her blood pressure was also low, and she refused food. However, staff at the health center assured her family that she was well. The following day, her condition further worsened, but the health center failed to perform any additional tests to determine what was wrong. Although she required referral to a hospital, she had to wait to be transferred for hours, as only one municipal public hospital had an available bed and refused to send its only ambulance to collect her. After she had been waiting in critical condition for eight hours, the municipal hospital finally agreed to authorize the use of their ambulance to transport her. On arrival at the hospital, she was placed in a corridor because there was no longer a bed available. She did not receive immediate medical attention. The hospital staff did not know that she had just delivered since her medical records had not been transferred with her; instead, the treating doctor was provided with a brief verbal account of her symptoms. Alyne died in hospital the following evening. Her death could have been prevented.

The case of *L.C. v. Peru* concerned a young girl from a very poor area of Peru. Over the course of four years, L.C. had been repeatedly raped by different men in her neighborhood. When in 2006, at the age of 13, she discovered that she was pregnant, she became seriously distressed and threw herself from the roof of a building, but her suicide attempt failed and she was taken to hospital. The following day, L.C. was assessed to be at risk of permanent paralysis. The head of the neurosurgical department recommended immediate realignment of her spine, but the available surgeon refused to perform the surgery due to her pregnancy. The medical board of the hospital refused to perform an abortion, even though Peruvian law permits abortion in cases where a woman's health or life is at risk. It was only after she miscarried, three months after being admitted to hospital, that doctors were willing to perform the necessary surgery. The enormous delay dramatically diminished the success of the intervention, and, as a result, L.C. is now quadriplegic.

Alyne's death and L.C.'s tragedy involved circumstances which are all too common for pregnant women in many countries: a lack of access to appropriate emergency obstetric care; unjustifiable delays in referral and treatment; denial of access to safe and legal abortion; discrimination and inequalities faced by marginalized women, including women living in poverty, ethnic, and racial minority women, indigenous and afro-descendent women, and adolescents; and a lack of appropriate remedies and redress at the national level. These problems lead to poor health outcomes and deaths.

The families of both Alyne and L.C. pursued but failed to obtain appropriate remedies or redress at the domestic level. After Alyne's death, her family sought civil redress, but the case languished in court for over four and a half years. No preliminary hearing was ever held, and it took the court three years and 10 months to appoint a medical expert, although court rules require that this be done within 10 days. In the case of L.C., there was no protocol in place that would have allowed her to demand that medical personnel and the authorities guarantee her access to a legal abortion within the limited period of time that exists under such circumstances. For these reasons, two women's rights organisations, Advocaci (in Brazil), and Promsex (in Peru), with the families of Alyne and L.C. respectively, supported by the Center for Reproductive Rights, took their cases to the CEDAW Committee, using what is called the optional communications procedure under the Convention. This procedure allows individuals and groups of women or girls who believe that they have been victims of violations of the rights protected under the Convention to bring cases against states that have ratified the optional protocol.

The CEDAW Committee's decisions and recommendations

In their decisions on these cases, the CEDAW Committee made concrete recommendations to Brazil and Peru that highlight some of the important actions required of states to ensure the highest attainable standard of sexual and reproductive health and rights for women and girls.

The two decisions mark the first times that a UN treaty-monitoring body has established that states have violated the right of access to healthcare services as an aspect of non-discrimination on the basis of sex, by failing to provide adequate and quality reproductive health services in conditions of equality.

Ensuring women's right to safe pregnancy and childbirth

In the *Alyne* decision, the Committee examined whether the government had put in place adequate measures to ensure equitable access to good-quality maternity services. The Committee concluded that Brazil had failed to do so since it had not ensured timely emergency obstetric care or referral for Alyne. The Committee also established that Alyne had not only been discriminated against because she was a woman, but also because she was poor and of African descent, thereby exposing the multiple forms of discrimination that women may experience when accessing maternity services. In the decision, the CEDAW Committee stated that:

> The lack of appropriate maternal health services in the State party clearly fails to meet the specific, distinctive health needs and interests of women . . . [and] has a differential impact on the right to life of women. (para. 7.7)

The Committee had previously established that denying women health services that only they need constitutes sex-based discrimination. The case of Alyne is the first decision in which the Committee has specifically required that a state provide adequate and quality maternal healthcare services as part of its non-discrimination obligations. The Committee recommended that Brazil ensure women's right to safe motherhood and affordable access for all women to emergency obstetric care and reaffirmed that state policies should be action oriented as well as adequately funded. . .

Access to safe and legal abortion on the grounds of rape and health

Human rights treaties, UN treaty-monitoring bodies, regional and national courts have increasingly recognized—and have been producing a growing body of jurisprudence that establishes—that the respect, protection and fulfillment of sexual and reproductive health rights require states to:

- ensure that abortion is legal in cases where the health and life of the woman are at risk and/or where pregnancy results from rape and incest, and that in these cases states must ensure that women can access safe abortion services
- amend laws that criminalize medical procedures needed only by women and/or that punish women who undergo those procedures
- provide rapid access to post-abortion care regardless of the legal permissibility of abortion.

In L.C., the CEDAW Committee reinforced the above standards, calling on Peru to:

> Review its laws with a view to establish a mechanism for effective access to therapeutic abortion under conditions that protect women's physical and mental health, prevent further occurrences in the future of violations similar to the ones in the present case; and to review its legislation with a view to decriminalizing abortion when the pregnancy results from rape or sexual abuse. (para. 9(b)(i))

As in its *Alyne* decision, the Committee found L.C.'s rights were violated because the state had failed to take all appropriate measures to eliminate discrimination and to ensure men and women access to healthcare services on a basis of equality. L.C. did not have access to any effective, accessible procedure that would have allowed her to establish her entitlement to the medical services (spinal surgery and therapeutic abortion) that her physical and mental health condition required. The Committee found this even more serious because she was a minor, a victim of sexual abuse, and in poor mental health, as evidenced by her suicide attempt.

L.C. is the second decision by a UN human rights treaty-monitoring body in recent years that has focused on the denial of access to legal therapeutic abortion. The case of *K.L. v. Peru* (2005), decided by the Human Rights Committee, which monitors the International Covenant on Civil and Political Rights, concerned a 17-year-old who was diagnosed with an anencephalic fetus at 14 weeks of pregnancy. Even though her pregnancy endangered her physical and mental health, and Peru's law permits therapeutic abortion, she was denied a legal abortion and was forced to carry the pregnancy to term and breastfeed the baby until its death four days later. The Human Rights Committee found that Peru had violated the right to be free from cruel, inhuman, and degrading treatment and the right to privacy and special protection as a minor under the International Covenant in this case. However, Peru has yet to implement the recommendations which the Human Rights Committee made to them in this decision.

The *L.C.* decision reinforces the findings in *K.L.* by emphasizing that where abortion is legal, states have a duty to ensure access to it. The L.C. case additionally establishes that access to legally permitted abortion is a matter of non-discrimination against women. It also provides a refined analysis of selected requirements to guarantee accessibility of legal therapeutic abortion. The Committee considered that:

> [S]ince the state party has legalized therapeutic abortion, it must establish an appropriate legal framework that allows women to exercise their right to it under conditions that guarantee necessary legal security, both for those who have recourse to abortion and for the healthcare professionals that must perform it . . . It is essential for this legal framework to include a mechanism for rapid decision making, with a view to limiting to the extent possible, risk to the health of the pregnant woman, that her opinion is to be taken into account and that there is a right to appeal. (para. 8.17). . .

Accountability of the state for the private sector

According to international human rights standards, states have an obligation to protect human rights not only against violations by their representatives, but also against harmful acts by private persons or entities. Due diligence provides an entry point to ensuring the prevention, investigation, and punishment of those responsible for any harm caused by private persons and for the provision of effective remedies. States must also ensure that the privatization of health services does not threaten the availability, accessibility, acceptability, and quality of care in them, on the basis of equality and non-discrimination.

Evidence suggests that privatization and outsourcing of sexual and reproductive health services often results in an authority vacuum, without any state body sufficiently in charge of ensuring that the highest attainable standard of health is secured for all. In *Alyne*, the CEDAW Committee held that Brazil must exert due diligence to ensure that private healthcare facilities comply with relevant national and international standards for reproductive healthcare and ensure affordable access for all women to adequate emergency obstetric care. The Committee confirmed that the state is responsible for the actions of private institutions when it outsources its medical services, and always has a duty to regulate and monitor private healthcare institutions. The Committee's finding was based on the obligation of states parties under CEDAW to take all appropriate measures to eliminate discrimination against women by any person, organization, or enterprise (CEDAW, Article 2.e).

Accountability of healthcare providers

The CEDAW Committee observed in both cases that negligence by healthcare providers was involved and, in the case of L.C., also stereotyping. In *Alyne*, the Committee pointed out that there had been professional negligence and that Alyne did not receive the medical care that she required. In the case of L.C., doctors failed to recognize the risk of permanent disability and provide appropriate services that could have protected L.C.'s health, a right enshrined in the Peruvian Constitution. The Committee found that postponing the provision of abortion and surgery was "influenced by the stereotype that the protection of the fetus should prevail over the health of the mother." The Committee explained that the state failed to fulfill its obligation to eliminate all practices which are based on stereotyped roles of women, since the timely access to necessary medical treatment was made conditional on carrying to term an unwanted pregnancy. The "stereotype" concerned was explained as placing L.C.'s reproductive function above her fundamental human rights (paras 8.15 and 9).

The CEDAW Committee's recommendations in both decisions highlighted states parties' obligation to provide adequate professional training for health workers, including for care involving women's sexual and reproductive health rights. This helps to ensure quality medical treatment during pregnancy and delivery, as well as timely emergency obstetric care. In *L.C.*, the Committee called on Peru to take measures to ensure that reproductive rights are understood and observed in all healthcare facilities:

> Such measures should include education and training programs to encourage health providers to change their attitudes and behavior in relation to adolescent women seeking reproductive health services and respond to specific health needs related to sexual violence. They should also include guidelines or protocols to ensure health services are available and accessible in public facilities. (para. 9(b)(2))

Monitoring and review

In *Alyne*, the CEDAW Committee recommended that Brazil implement its National Pact to Reduce Maternal and Neonatal Death, including through establishing more maternal mortality committees to monitor the number and causes of maternal deaths. Maternal death audits and reviews are conducted in many countries worldwide. The data generated provide an important basis for determining policy and funding priorities for addressing these causes and reducing maternal deaths. A strong capacity in countries to collect such data, including on the health of women, is essential to determine where investments should be focused and whether progress is being made.

Access to justice, remedies, and redress

The inaccessibility of justice and effective remedies impedes the realization of sexual and reproductive health and rights. Often when a pregnant woman is denied access to urgent life-saving and health-preserving medical services, there are also multiple obstacles to accessing justice and remedies afterwards. . . .

Victims of human rights violations have a right to effective remedy and reparation. Remedies take a variety of forms, including: restitution (re-establishing the situation before the violation took place); rehabilitation (e.g., medical or psychological care or social or legal services); compensation (payment for financially assessable damages); satisfaction (e.g., acknowledgement of a breach or an apology); and guarantees of non-repetition (e.g., legislation, organizational improvements). Some of these measures primarily address the individual victims of violations, others are more directed at the general population, to proactively protect their rights. Depending on the situation, full reparation for a violation may require a combination of these measures.

In both decisions, the CEDAW Committee recommended remedies that not only addressed the violations suffered by Alyne and L.C., but also called for systemic changes in the healthcare and justice sectors, and in the law itself, to prevent similar abuses occurring in the future. In *Alyne*, the Committee recommended that Brazil provide appropriate reparation, including financial compensation, to the daughter of Alyne, commensurate with the gravity of the violations against her. The Committee also recommended that Brazil ensure access to effective remedies in cases where women's reproductive health rights have been violated, and provide training for judiciary and law enforcement personnel.

In *L.C.*, the Committee recommended that Peru:

> [P]rovide reparation that includes adequate compensation for material and moral damages and measures of rehabilitation, commensurate with the gravity of the violation of her rights and the condition of her health, in order to ensure that she enjoys the best possible quality of life . . .

> [and] review its laws with a view to establishing a mechanism for effective access to therapeutic abortion under conditions that protect women's physical and mental health and prevent further occurrences in the future of violations similar to the ones in the present case. (paras 12a, b)

Further, the Committee also recommended that Peru "review its legislation with a view to decriminalizing abortion when the pregnancy results from rape or sexual abuse." The Committee also made recommendations to Peru to take steps to increase awareness about reproductive rights in all healthcare facilities, including through training of healthcare providers, and implementation of guidelines and protocols to ensure health services are available and accessible in public facilities. These recommendations require Peru to take proactive measures to ensure that similar violations can be avoided in the future and women and girls in similar situations to L.C. can have better access to services.

The global relevance of these cases

. . . These cases highlight that international human rights mechanisms can be used to hold states to account for sexual and reproductive health rights, including where domestic accountability is absent, inaccessible or ineffective, as it was for L.C. and the family of Alyne. As well as CEDAW, other UN human rights treaty bodies, the UN Human Rights Council and regional human rights mechanisms are among the key bodies that may play a role. Most of these bodies operate periodic reporting procedures involving the scrutiny of states' human rights performance. Some of these bodies, like CEDAW, also have complaints procedures that can be used by individuals and/or groups.

A new independent expert review group was established in September 2011, with responsibility for reporting to the UN Secretary-General on progress towards implementing the *Global strategy* on women's and children's health. It has also been tasked with following up on the recommendations of the Commission on Information and Accountability, which identified accountability as a missing element for the improvement of women's and children's health worldwide. The review group has a human rights purview and this provides a new, potentially important opportunity for improving maternal health in a broader women's rights and sexual and reproductive health framework.

Conclusion

. . . The decisions highlight the key role that human rights can play in seeking to hold states accountable for sexual and reproductive health, in order to protect the health and lives of women like Alyne and adolescent girls like

L.C. Brazil and Peru need to take urgent steps to implement the recommendations of the Committee.

Implementation of these decisions will not only have significance from the domestic perspective and the perspectives of the families affected, but would also impact global normative developments in this regard.

Index